QUANTITATIVE INVESTMENT ANALYSIS WORKBOOK

CFA Institute is the premier association for investment professionals around the world, with over 85,000 members in 129 countries. Since 1963 the organization has developed and administered the renowned Chartered Financial Analyst® Program. With a rich history of leading the investment profession, CFA Institute has set the highest standards in ethics, education, and professional excellence within the global investment community, and is the foremost authority on investment profession conduct and practice.

Each book in the CFA Institute Investment Series is geared toward industry practitioners along with graduate-level finance students and covers the most important topics in the industry. The authors of these cutting-edge books are themselves industry professionals and academics and bring their wealth of knowledge and expertise to this series.

QUANTITATIVE INVESTMENT ANALYSIS WORKBOOK

Second Edition

Richard A. DeFusco, CFA

Dennis W. McLeavey, CFA

Jerald E. Pinto, CFA

David E. Runkle, CFA

John Wiley & Sons, Inc.

Published by John Wiley & Sons, Inc., Hoboken, New Jersey.
Published simultaneously in Canada.

For general information on our other products and services or for technical support, please contact our Customer Care Department within the United States at (800) 762-2974, outside the United States at (317) 572-3993 or fax (317) 572-4002.

Wiley also publishes its books in a variety of electronic formats. Some content that appears in print may not be available in electronic formats. For more information about Wiley products, visit our Web site at www.wiley.com.

Library of Congress Cataloging-in-Publication Data:

Quantitative investment analysis workbook / Richard A. DeFusco . . . [et al.]. — 2nd ed.
        p. cm. — (The CFA Institute investment series)
    Includes bibliographical references.
    ISBN-13 978-0-470-06918-9 (paper)
    ISBN-10 0-470-06918-X (paper)
    1. Investment analysis — Mathematical models.   I. DeFusco, Richard
Armand.
        HG4529.Q35 2006
        332.601′5195 — dc22

                                                                2006052578

10   9   8   7   6   5   4   3

CONTENTS

CHAPTER 1

THE TIME VALUE OF MONEY

LEARNING OUTCOMES

After reading chapter 1, you should be able to do the following:

- Explain an interest rate as the sum of a real risk-free rate and premiums that compensate investors for distinct types of risk.
- Calculate the future value (FV) or present value (PV) of a single sum of money.
- Distinguish between the stated annual interest rate and the effective annual rate.
- Calculate the effective annual rate, given the stated annual interest rate and the frequency of compounding.
- Solve time value of money problems when compounding periods are other than annual.
- Calculate the FV or PV of an ordinary annuity and an annuity due.
- Calculate the PV of a perpetuity.
- Calculate an unknown variable, given the other relevant variables, in time value of money problems.
- Calculate the FV or the PV of a series of uneven cash flows.
- Draw a time line, specify a time index, and solve problems involving the time value of money as applied, for example, to mortgages and savings for college tuition or retirement.
- Explain the cash flow additivity principle in time value of money applications.

SUMMARY OVERVIEW

In chapter 1, we have explored a foundation topic in investment mathematics, the time value of money. We have developed and reviewed the following concepts for use in financial applications:

- The interest rate, r, is the required rate of return; r is also called the discount rate or opportunity cost.
- An interest rate can be viewed as the sum of the real risk-free interest rate and a set of premiums that compensate lenders for risk: an inflation premium, a default risk premium, a liquidity premium, and a maturity premium.
- The future value, FV, is the present value, PV, times the future value factor, $(1 + r)^N$.
- The interest rate, r, makes current and future currency amounts equivalent based on their time value.

- The stated annual interest rate is a quoted interest rate that does not account for compounding within the year.
- The periodic rate is the quoted interest rate per period; it equals the stated annual interest rate divided by the number of compounding periods per year.
- The effective annual rate is the amount by which a unit of currency will grow in a year with interest on interest included.
- An annuity is a finite set of level sequential cash flows.
- There are two types of annuities, the annuity due and the ordinary annuity. The annuity due has a first cash flow that occurs immediately; the ordinary annuity has a first cash flow that occurs one period from the present (indexed at $t = 1$).
- On a time line, we can index the present as 0 and then display equally spaced hash marks to represent a number of periods into the future. This representation allows us to index how many periods away each cash flow will be paid.
- Annuities may be handled in a similar fashion as single payments if we use annuity factors instead of single-payment factors.
- The present value, PV, is the future value, FV, times the present value factor, $(1 + r)^{-N}$.
- The present value of a perpetuity is A/r, where A is the periodic payment to be received forever.
- It is possible to calculate an unknown variable, given the other relevant variables in time value of money problems.
- The cash flow additivity principle can be used to solve problems with uneven cash flows by combining single payments and annuities.

PROBLEMS

1. The table below gives current information on the interest rates for two two-year and two eight-year maturity investments. The table also gives the maturity, liquidity, and default risk characteristics of a new investment possibility (Investment 3). All investments promise only a single payment (a payment at maturity). Assume that premiums relating to inflation, liquidity, and default risk are constant across all time horizons.

Investment	Maturity (in years)	Liquidity	Default Risk	Interest Rate (%)
1	2	High	Low	2.0
2	2	Low	Low	2.5
3	7	Low	Low	r_3
4	8	High	Low	4.0
5	8	Low	High	6.5

Based on the information in the above table, address the following:

A. Explain the difference between the interest rates on Investment 1 and Investment 2.
B. Estimate the default risk premium.
C. Calculate upper and lower limits for the interest rate on Investment 3, r_3.

2. A client has a $5 million portfolio and invests 5 percent of it in a money market fund projected to earn 3 percent annually. Estimate the value of this portion of his portfolio after seven years.

3. A client invests $500,000 in a bond fund projected to earn 7 percent annually. Estimate the value of her investment after 10 years.

4. For liquidity purposes, a client keeps $100,000 in a bank account. The bank quotes a stated annual interest rate of 7 percent. The bank's service representative explains that the stated rate is the rate one would earn if one were to cash out rather than invest the interest payments. How much will your client have in his account at the end of one year, assuming no additions or withdrawals, using the following types of compounding?

   A. Quarterly
   B. Monthly
   C. Continuous

5. A bank quotes a rate of 5.89 percent with an effective annual rate of 6.05 percent. Does the bank use annual, quarterly, or monthly compounding?

6. A bank pays a stated annual interest rate of 8 percent. What is the effective annual rate using the following types of compounding?

   A. Quarterly
   B. Monthly
   C. Continuous

7. A couple plans to set aside $20,000 per year in a conservative portfolio projected to earn 7 percent a year. If they make their first savings contribution one year from now, how much will they have at the end of 20 years?

8. Two years from now, a client will receive the first of three annual payments of $20,000 from a small business project. If she can earn 9 percent annually on her investments and plans to retire in six years, how much will the three business project payments be worth at the time of her retirement?

9. To cover the first year's total college tuition payments for his two children, a father will make a $75,000 payment five years from now. How much will he need to invest today to meet his first tuition goal if the investment earns 6 percent annually?

10. A client has agreed to invest €100,000 one year from now in a business planning to expand, and she has decided to set aside the funds today in a bank account that pays 7 percent compounded quarterly. How much does she need to set aside?

11. A client can choose between receiving 10 annual $100,000 retirement payments, starting one year from today, or receiving a lump sum today. Knowing that he can invest at a rate of 5 percent annually, he has decided to take the lump sum. What lump sum today will be equivalent to the future annual payments?

12. A perpetual preferred stock position pays quarterly dividends of $1,000 indefinitely (forever). If an investor has a required rate of return of 12 percent per year on this type of investment, how much should he be willing to pay for this dividend stream?

13. At retirement, a client has two payment options: a 20-year annuity at €50,000 per year starting after one year or a lump sum of €500,000 today. If the client's required rate of return on retirement fund investments is 6 percent per year, which plan has the higher present value and by how much?

14. You are considering investing in two different instruments. The first instrument will pay nothing for three years, but then it will pay $20,000 per year for four years. The second instrument will pay $20,000 for three years and $30,000 in the fourth year. All payments are made at year-end. If your required rate of return on these investments is 8 percent annually, what should you be willing to pay for:

   A. The first instrument
   B. The second instrument (use the formula for a four-year annuity)

15. Suppose you plan to send your daughter to college in three years. You expect her to earn two-thirds of her tuition payment in scholarship money, so you estimate that your payments will be $10,000 a year for four years. To estimate whether you have set aside enough money, you ignore possible inflation in tuition payments and assume that you can earn 8 percent annually on your investments. How much should you set aside now to cover these payments?

16. A client is confused about two terms on some certificate-of-deposit rates quoted at his bank in the United States. You explain that the stated annual interest rate is an annual rate that does not take into account compounding within a year. The rate his bank calls APY (annual percentage yield) is the effective annual rate taking into account compounding. The bank's customer service representative mentioned monthly compounding, with $1,000 becoming $1,061.68 at the end of a year. To prepare to explain the terms to your client, calculate the stated annual interest rate that the bank must be quoting.

17. A client seeking liquidity sets aside €35,000 in a bank account today. The account pays 5 percent compounded monthly. Because the client is concerned about the fact that deposit insurance covers the account for only up to €100,000, calculate how many months it will take to reach that amount.

18. A client plans to send a child to college for 4 years starting 18 years from now. Having set aside money for tuition, she decides to plan for room and board also. She estimates these costs at $20,000 per year, payable at the beginning of each year, by the time her child goes to college. If she starts next year and makes 17 payments into a savings account paying 5 percent annually, what annual payments must she make?

19. A couple plans to pay their child's college tuition for 4 years starting 18 years from now. The current annual cost of college is C$7,000, and they expect this cost to rise at an annual rate of 5 percent. In their planning, they assume that they can earn 6 percent annually. How much must they put aside each year, starting next year, if they plan to make 17 equal payments?

20. You are analyzing the last five years of earnings per share data for a company. The figures are $4.00, $4.50, $5.00, $6.00, and $7.00. At what compound annual rate did EPS grow during these years?

CHAPTER 2

DISCOUNTED CASH FLOW APPLICATIONS

LEARNING OUTCOMES

After reading chapter 2, you should be able to do the following:

- Calculate and interpret the net present value (NPV) and the internal rate of return (IRR) of an investment.
- Contrast the NPV rule to the IRR rule.
- Distinguish between money-weighted and time-weighted rates of return.
- Calculate the money-weighted and time-weighted rates of return of a portfolio.
- Calculate bank discount yield, holding period yield, effective annual yield, and money market yield for a U.S. Treasury bill.
- Convert among holding period yields, money market yields, and effective annual yields.
- Calculate bond-equivalent yield.

SUMMARY OVERVIEW

In chapter 2, we applied the concepts of present value, net present value, and internal rate of return to the fundamental problem of valuing investments. We applied these concepts first to corporate investment, the well-known capital budgeting problem. We then examined the fundamental problem of calculating the return on a portfolio subject to cash inflows and outflows. Finally we discussed money market yields and basic bond market terminology. The following summarizes the chapter's key concepts:

- The net present value (NPV) of a project is the present value of its cash inflows minus the present value of its cash outflows. The internal rate of return (IRR) is the discount rate that makes NPV equal to 0. We can interpret IRR as an expected compound return only when all interim cash flows can be reinvested at the internal rate of return and the investment is maintained to maturity.
- The NPV rule for decision making is to accept all projects with positive NPV or, if projects are mutually exclusive, to accept the project with the higher positive NPV. With mutually exclusive projects, we rely on the NPV rule. The IRR rule is to accept all projects with an internal rate of return exceeding the required rate of return. The IRR rule can be affected by problems of scale and timing of cash flows.
- Money-weighted rate of return and time-weighted rate of return are two alternative methods for calculating portfolio returns in a multiperiod setting when the portfolio is subject to

additions and withdrawals. Time-weighted rate of return is the standard in the investment management industry. Money-weighted rate of return can be appropriate if the investor exercises control over additions and withdrawals to the portfolio.

- The money-weighted rate of return is the internal rate of return on a portfolio, taking account of all cash flows.
- The time-weighted rate of return removes the effects of timing and amount of withdrawals and additions to the portfolio and reflects the compound rate of growth of one unit of currency invested over a stated measurement period.
- The bank discount yield for U.S. Treasury bills (and other money-market instruments sold on a discount basis) is given by $r_{BD} = (F - P_0)/F \times 360/t = D/F \times 360/t$, where F is the face amount to be received at maturity, P_0 is the price of the Treasury bill, t is the number of days to maturity, and D is the dollar discount.
- For a stated holding period or horizon, holding period yield (HPY) = (Ending price − Beginning price + Cash distributions)/(Beginning price). For a U.S. Treasury bill, HPY = D/P_0.
- The effective annual yield (EAY) is $(1 + HPY)^{365/t} - 1$.
- The money market yield is given by $r_{MM} = HPY \times 360/t$, where t is the number of days to maturity.
- For a Treasury bill, money market yield can be obtained from the bank discount yield using $r_{MM} = (360 \times r_{BD})/(360 - t \times r_{BD})$.
- We can convert back and forth between holding period yields, money market yields, and equivalent annual yields by using the holding period yield, which is common to all the calculations.
- The bond-equivalent yield of a yield stated on a semiannual basis is that yield multiplied by 2.

PROBLEMS

1. Waldrup Industries is considering a proposal for a joint venture that will require an investment of C$13 million. At the end of the fifth year, Waldrup's joint venture partner will buy out Waldrup's interest for C$10 million. Waldrup's chief financial officer has estimated that the appropriate discount rate for this proposal is 12 percent. The expected cash flows are given below.

Year	Cash Flow
0	− C$13,000,000
1	C$3,000,000
2	C$3,000,000
3	C$3,000,000
4	C$3,000,000
5	C$10,000,000

A. Calculate this proposal's NPV.
B. Make a recommendation to the CFO (chief financial officer) concerning whether Waldrup should enter into this joint venture.

2. Waldrup Industries has committed to investing C$5,500,000 in a project with expected cash flows of C$1,000,000 at the end of Year 1, C$1,500,000 at the end of Year 4, and C$7,000,000 at the end of Year 5.

   A. Demonstrate that the internal rate of return of the investment is 13.51 percent.
   B. State how the internal rate of return of the investment would change if Waldrup's opportunity cost of capital were to increase by 5 percentage points.

3. Bestfoods, Inc. is planning to spend $10 million on advertising. The company expects this expenditure to result in annual incremental cash flows of $1.6 million in perpetuity. The corporate opportunity cost of capital for this type of project is 12.5 percent.

   A. Calculate the NPV for the planned advertising.
   B. Calculate the internal rate of return.
   C. Should the company go forward with the planned advertising? Explain.

4. Trilever is planning to establish a new factory overseas. The project requires an initial investment of $15 million. Management intends to run this factory for six years and then sell it to a local entity. Trilever's finance department has estimated the following yearly cash flows:

Year	Cash Flow
0	−$15,000,000
1	$4,000,000
2	$4,000,000
3	$4,000,000
4	$4,000,000
5	$4,000,000
6	$7,000,000

   Trilever's CFO decides that the company's cost of capital of 19 percent is an appropriate hurdle rate for this project.

   A. Calculate the internal rate of return of this project.
   B. Make a recommendation to the CFO concerning whether to undertake this project.

5. Westcott–Smith is a privately held investment management company. Two other investment counseling companies, which want to be acquired, have contacted Westcott–Smith about purchasing their business. Company A's price is £2 million. Company B's price is £3 million. After analysis, Westcott–Smith estimates that Company A's profitability is consistent with a perpetuity of £300,000 a year. Company B's prospects are consistent with a perpetuity of £435,000 a year. Westcott–Smith has a budget that limits acquisitions to a maximum purchase cost of £4 million. Its opportunity cost of capital relative to undertaking either project is 12 percent.

   A. Determine which company or companies (if any) Westcott–Smith should purchase according to the NPV rule.

B. Determine which company or companies (if any) Westcott–Smith should purchase according to the IRR rule.

C. State which company or companies (if any) Westcott–Smith should purchase. Justify your answer.

6. John Wilson buys 150 shares of ABM on 1 January 2002 at a price of $156.30 per share. A dividend of $10 per share is paid on 1 January 2003. Assume that this dividend is not reinvested. Also on 1 January 2003, Wilson sells 100 shares at a price of $165 per share. On 1 January 2004, he collects a dividend of $15 per share (on 50 shares) and sells his remaining 50 shares at $170 per share. $\left(\text{11.96\%} \right) \left(\text{12.12\%} \right)$

A. Write the formula to calculate the money-weighted rate of return on Wilson's portfolio.

B. Using any method, compute the money-weighted rate of return.

C. Calculate the time-weighted rate of return on Wilson's portfolio. $\text{— 12.04\%}$

D. Describe a set of circumstances for which the money-weighted rate of return is an appropriate return measure for Wilson's portfolio.

E. Describe a set of circumstances for which the time-weighted rate of return is an appropriate return measure for Wilson's portfolio.

7. Mario Luongo and Bob Weaver both purchase the same stock for €100. One year later, the stock price is €110 and it pays a dividend of €5 per share. Weaver decides to buy another share at €110 (he does not reinvest the €5 dividend, however). Luongo also spends the €5 per share dividend but does not transact in the stock. At the end of the second year, the stock pays a dividend of €5 per share but its price has fallen back to €100. Luongo and Weaver then decide to sell their entire holdings of this stock. The performance for Luongo and Weaver's investments are as follows:

Luongo: Time-weighted return = 4.77 percent

Money-weighted return = 5.00 percent

Weaver: Money-weighted return = 1.63 percent

Briefly explain any similarities and differences between the performance of Luongo's and Weaver's investments.

8. A Treasury bill with a face value of $100,000 and 120 days until maturity is selling for $98,500.

A. What is the T-bill's bank discount yield?

B. What is the T-bill's money market yield?

C. What is the T-bill's effective annual yield?

9. Jane Cavell has just purchased a 90-day U.S. Treasury bill. She is familiar with yield quotes on German Treasury discount paper but confused about the bank discount quoting convention for the U.S. T-bill she just purchased.

A. Discuss three reasons why bank discount yield is not a meaningful measure of return.

B. Discuss the advantage of money market yield compared with bank discount yield as a measure of return.

C. Explain how the bank discount yield can be converted to an estimate of the holding period return Cavell can expect if she holds the T-bill to maturity.

CHAPTER 3

STATISTICAL CONCEPTS AND MARKET RETURNS

LEARNING OUTCOMES

After reading chapter 3, you should be able to do the following:

- Differentiate between a population and a sample.
- Explain the concepts of a parameter and a sample statistic.
- Explain the differences among the types of measurement scales.
- Define and interpret a frequency distribution.
- Define, calculate, and interpret a holding period return (total return).
- Calculate relative frequencies and cumulative relative frequencies, given a frequency distribution.
- Describe the properties of data presented as a histogram or a frequency polygon.
- Define, calculate, and interpret measures of central tendency, including the arithmetic mean, population mean, sample mean, weighted mean, geometric mean, harmonic mean, median, and mode.
- Describe and interpret quartiles, quintiles, deciles, and percentiles.
- Define, calculate, and interpret (1) a weighted average or mean (including portfolio return viewed as weighted mean), (2) a range and mean absolute deviation, (3) a sample and a population variance and standard deviation.
- Contrast variance with semivariance and target semivariance.
- Calculate the proportion of observations falling within a certain number of standard deviations of the mean, using Chebyshev's inequality.
- Define, calculate, and interpret the coefficient of variation.
- Define, calculate, and interpret the Sharpe ratio.
- Describe the relative locations of the mean, median, and mode for a nonsymmetrical distribution.
- Define and interpret skew, and explain the meaning of a positively or negatively skewed return distribution.
- Define and interpret kurtosis and explain the meaning of kurtosis in excess of 3.
- Describe and interpret sample measures of skew and kurtosis.

SUMMARY OVERVIEW

In chapter 3, we have presented descriptive statistics, the set of methods that permit us to convert raw data into useful information for investment analysis.

- A population is defined as all members of a specified group. A sample is a subset of a population.
- A parameter is any descriptive measure of a population. A sample statistic (statistic, for short) is a quantity computed from or used to describe a sample.
- Data measurements are taken using one of four major scales: nominal, ordinal, interval, or ratio. Nominal scales categorize data but do not rank them. Ordinal scales sort data into categories that are ordered with respect to some characteristic. Interval scales provide not only ranking but also assurance that the differences between scale values are equal. Ratio scales have all the characteristics of interval scales as well as a true zero point as the origin. The scale on which data are measured determines the type of analysis that can be performed on the data.
- A frequency distribution is a tabular display of data summarized into a relatively small number of intervals. Frequency distributions permit us to evaluate how data are distributed.
- The relative frequency of observations in an interval is the number of observations in the interval divided by the total number of observations. The cumulative relative frequency cumulates (adds up) the relative frequencies as we move from the first interval to the last, thus giving the fraction of the observations that are less than the upper limit of each interval.
- A histogram is a bar chart of data that have been grouped into a frequency distribution. A frequency polygon is a graph of frequency distributions obtained by drawing straight lines joining successive points representing the class frequencies.
- Sample statistics such as measures of central tendency, measures of dispersion, skewness, and kurtosis help with investment analysis, particularly in making probabilistic statements about returns.
- Measures of central tendency specify where data are centered and include the (arithmetic) mean, median, and mode (most frequently occurring value). The mean is the sum of the observations divided by the number of observations. The median is the value of the middle item (or the mean of the values of the two middle items) when the items in a set are sorted into ascending or descending order. The mean is the most frequently used measure of central tendency. The median is not influenced by extreme values and is most useful in the case of skewed distributions. The mode is the only measure of central tendency that can be used with nominal data.
- A portfolio's return is a weighted mean return computed from the returns on the individual assets, where the weight applied to each asset's return is the fraction of the portfolio invested in that asset.
- The geometric mean, G, of a set of observations $X_1, X_2, \ldots X_n$ is $G = \sqrt[n]{X_1 X_2 X_3 \ldots X_n}$ with $X_i \geq 0$ for $i = 1, 2, \ldots, n$. The geometric mean is especially important in reporting compound growth rates for time series data.
- Quantiles such as the median, quartiles, quintiles, deciles, and percentiles are location parameters that divide a distribution into halves, quarters, fifths, tenths, and hundredths, respectively.
- Dispersion measures such as the variance, standard deviation, and mean absolute deviation (MAD) describe the variability of outcomes around the arithmetic mean.
- Range is defined as the maximum value minus the minimum value. Range has only a limited scope because it uses information from only two observations.
- MAD for a sample is $\dfrac{\sum_{i=1}^{n} |X_i - \overline{X}|}{n}$ where $\overline{X}$ is the sample mean and n is the number of observations in the sample.

- The variance is the average of the squared deviations around the mean, and the standard deviation is the positive square root of variance. In computing sample variance (s^2) and sample standard deviation, the average squared deviation is computed using a divisor equal to the sample size minus 1.
- The semivariance is the average squared deviation below the mean; semideviation is the positive square root of semivariance. Target semivariance is the average squared deviation below a target level; target semideviation is its positive square root. All these measures quantify downside risk.
- According to Chebyshev's inequality, the proportion of the observations within k standard deviations of the arithmetic mean is at least $1 - 1/k^2$ for all $k > 1$. Chebyshev's inequality permits us to make probabilistic statements about the proportion of observations within various intervals around the mean for any distribution. As a result of Chebyshev's inequality, a two-standard-deviation interval around the mean must contain at least 75 percent of the observations, and a three-standard-deviation interval around the mean must contain at least 89 percent of the observations, no matter how the data are distributed.
- The coefficient of variation, CV, is the ratio of the standard deviation of a set of observations to their mean value. A scale-free measure of relative dispersion, by expressing the magnitude of variation among observations relative to their average size, the CV permits direct comparisons of dispersion across different data sets.
- The Sharpe ratio for a portfolio, p, based on historical returns, is defined as $S_h = \dfrac{\overline{R}_p - \overline{R}_F}{s_p}$, where $\overline{R}_p$ is the mean return to the portfolio, $\overline{R}_F$ is the mean return to a risk-free and asset, and s_p is the standard deviation of return on the portfolio.
- Skew describes the degree to which a distribution is not symmetric about its mean. A return distribution with positive skewness has frequent small losses and a few extreme gains. A return distribution with negative skewness has frequent small gains and a few extreme losses. Zero skewness indicates a symmetric distribution of returns.
- Kurtosis measures the peakedness of a distribution and provides information about the probability of extreme outcomes. A distribution that is more peaked than the normal distribution is called leptokurtic; a distribution that is less peaked than the normal distribution is called platykurtic; and a distribution identical to the normal distribution in this respect is called mesokurtic. The calculation for kurtosis involves finding the average of deviations from the mean raised to the fourth power and then standardizing that average by the standard deviation raised to the fourth power. Excess kurtosis is kurtosis minus 3, the value of kurtosis for all normal distributions.

PROBLEMS

1. Identify each of the following groups as a population or a sample. If the group is a sample, identify the population to which the sample is related.

   A. The S&P MidCap 400 Index viewed as representing U.S. stocks with market capitalization falling within a stated range.
   B. U.K. shares that traded on 11 August 2003 and that also closed above £100/share as of the close of the London Stock Exchange on that day.
   C. Marsh & McLennan Companies, Inc. (NYSE: MMC) and AON Corporation (NYSE: AON). This group is part of Standard & Poor's Insurance Brokers Index.

D. The set of 31 estimates for Microsoft EPS for fiscal year 2003, as of the 4 June 2003 date of a First Call/Thomson Financial report.

2. State the type of scale used to measure the following sets of data.

A. Sales in euros.
B. The investment style of mutual funds.
C. An analyst's rating of a stock as *underweight, market weight,* or *overweight,* referring to the analyst's suggested weighting of the stock in a portfolio.
D. A measure of the risk of portfolios on a scale of whole numbers from 1 (very conservative) to 5 (very risky) where the difference between 1 and 2 represents the same increment in risk as the difference between 4 and 5.

The table below gives the deviations of a hypothetical portfolio's annual total returns (gross of fees) from its benchmark's annual returns, for a 12-year period ending in 2003. Use this information to answer Problems 3 and 4.

Portfolio's Deviations from Benchmark Return, 1992–2003

1992	−7.14%
1993	1.62%
1994	2.48%
1995	−2.59%
1996	9.37%
1997	−0.55%
1998	−0.89%
1999	−9.19%
2000	−5.11%
2001	−0.49%
2002	6.84%
2003	3.04%

3. A. Calculate the frequency, cumulative frequency, relative frequency, and cumulative relative frequency for the portfolio's deviations from benchmark return, given the set of intervals in the table below.

Return Interval	Frequency	Cumulative Frequency	Relative Frequency	Cumulative Relative Frequency
$-9.19 \leq A < -4.55$				
$-4.55 \leq B < 0.09$				
$0.09 \leq C < 4.73$				
$4.73 \leq D \leq 9.37$				

B. Construct a histogram using the data.
C. Identify the modal interval of the grouped data.

4. Tracking risk (also called tracking error) is the standard deviation of the deviation of a portfolio's gross-of-fees total returns from benchmark return. Calculate the tracking risk of the portfolio, stated in percent (give the answer to two decimal places).

The table below gives the annual total returns on the MSCI Germany Index from 1993 to 2002. The returns are in the local currency. Use the information in this table to answer Problems 5 through 10.

MSCI Germany Index Total Returns, 1993–2002

Year	Return
1993	46.21%
1994	−6.18%
1995	8.04%
1996	22.87%
1997	45.90%
1998	20.32%
1999	41.20%
2000	−9.53%
2001	−17.75%
2002	−43.06%

Source: Ibbotson EnCorr Analyzer.

5. To describe the distribution of observations, perform the following:

   A. Create a frequency distribution with five equally spaced classes (round up at the second decimal place in computing the width of class intervals).
   B. Calculate the cumulative frequency of the data.
   C. Calculate the relative frequency and cumulative relative frequency of the data.
   D. State whether the frequency distribution is symmetric or asymmetric. If the distribution is asymmetric, characterize the nature of the asymmetry.

6. To describe the central tendency of the distribution, perform the following:

   A. Calculate the sample mean return.
   B. Calculate the median return.
   C. Identify the modal interval (or intervals) of the grouped returns.

7. To describe the compound rate of growth of the MSCI Germany Index, calculate the geometric mean return.
8. To describe the values at which certain returns fall, calculate the 30th percentile.
9. To describe the dispersion of the distribution, perform the following:

   A. Calculate the range.
   B. Calculate the mean absolute deviation (MAD).
   C. Calculate the variance.
   D. Calculate the standard deviation.
   E. Calculate the semivariance.
   F. Calculate the semideviation.

10. To describe the degree to which the distribution may depart from normality, perform the following:

    A. Calculate the skewness.
    B. Explain the finding for skewness in terms of the location of the median and mean returns.
    C. Calculate excess kurtosis.
    D. Contrast the distribution of annual returns on the MSCI Germany Index to a normal distribution model for returns.

11. A. Explain the relationship among arithmetic mean return, geometric mean return, and variability of returns.
    B. Contrast the use of the arithmetic mean return to the geometric mean return of an investment from the perspective of an investor concerned with the investment's terminal value.
    C. Contrast the use of the arithmetic mean return to the geometric mean return of an investment from the perspective of an investor concerned with the investment's average one-year return.

The following table repeats the annual total returns on the MSCI Germany Index previously given and also gives the annual total returns on the JP Morgan Germany five- to seven-year government bond index (JPM 5–7 Year GBI, for short). During the period given in the table, the International Monetary Fund Germany Money Market Index (IMF Germany MMI, for short) had a mean annual total return of 4.33 percent. Use that information and the information in the table to answer Problems 12 through 14.

Year	MSCI Germany Index	JPM Germany 5–7 Year GBI
1993	46.21%	15.74%
1994	−6.18%	−3.40%
1995	8.04%	18.30%
1996	22.87%	8.35%
1997	45.90%	6.65%
1998	20.32%	12.45%
1999	41.20%	−2.19%
2000	−9.53%	7.44%
2001	−17.75%	5.55%
2002	−43.06%	10.27%

Source: Ibbotson EnCorr Analyzer.

12. Calculate the annual returns and the mean annual return on a portfolio 60 percent invested in the MSCI Germany Index and 40 percent invested in the JPM Germany GBI.

13. A. Calculate the coefficient of variation for

    i. the 60/40 equity/bond portfolio described in Problem 12.
    ii. the MSCI Germany Index.
    iii. the JPM Germany 5–7 Year GBI.

B. Contrast the risk of the 60/40 equity/bond portfolio, the MSCI Germany Index, and the JPM Germany 5–7 Year GBI, as measured by the coefficient of variation.

14. A. Using the IMF Germany MMI as a proxy for the risk-free return, calculate the Sharpe ratio for

    i. the 60/40 equity/bond portfolio described in Problem 12.
    ii. the MSCI Germany Index.
    iii. the JPM Germany 5–7 Year GBI.

B. Contrast the risk-adjusted performance of the 60/40 equity/bond portfolio, the MSCI Germany Index, and the JPM Germany 5–7 Year GBI, as measured by the Sharpe ratio.

15. Suppose a client asks you for a valuation analysis on the eight-stock U.S. common stock portfolio given in the table below. The stocks are equally weighted in the portfolio. You are evaluating the portfolio using three price multiples. The trailing 12 months (TTM) price-to-earnings ratio (P/E) is current price divided by diluted EPS over the past four quarters.[1] The TTM price-to-sales ratio (P/S) is current price divided by sales per share over the last four quarters. The price-to-book ratio (P/B) is the current price divided by book value per share as given in the most recent quarterly statement. The data in the table are as of 12 September 2003.

Client Portfolio

Common Stock	TTM P/E	TTM P/S	P/B
Abercrombie & Fitch (NYSE: AFN)	13.67	1.66	3.43
Albemarle Corporation (NYSE: ALB)	14.43	1.13	1.96
Avon Products, Inc. (NYSE: AVP)	28.06	2.45	382.72
Berkshire Hathaway (NYSE: BRK.A)	18.46	2.39	1.65
Everest Re Group Ltd (NYSE: RE)	11.91	1.34	1.30
FPL Group, Inc. (NYSE: FPL)	15.80	1.04	1.70
Johnson Controls, Inc. (NYSE: JCI)	14.24	0.40	2.13
Tenneco Automotive, Inc. (NYSE: TEN)	6.44	0.07	41.31

Source: www.multexinvestor.com.

---

[1] In particular, diluted EPS is for continuing operations and before extraordinary items and accounting changes.

Based only on the information in the above table, calculate the following for the portfolio:

A. i. Arithmetic mean P/E
    ii. Median P/E
B. i. Arithmetic mean P/S
    ii. Median P/S
C. i. Arithmetic mean P/B
    ii. Median P/B
D. Based on your answers to Parts A, B, and C, characterize the appropriateness of using the following valuation measures:

    i. Mean and median P/E
    ii. Mean and median P/S
    iii. Mean and median P/B

16. The table below gives statistics relating to a hypothetical 10-year record of two portfolios.

	Mean Annual Return	Standard Deviation of Return	Skewness
Portfolio A	8.3%	19.5%	−1.9
Portfolio B	8.3%	18.0%	3.0

Based only on the information in the above table, perform the following:

A. Contrast the distributions of returns of Portfolios A and B.
B. Evaluate the relative attractiveness of Portfolios A and B.

17. The table below gives statistics relating to a hypothetical three-year record of two portfolios.

	Mean Monthly Return	Standard Deviation	Skewness	Excess Kurtosis
Portfolio A	1.1994%	5.5461%	−2.2603	6.2584
Portfolio B	1.1994%	6.4011%	−2.2603	8.0497

Based only on the information in the above table, perform the following:

A. Contrast the distributions of returns of Portfolios A and B.
B. Evaluate the relative attractiveness of Portfolios A and B.

18. The table below gives statistics relating to a hypothetical five-year record of two portfolios.

	Mean Monthly Return	Standard Deviation	Skewness	Excess Kurtosis
Portfolio A	1.6792%	5.3086%	−0.1395	−0.0187
Portfolio B	1.8375%	5.9047%	0.4934	−0.8525

Based only on the information in the above table, perform the following:

A. Contrast the distributions of returns of Portfolios A and B.
B. Evaluate the relative attractiveness of Portfolios A and B.

19. At the UXI Foundation, portfolio managers are normally kept on only if their annual rate of return meets or exceeds the mean annual return for portfolio managers of a similar investment style. Recently, the UXI Foundation has also been considering two other evaluation criteria: the median annual return of funds with the same investment style, and two-thirds of the return performance of the top fund with the same investment style. The table below gives the returns for nine funds with the same investment style as the UXI Foundation.

Fund	Return
1	17.8%
2	21.0%
3	38.0%
4	19.2%
5	2.5%
6	24.3%
7	18.7%
8	16.9%
9	12.6%

With the above distribution of fund performance, which of the three evaluation criteria is the most difficult to achieve?

CHAPTER 4

PROBABILITY CONCEPTS

LEARNING OUTCOMES

After reading chapter 4, you should be able to do the following:

- Define a random variable, an outcome, an event, mutually exclusive events, and exhaustive events.
- Explain the two defining properties of probability.
- Distinguish among empirical, subjective, and a priori probabilities.
- State the probability of an event in terms of odds for or against the event.
- Describe the investment consequences of probabilities that are mutually inconsistent.
- Distinguish between unconditional and conditional probabilities.
- Define a joint probability.
- Calculate, using the multiplication rule, the joint probability of two events.
- Calculate, using the addition rule, the probability that at least one of two events will occur.
- Distinguish between dependent and independent events.
- Calculate a joint probability of any number of independent events.
- Calculate, using the total probability rule, an unconditional probability.
- Define, calculate, and interpret expected value, variance, and standard deviation.
- Explain the use of conditional expectation in investment applications.
- Calculate an expected value using the total probability rule for expected value.
- Diagram an investment problem, using a tree diagram.
- Define, calculate, and interpret covariance and correlation.
- Calculate the expected return, variance of return, and standard deviation of return on a portfolio.
- Calculate covariance, given a joint probability function.
- Calculate an updated probability, using Bayes' formula.
- Calculate the number of ways a specified number of tasks can be performed, using the multiplication rule of counting.
- Solve counting problems using the factorial, combination, and permutation notations.
- Calculate the number of ways to choose r objects from a total of n objects when the order in which the r objects are listed matters, and calculate the number of ways to do so when the order does not matter.
- Identify which counting method is appropriate to solve a particular counting problem.

SUMMARY OVERVIEW

In chapter 4, we have discussed the essential concepts and tools of probability. We have applied probability, expected value, and variance to a range of investment problems.

- A random variable is a quantity whose outcome is uncertain.
- Probability is a number between 0 and 1 that describes the chance that a stated event will occur.
- An event is a specified set of outcomes of a random variable.
- Mutually exclusive events can occur only one at a time. Exhaustive events cover or contain all possible outcomes.
- The two defining properties of a probability are, first, that $0 \leq P(E) \leq 1$ (where $P(E)$ denotes the probability of an event E), and second, that the sum of the probabilities of any set of mutually exclusive and exhaustive events equals 1.
- A probability estimated from data as a relative frequency of occurrence is an empirical probability. A probability drawing on personal or subjective judgment is a subjective probability. A probability obtained based on logical analysis is an a priori probability.
- A probability of an event E, $P(E)$, can be stated as odds for $E = P(E)/[1 - P(E)]$ or odds against $E = [1 - P(E)]/P(E)$.
- Probabilities that are inconsistent create profit opportunities, according to the Dutch Book Theorem.
- A probability of an event *not* conditioned on another event is an unconditional probability. The unconditional probability of an event A is denoted $P(A)$. Unconditional probabilities are also called marginal probabilities.
- A probability of an event given (conditioned on) another event is a conditional probability. The probability of an event A given an event B is denoted $P(A \mid B)$.
- The probability of both A and B occurring is the joint probability of A and B, denoted $P(AB)$.
- $P(A \mid B) = P(AB)/P(B)$, $P(B) \neq 0$.
- The multiplication rule for probabilities is $P(AB) = P(A \mid B)P(B)$.
- The probability that A or B occurs, or both occur, is denoted by $P(A \text{ or } B)$.
- The addition rule for probabilities is $P(A \text{ or } B) = P(A) + P(B) - P(AB)$.
- When events are independent, the occurrence of one event does not affect the probability of occurrence of the other event. Otherwise, the events are dependent.
- The multiplication rule for independent events states that if A and B are independent events, $P(AB) = P(A)P(B)$. The rule generalizes in similar fashion to more than two events.
- According to the total probability rule, if $S_1, S_2, \ldots, S_n$ are mutually exclusive and exhaustive scenarios or events, then $P(A) = P(A \mid S_1)P(S_1) + P(A \mid S_2)P(S_2) + \cdots + P(A \mid S_n)P(S_n)$.
- The expected value of a random variable is a probability-weighted average of the possible outcomes of the random variable. For a random variable X, the expected value of X is denoted $E(X)$.
- The total probability rule for expected value states that $E(X) = E(X|S_1)P(S_1) + E(X|S_2)P(S_2) + \cdots + E(X|S_n)P(S_n)$, where $S_1, S_2, \ldots, S_n$ are mutually exclusive and exhaustive scenarios or events.
- The variance of a random variable is the expected value (the probability-weighted average) of squared deviations from the random variable's expected value $E(X)$: $\sigma^2(X) = E\{[X - E(X)]^2\}$, where $\sigma^2(X)$ stands for the variance of X.
- Variance is a measure of dispersion about the mean. Increasing variance indicates increasing dispersion. Variance is measured in squared units of the original variable.
- Standard deviation is the positive square root of variance. Standard deviation measures dispersion (as does variance), but it is measured in the same units as the variable.
- Covariance is a measure of the co-movement between random variables.

- The covariance between two random variables R_i and R_j is the expected value of the cross-product of the deviations of the two random variables from their respective means: $\text{Cov}(R_i, R_j) = E\{[R_i - E(R_i)][R_j - E(R_j)]\}$. The covariance of a random variable with itself is its own variance.
- Correlation is a number between -1 and $+1$ that measures the co-movement (linear association) between two random variables: $\rho(R_i, R_j) = \text{Cov}(R_i, R_j)/[\sigma(R_i)\sigma(R_j)]$.
- To calculate the variance of return on a portfolio of n assets, the inputs needed are the n expected returns on the individual assets, n variances of return on the individual assets, and $n(n-1)/2$ distinct covariances.
- Portfolio variance of return is $\sigma^2(R_p) = \sum_{i=1}^{n} \sum_{j=1}^{n} w_i w_j \text{Cov}(R_i, R_j)$.
- The calculation of covariance in a forward-looking sense requires the specification of a joint probability function, which gives the probability of joint occurrences of values of the two random variables.
- When two random variables are independent, the joint probability function is the product of the individual probability functions of the random variables.
- Bayes' formula is a method for updating probabilities based on new information.
- Bayes' formula is expressed as follows: Updated probability of event given the new information = [(Probability of the new information given event)/(Unconditional probability of the new information)] × Prior probability of event.
- The multiplication rule of counting says, for example, that if the first step in a process can be done in 10 ways, the second step, given the first, can be done in 5 ways, and the third step, given the first two, can be done in 7 ways, then the steps can be carried out in $(10)(5)(7) = 350$ ways.
- The number of ways to assign every member of a group of size n to n slots is $n! = n(n-1)(n-2)(n-3)\ldots 1$. (By convention, $0! = 1$.)
- The number of ways that n objects can be labeled with k different labels, with n_1 of the first type, n_2 of the second type, and so on, with $n_1 + n_2 + \cdots + n_k = n$, is given by $n!/(n_1!n_2!\ldots n_k!)$ This expression is the multinomial formula.
- A special case of the multinomial formula is the combination formula. The number of ways to choose r objects from a total of n objects, when the order in which the r objects are listed does not matter, is

$$_nC_r = \binom{n}{r} = \frac{n!}{(n-r)!r!}$$

- The number of ways to choose r objects from a total of n objects, when the order in which the r objects are listed does matter, is

$$_nP_r = \frac{n!}{(n-r)!}$$

This expression is the permutation formula.

PROBLEMS

1. Define the following terms:

   A. Probability
   B. Conditional probability

    C. Event
    D. Independent events
    E. Variance

2. State three mutually exclusive and exhaustive events describing the reaction of a company's stock price to a corporate earnings announcement on the day of the announcement.
3. Label each of the following as an empirical, a priori, or subjective probability.

    A. The probability that U.S. stock returns exceed long-term corporate bond returns over a 10-year period, based on Ibbotson Associates data.
    B. An updated (posterior) probability of an event arrived at using Bayes' formula and the perceived prior probability of the event.
    C. The probability of a particular outcome when exactly 12 equally likely possible outcomes exist.
    D. A historical probability of default for double-B rated bonds, adjusted to reflect your perceptions of changes in the quality of double-B rated issuance.

4. You are comparing two companies, BestRest Corporation and Relaxin, Inc. The exports of both companies stand to benefit substantially from the removal of import restrictions on their products in a large export market. The price of BestRest shares reflects a probability of 0.90 that the restrictions will be removed within the year. The price of Relaxin stock, however, reflects a 0.50 probability that the restrictions will be removed within that time frame. By all other information related to valuation, the two stocks appear comparably valued. How would you characterize the implied probabilities reflected in share prices? Which stock is relatively overvalued compared to the other?
5. Suppose you have two limit orders outstanding on two different stocks. The probability that the first limit order executes before the close of trading is 0.45. The probability that the second limit order executes before the close of trading is 0.20. The probability that the two orders both execute before the close of trading is 0.10. What is the probability that at least one of the two limit orders executes before the close of trading?
6. Suppose that 5 percent of the stocks meeting your stock-selection criteria are in the telecommunications (telecom) industry. Also, dividend-paying telecom stocks are 1 percent of the total number of stocks meeting your selection criteria. What is the probability that a stock is dividend paying, given that it is a telecom stock that has met your stock selection criteria?
7. You are using the following three criteria to screen potential acquisition targets from a list of 500 companies:

Criterion	Fraction of the 500 Companies Meeting the Criterion
Product lines compatible	0.20
Company will increase combined sales growth rate	0.45
Balance sheet impact manageable	0.78

If the criteria are independent, how many companies will pass the screen?

8. You apply both valuation criteria and financial strength criteria in choosing stocks. The probability that a randomly selected stock (from your investment universe) meets your valuation criteria is 0.25. Given that a stock meets your valuation criteria, the probability that the stock meets your financial strength criteria is 0.40. What is the probability that a stock meets both your valuation and financial strength criteria?

9. A report from Fitch data service states the following two facts:[1]

   - In 2002, the volume of defaulted U.S. high-yield debt was $109.8 billion. The average market size of the high-yield bond market during 2002 was $669.5 billion.
   - The average recovery rate for defaulted U.S. high-yield bonds in 2002 (defined as average price one month after default) was $0.22 on the dollar.

   Address the following three tasks:

   A. On the basis of the first fact given above, calculate the default rate on U.S. high-yield debt in 2002. Interpret this default rate as a probability.
   B. State the probability computed in Part A as an odds against default.
   C. The quantity 1 minus the recovery rate given in the second fact above is the expected loss per $1 of principal value, given that default has occurred. Suppose you are told that an institution held a diversified high-yield bond portfolio in 2002. Using the information in both facts, what was the institution's expected loss in 2002, per $1 of principal value of the bond portfolio?

10. You are given the following probability distribution for the annual sales of ElStop Corporation:

    Probability Distribution for ElStop Annual Sales

Probability	Sales (millions)
0.20	$275
0.40	$250
0.25	$200
0.10	$190
0.05	$180
Sum = 1.00	

    A. Calculate the expected value of ElStop's annual sales.
    B. Calculate the variance of ElStop's annual sales.
    C. Calculate the standard deviation of ElStop's annual sales.

11. Suppose the prospects for recovering principal for a defaulted bond issue depend on which of two economic scenarios prevails. Scenario 1 has probability 0.75 and will result in recovery of $0.90 per $1 principal value with probability 0.45, or in recovery of $0.80 per $1 principal value with probability 0.55. Scenario 2 has probability 0.25 and will

---

[1]"High Yield Defaults 2002: The Perfect Storm," 19 February, 2003.

result in recovery of $0.50 per $1 principal value with probability 0.85, or in recovery of $0.40 per $1 principal value with probability 0.15.

A. Compute the probability of each of the four possible recovery amounts: $0.90, $0.80, $0.50, and $0.40.
B. Compute the expected recovery, given the first scenario.
C. Compute the expected recovery, given the second scenario.
D. Compute the expected recovery.
E. Graph the information in a tree diagram.

12. Suppose we have the expected daily returns (in terms of U.S. dollars), standard deviations, and correlations shown in the table below.

U.S., German, and Italian Bond Returns

U.S. Dollar Daily Returns in Percent		
	U.S. Bonds	German Bonds	Italian Bonds
Expected Return	0.029	0.021	0.073
Standard Deviation	0.409	0.606	0.635

Correlation Matrix		
	U.S. Bonds	German Bonds	Italian Bonds
U.S. Bonds	1	0.09	0.10
German Bonds		1	0.70
Italian Bonds			1

Source: Kool (2000), Table 1 (excerpted and adapted).

A. Using the data given above, construct a covariance matrix for the daily returns on U.S., German, and Italian bonds.
B. State the expected return and variance of return on a portfolio 70 percent invested in U.S. bonds, 20 percent in German bonds, and 10 percent in Italian bonds.
C. Calculate the standard deviation of return for the portfolio in Part B.

13. The variance of a stock portfolio depends on the variances of each individual stock in the portfolio and also the covariances among the stocks in the portfolio. If you have five stocks, how many unique covariances (excluding variances) must you use in order to compute the variance of return on your portfolio? (Recall that the covariance of a stock with itself is the stock's variance.)

14. Calculate the covariance of the returns on Bedolf Corporation (R_B) with the returns on Zedock Corporation (R_Z), using the following data.

Probability Function of Bedolf and Zedock Returns

	$R_Z = 15\%$	$R_Z = 10\%$	$R_Z = 5\%$
$R_B = 30\%$	0.25	0	0
$R_B = 15\%$	0	0.50	0
$R_B = 10\%$	0	0	0.25

Note: Entries are joint probabilities.

15. You have developed a set of criteria for evaluating distressed credits. Companies that do not receive a passing score are classed as likely to go bankrupt within 12 months. You gathered the following information when validating the criteria:

    - Forty percent of the companies to which the test is administered will go bankrupt within 12 months: $P(nonsurvivor) = 0.40$.
    - Fifty-five percent of the companies to which the test is administered pass it: $P(pass\ test) = 0.55$.
    - The probability that a company will pass the test given that it will subsequently survive 12 months, is 0.85: $P(pass\ test \mid survivor) = 0.85$.

    A. What is $P(pass\ test \mid nonsurvivor)$?
    B. Using Bayes' formula, calculate the probability that a company is a survivor, given that it passes the test; that is, calculate $P(survivor \mid pass\ test)$.
    C. What is the probability that a company is a *nonsurvivor*, given that it fails the test?
    D. Is the test effective?

16. On one day in March, 3,292 issues traded on the NYSE: 1,303 advanced, 1,764 declined, and 225 were unchanged. In how many ways could this set of outcomes have happened? (Set up the problem but do not solve it.)

17. Your firm intends to select 4 of 10 vice presidents for the investment committee. How many different groups of four are possible?

18. As in Example 4-11, you are reviewing the pricing of a speculative-grade, one-year-maturity, zero-coupon bond. Your goal is to estimate an appropriate default risk premium for this bond. The default risk premium is defined as the extra return above the risk-free return that will compensate investors for default risk. If R is the promised return (yield-to-maturity) on the debt instrument and R_F is the risk-free rate, the default risk premium is $R - R_F$. You assess that the probability that the bond defaults is 0.06: $P(the\ bond\ defaults) = 0.06$. One-year U.S. T-bills are offering a return of 5.8 percent, an estimate of R_F. In contrast to your approach in Example 4-11, you no longer make the simplifying assumption that bondholders will recover nothing in the event of a default. Rather, you now assume that recovery will be $0.35 on the dollar, given default.

    A. Denote the fraction of principal recovered in default as θ. Following the model of Example 4-11, develop a general expression for the promised return R on this bond.
    B. Given your expression for R and the estimate of R_F, state the minimum default risk premium you should require for this instrument.

CHAPTER 5

COMMON PROBABILITY DISTRIBUTIONS

LEARNING OUTCOMES

After reading chapter 5, you should be able to do the following:

- Define and explain a probability distribution.
- Distinguish between and give examples of discrete and continuous random variables.
- Describe the set of possible outcomes of a specified random variable.
- Define a probability function, state its two key properties, and determine whether a given function satisfies those properties.
- Define a probability density function.
- Define a cumulative distribution function and calculate probabilities for a random variable, given its cumulative distribution function.
- Define a discrete uniform random variable and calculate probabilities, given a discrete uniform distribution.
- Define a binomial random variable and calculate probabilities, given a binomial distribution.
- Calculate the expected value and variance of a binomial random variable.
- Construct a binomial tree to describe stock price movement.
- Describe the continuous uniform distribution and calculate probabilities, given a continuous uniform distribution.
- Explain the key properties of the normal distribution.
- Distinguish between a univariate and a multivariate distribution.
- Explain the role of correlation in the multivariate normal distribution.
- Construct and explain confidence intervals for a normally distributed random variable.
- Define the standard normal distribution and explain how to standardize a normal random variable.
- Calculate probabilities using the standard normal distribution.
- Define shortfall risk.
- Calculate the safety-first ratio and select an optimal portfolio using Roy's safety-first criterion.
- Explain the relationship between the lognormal and normal distributions.
- Explain the use of the lognormal distribution in modeling asset prices.
- Distinguish between discretely and continuously compounded rates of return.
- Calculate the continuously compounded rate of return, given a specific holding period return.

- Explain Monte Carlo simulation and historical simulation and describe their major applications and limitations.

SUMMARY OVERVIEW

In chapter 5, we have presented the most frequently used probability distributions in investment analysis and the Monte Carlo simulation.

- A probability distribution specifies the probabilities of the possible outcomes of a random variable.
- The two basic types of random variables are discrete random variables and continuous random variables. Discrete random variables take on at most a countable number of possible outcomes that we can list as $x_1, x_2, \ldots$. In contrast, we cannot describe the possible outcomes of a continuous random variable Z with a list $z_1, z_2, \ldots$ because the outcome $(z_1 + z_2)/2$, not in the list, would always be possible.
- The probability function specifies the probability that the random variable will take on a specific value. The probability function is denoted $p(x)$ for a discrete random variable and $f(x)$ for a continuous random variable. For any probability function $p(x)$, $0 \leq p(x) \leq 1$, and the sum of $p(x)$ over all values of X equals 1.
- The cumulative distribution function, denoted $F(x)$ for both continuous and discrete random variables, gives the probability that the random variable is less than or equal to x.
- The discrete uniform and the continuous uniform distributions are the distributions of equally likely outcomes.
- The binomial random variable is defined as the number of successes in n Bernoulli trials, where the probability of success, p, is constant for all trials and the trials are independent. A Bernoulli trial is an experiment with two outcomes, which can represent success or failure, an up move or a down move, or another binary (two-fold) outcome.
- A binomial random variable has an expected value or mean equal to np and variance equal to $np(1 - p)$.
- A binomial tree is the graphical representation of a model of asset price dynamics in which, at each period, the asset moves up with probability p or down with probability $(1 - p)$. The binomial tree is a flexible method for modeling asset price movement and is widely used in pricing options.
- The normal distribution is a continuous symmetric probability distribution that is completely described by two parameters: its mean, μ, and its variance, σ^2.
- A univariate distribution specifies the probabilities for a single random variable. A multivariate distribution specifies the probabilities for a group of related random variables.
- To specify the normal distribution for a portfolio when its component securities are normally distributed, we need the means, standard deviations, and all the distinct pairwise correlations of the securities. When we have those statistics, we have also specified a multivariate normal distribution for the securities.
- For a normal random variable, approximately 68 percent of all possible outcomes are within a one standard deviation interval about the mean, approximately 95 percent are within a two standard deviation interval about the mean, and approximately 99 percent are within a three standard deviation interval about the mean.
- A normal random variable, X, is standardized using the expression $Z = (X - \mu)/\sigma$, where μ and σ are the mean and standard deviation of X. Generally, we use the sample mean $\overline{X}$ as an estimate of μ and the sample standard deviation s as an estimate of σ in this expression.

- The standard normal random variable, denoted Z, has a mean equal to 0 and variance equal to 1. All questions about any normal random variable can be answered by referring to the cumulative distribution function of a standard normal random variable, denoted $N(x)$ or $N(z)$.
- Shortfall risk is the risk that portfolio value will fall below some minimum acceptable level over some time horizon.
- Roy's safety-first criterion, addressing shortfall risk, asserts that the optimal portfolio is the one that minimizes the probability that portfolio return falls below a threshold level. According to Roy's safety-first criterion, if returns are normally distributed, the safety-first optimal portfolio P is the one that maximizes the quantity $[E(R_P) - R_L]/\sigma_P$, where R_L is the minimum acceptable level of return.
- A random variable follows a lognormal distribution if the natural logarithm of the random variable is normally distributed. The lognormal distribution is defined in terms of the mean and variance of its associated normal distribution. The lognormal distribution is bounded below by 0 and skewed to the right (it has a long right tail).
- The lognormal distribution is frequently used to model the probability distribution of asset prices because it is bounded below by zero.
- Continuous compounding views time as essentially continuous or unbroken; discrete compounding views time as advancing in discrete finite intervals.
- The continuously compounded return associated with a holding period is the natural log of 1 plus the holding period return, or equivalently, the natural log of ending price over beginning price.
- If continuously compounded returns are normally distributed, asset prices are lognormally distributed. This relationship is used to move back and forth between the distributions for return and price. Because of the central limit theorem, continuously compounded returns need not be normally distributed for asset prices to be reasonably well described by a lognormal distribution.
- Monte Carlo simulation involves the use of a computer to represent the operation of a complex financial system. A characteristic feature of Monte Carlo simulation is the generation of a large number of random samples from specified probability distribution(s) to represent the operation of risk in the system. Monte Carlo simulation is used in planning, in financial risk management, and in valuing complex securities. Monte Carlo simulation is a complement to analytical methods but provides only statistical estimates, not exact results.
- Historical simulation is an established alternative to Monte Carlo simulation that in one implementation involves repeated sampling from a historical data series. Historical simulation is grounded in actual data but can reflect only risks represented in the sample historical data. Compared with Monte Carlo simulation, historical simulation does not lend itself to "what if" analyses.

PROBLEMS

1. A European put option on stock conveys the right to sell the stock at a prespecified price, called the exercise price, at the maturity date of the option. The value of this put at maturity is (Exercise price − Stock price) or $0, whichever is greater. Suppose the exercise price is $100 and the underlying stock trades in ticks of $0.01. At any time before maturity, the terminal value of the put is a random variable.

A. Describe the distinct possible outcomes for terminal put value. (Think of the put's maximum and minimum values and its minimum price increments.)

B. Is terminal put value, at a time before maturity, a discrete or continuous random variable?

C. Letting Y stand for terminal put value, express in standard notation the probability that terminal put value is less than or equal to $24. No calculations or formulas are necessary.

2. Suppose X, Y, and Z are discrete random variables with these sets of possible outcomes: $X = \{2, 2.5, 3\}$, $Y = \{0, 1, 2, 3\}$, and $Z = \{10, 11, 12\}$. For each of the functions $f(X)$, $g(Y)$, and $h(Z)$, state whether the function satisfies the conditions for a probability function.

A. $f(2) = -0.01$ $f(2.5) = -0.50$ $f(3) = -0.51$

B. $g(0) = 0.25$ $g(1) = 0.50$ $g(2) = 0.125$ $g(3) = 0.125$

C. $h(10) = 0.35$ $h(11) = 0.15$ $h(12) = 0.52$

3. Define the term "binomial random variable." Describe the types of problems for which the binomial distribution is used.

4. Over the last 10 years, a company's annual earnings increased year over year seven times and decreased year over year three times. You decide to model the number of earnings increases for the next decade as a binomial random variable.

A. What is your estimate of the probability of success, defined as an increase in annual earnings?

For Parts B, C, and D of this problem, assume the estimated probability is the actual probability for the next decade.

B. What is the probability that earnings will increase in exactly 5 of the next 10 years?

C. Calculate the expected number of yearly earnings increases during the next 10 years.

D. Calculate the variance and standard deviation of the number of yearly earnings increases during the next 10 years.

E. The expression for the probability function of a binomial random variable depends on two major assumptions. In the context of this problem, what must you assume about annual earnings increases to apply the binomial distribution in Part B? What reservations might you have about the validity of these assumptions?

5. You are examining the record of an investment newsletter writer who claims a 70 percent success rate in making investment recommendations that are profitable over a one-year time horizon. You have the one-year record of the newsletter's seven most recent recommendations. Four of those recommendations were profitable. If all the recommendations are independent and the newsletter writer's skill is as claimed, what is the probability of observing four or fewer profitable recommendations out of seven in total?

6. By definition, a down-and-out call option on stock becomes worthless and terminates if the price of the underlying stock moves down and touches a prespecified point during the life of the call. If the prespecified level is $75, for example, the call expires worthless if and when the stock price falls to $75. Describe, without a diagram, how a binomial tree can be used to value a down-and-out call option.

7. You are forecasting sales for a company in the fourth quarter of its fiscal year. Your low-end estimate of sales is €14 million, and your high-end estimate is €15 million. You decide to treat all outcomes for sales between these two values as equally likely, using a continuous uniform distribution.

   A. What is the expected value of sales for the fourth quarter?
   B. What is the probability that fourth-quarter sales will be less than or equal to €14, 125, 000?

8. State the approximate probability that a normal random variable will fall within the following intervals:

   A. Mean plus or minus one standard deviation
   B. Mean plus or minus two standard deviations
   C. Mean plus or minus three standard deviations

9. You are evaluating a diversified equity portfolio. The portfolio's mean monthly return is 0.56 percent, and its standard deviation of monthly returns is 8.86 percent.

   A. Calculate a one standard deviation confidence interval for the return on this portfolio. Interpret this interval, with a normality assumption for returns.
   B. Calculate an exact 95 percent confidence interval for portfolio return, assuming portfolio returns are described by a normal distribution.
   C. Calculate an exact 99 percent confidence interval for portfolio return, assuming portfolio returns are described by a normal distribution.

10. Find the area under the normal curve up to $z = 0.36$; that is, find $P(Z \leq 0.36)$. Interpret this value.

11. In futures markets, profits or losses on contracts are settled at the end of each trading day. This procedure is called marking to market or daily resettlement. By preventing a trader's losses from accumulating over many days, marking to market reduces the risk that traders will default on their obligations. A futures markets trader needs a liquidity pool to meet the daily mark to market. If liquidity is exhausted, the trader may be forced to unwind his position at an unfavorable time.

    Suppose you are using financial futures contracts to hedge a risk in your portfolio. You have a liquidity pool (cash and cash equivalents) of λ dollars per contract and a time horizon of T trading days. For a given size liquidity pool, λ, Kolb, Gay, and Hunter (1985) developed an expression for the probability stating that you will exhaust your liquidity pool within a T-day horizon as a result of the daily mark to market. Kolb et al. assumed that the expected change in futures price is 0 and that futures price changes are normally distributed. With σ representing the standard deviation of daily futures price changes, the standard deviation of price changes over a time horizon to day T is $\sigma\sqrt{T}$, given continuous compounding. With that background, the Kolb et al. expression is

$$\text{Probability of exhausting liquidity pool} = 2[1 - N(x)]$$

where $x = \lambda/(\sigma\sqrt{T})$. Here x is a standardized value of λ. $N(x)$ is the standard normal cumulative distribution function. For some intuition about $1 - N(x)$ in the expression, note that the liquidity pool is exhausted if losses exceed the size of the liquidity pool at any time up to and including T; the probability of that event happening can be shown to be proportional to an area in the right tail of a standard normal distribution, $1 - N(x)$.

Using the Kolb et al. expression, answer the following questions:

A. Your hedging horizon is five days, and your liquidity pool is $2,000 per contract. You estimate that the standard deviation of daily price changes for the contract is $450. What is the probability that you will exhaust your liquidity pool in the five-day period?

B. Suppose your hedging horizon is 20 days, but all the other facts given in Part A remain the same. What is the probability that you will exhaust your liquidity pool in the 20-day period?

Use the information and table below to solve Problems 12 through 14.

As reported by Liang (1999), U.S. equity funds in three style categories had the following mean monthly returns, standard deviations of return, and Sharpe ratios during the period January 1994 to December 1996:

Strategy	January 1994 to December 1996		
	Mean Return	Standard Deviation	Sharpe Ratio
Large-cap growth	1.15%	2.89%	0.26
Large-cap value	1.08%	2.20%	0.31
Large-cap blend	1.07%	2.38%	0.28

Source: Liang (1999), Table 5 (excerpt).

12. Basing your estimate of future-period monthly return parameters on the sample mean and standard deviation for the period January 1994 to December 1996, construct a 90 percent confidence interval for the monthly return on a large-cap blend fund. Assume fund returns are normally distributed.

13. Basing your estimate of future-period monthly return parameters on the sample mean and standard deviation for the period January 1994 to December 1996, calculate the probability that a large-cap growth fund will earn a monthly return of 0 percent or less. Assume fund returns are normally distributed.

14. Assuming fund returns are normally distributed, which fund category minimized the probability of earning less than the risk-free rate for the period January 1994 to December 1996?

15. A client has a portfolio of common stocks and fixed-income instruments with a current value of £1,350,000. She intends to liquidate £50,000 from the portfolio at the end of the year to purchase a partnership share in a business. Furthermore, the client would like to be able to withdraw the £50,000 without reducing the initial capital of £1,350,000. The following table shows four alternative asset allocations.

Mean and Standard Deviation for Four Allocations (in percent)

	A	B	C	D
Expected annual return	16	12	10	9
Standard deviation of return	24	17	12	11

Address the following questions (assume normality for Parts B and C):

A. Given the client's desire not to invade the £1, 350, 000 principal, what is the shortfall level, R_L? Use this shortfall level to answer Part B.

B. According to the safety-first criterion, which of the three allocations is the best?

C. What is the probability that the return on the safety-first optimal portfolio will be less than the shortfall level, R_L?

16. A. Describe two important characteristics of the lognormal distribution.

B. Compared with the normal distribution, why is the lognormal distribution a more reasonable model for the distribution of asset prices?

C. What are the two parameters of a lognormal distribution?

17. The basic calculation for volatility (denoted σ) as used in option pricing is the annualized standard deviation of continuously compounded daily returns. Calculate volatility for Dollar General Corporation (NYSE: DG) based on its closing prices for two weeks, given in the table below. (Annualize based on 250 days in a year.)

**Dollar General Corporation
Daily Closing Stock Price**

Date	Closing Price
27 January 2003	$10.68
28 January 2003	$10.87
29 January 2003	$11.00
30 January 2003	$10.95
31 January 2003	$11.26
3 February 2003	$11.31
4 February 2003	$11.23
5 February 2003	$10.91
6 February 2003	$10.80
7 February 2003	$10.47

Source: http://finance.yahoo.com.

18. A. Define Monte Carlo simulation and explain its use in finance.

B. Compared with analytical methods, what are the strengths and weaknesses of Monte Carlo simulation for use in valuing securities?

19. A standard lookback call option on stock has a value at maturity equal to (Value of the stock at maturity − Minimum value of stock during the life of the option prior to maturity) or $0, whichever is greater. If the minimum value reached prior to maturity was $20.11 and the value of the stock at maturity is $23, for example, the call is worth $23 − $20.11 = $2.89. Briefly discuss how you might use Monte Carlo simulation in valuing a lookback call option.

CHAPTER 6

SAMPLING AND ESTIMATION

LEARNING OUTCOMES

After reading chapter 6, you should able to do the following:

- Define simple random sampling.
- Define and interpret sampling error.
- Define a sampling distribution.
- Distinguish between simple random and stratified random sampling.
- Distinguish between time-series and cross-sectional data.
- State the central limit theorem and describe its importance.
- Calculate and interpret the standard error of the sample mean.
- Distinguish between a point estimate and a confidence interval estimate of a population parameter.
- Identify and describe the desirable properties of an estimator.
- Explain the construction of confidence intervals.
- Describe the properties of Student's *t*-distribution.
- Calculate and explain degrees of freedom.
- Calculate and interpret a confidence interval for a population mean when sampling from a normal distribution with (1) a known population variance, (2) an unknown population variance, or (3) when sampling from a population with an unknown variance and the sample size is large.
- Discuss the issues surrounding selection of the appropriate sample size.
- Define and discuss data-mining bias.
- Define and discuss sample selection bias, survivorship bias, look-ahead bias, and time-period bias.

SUMMARY OVERVIEW

In chapter 6, we have presented basic concepts and results in sampling and estimation. We have also emphasized the challenges faced by analysts in appropriately using and interpreting financial data. As analysts, we should always use a critical eye when evaluating the results from any study. The quality of the sample is of the utmost importance: If the sample is biased, the conclusions drawn from the sample will be in error.

- To draw valid inferences from a sample, the sample should be random.
- In simple random sampling, each observation has an equal chance of being selected. In stratified random sampling, the population is divided into subpopulations, called strata or cells, based on one or more classification criteria; simple random samples are then drawn from each stratum.
- Stratified random sampling ensures that population subdivisions of interest are represented in the sample. Stratified random sampling also produces more-precise parameter estimates than simple random sampling.
- Time-series data are a collection of observations at equally spaced intervals of time. Cross-sectional data are observations that represent individuals, groups, geographical regions, or companies at a single point in time.
- The central limit theorem states that for large sample sizes, for any underlying distribution for a random variable, the sampling distribution of the sample mean for that variable will be approximately normal, with mean equal to the population mean for that random variable and variance equal to the population variance of the variable divided by sample size.
- Based on the central limit theorem, when the sample size is large, we can compute confidence intervals for the population mean based on the normal distribution regardless of the distribution of the underlying population. In general, a sample size of 30 or larger can be considered large.
- An estimator is a formula for estimating a parameter. An estimate is a particular value that we calculate from a sample by using an estimator.
- Because an estimator or statistic is a random variable, it is described by some probability distribution. We refer to the distribution of an estimator as its sampling distribution. The standard deviation of the sampling distribution of the sample mean is called the standard error of the sample mean.
- The desirable properties of an estimator are unbiasedness (the expected value of the estimator equals the population parameter), efficiency (the estimator has the smallest variance), and consistency (the probability of accurate estimates increases as sample size increases).
- The two types of estimates of a parameter are point estimates and interval estimates. A point estimate is a single number that we use to estimate a parameter. An interval estimate is a range of values that brackets the population parameter with some probability.
- A confidence interval is an interval for which we can assert with a given probability $1 - \alpha$, called the degree of confidence, that it will contain the parameter it is intended to estimate. This measure is often referred to as the $(1 - \alpha)\%$ confidence interval for the parameter.
- A $(1 - \alpha)\%$ confidence interval for a parameter has the following structure: Point estimate $\pm$ Reliability factor $\times$ Standard error, where the reliability factor is a number based on the assumed distribution of the point estimate and the degree of confidence $(1 - \alpha)$ for the confidence interval and where standard error is the standard error of the sample statistic providing the point estimate.
- A $(1 - \alpha)\%$ confidence interval for population mean μ when sampling from a normal distribution with known variance σ^2 is given by $\overline{X} \pm z_{\alpha/2}(\sigma/\sqrt{n})$, where $z_{\alpha/2}$ is the point of the standard normal distribution such that $\alpha/2$ remains in the right tail.
- Student's t-distribution is a family of symmetrical distributions defined by a single parameter, degrees of freedom.
- A random sample of size n is said to have $n - 1$ degrees of freedom for estimating the population variance, in the sense that there are only $n - 1$ independent deviations from the mean on which to base the estimate.
- The degrees of freedom number for use with the t-distribution is also $n - 1$.

- The t-distribution has fatter tails than the standard normal distribution but converges to the standard normal distribution as degrees of freedom go to infinity.
- A $(1 - \alpha)$% confidence interval for the population mean μ when sampling from a normal distribution with unknown variance (a t-distribution confidence interval) is given by $\overline{X} \pm t_{\alpha/2}(s/\sqrt{n})$, where $t_{\alpha/2}$ is the point of the t-distribution such that $\alpha/2$ remains in the right tail and s is the sample standard deviation. This confidence interval can also be used, because of the central limit theorem, when dealing with a large sample from a population with unknown variance that may not be normal.
- We may use the confidence interval $\overline{X} \pm z_{\alpha/2}(s/\sqrt{n})$ as an alternative to the t-distribution confidence interval for the population mean when using a large sample from a population with unknown variance. The confidence interval based on the z-statistic is less conservative (narrower) than the corresponding confidence interval based on a t-distribution.
- Three issues in the selection of sample size are the need for precision, the risk of sampling from more than one population, and the expenses of different sample sizes.
- Sample data in investments can have a variety of problems. Survivorship bias occurs if companies are excluded from the analysis because they have gone out of business or because of reasons related to poor performance. Data-mining bias comes from finding models by repeatedly searching through databases for patterns. Look-ahead bias exists if the model uses data not available to market participants at the time the market participants act in the model. Finally, time-period bias is present if the time period used makes the results time-period specific or if the time period used includes a point of structural change.

PROBLEMS

1. Peter Biggs wants to know how growth managers performed last year. Biggs assumes that the population cross-sectional standard deviation of growth manager returns is 6 percent and that the returns are independent across managers.

   A. How large a random sample does Biggs need if he wants the standard deviation of the sample means to be 1 percent?
   B. How large a random sample does Biggs need if he wants the standard deviation of the sample means to be 0.25 percent?

2. Petra Munzi wants to know how value managers performed last year. Munzi assumes that the population cross-sectional standard deviation of value manager returns is 4 percent and that the returns are independent across managers.

   A. Munzi wants to build a 95 percent confidence interval for the mean return. How large a random sample does Munzi need if she wants the 95 percent confidence interval to have a total width of 1 percent?
   B. Munzi expects a cost of about $10 to collect each observation. If she has a $1,000 budget, will she be able to construct the confidence interval she wants?

3. Assume that the equity risk premium is normally distributed with a population mean of 6 percent and a population standard deviation of 18 percent. Over the last four years, equity returns (relative to the risk-free rate) have averaged -2.0 percent. You have a large client who is very upset and claims that results this poor should *never* occur. Evaluate your client's concerns.

A. Construct a 95 percent confidence interval for the population mean for a sample of four-year returns.

B. What is the probability of the -2.0 percent returns over a four-year period?

4. Compare the standard normal distribution and Student's t-distribution.
5. Find the reliability factors based on the t-distribution for the following confidence intervals for the population mean (df = degrees of freedom, n = sample size):

A. A 99 percent confidence interval, df = 20
B. A 90 percent confidence interval, df = 20
C. A 95 percent confidence interval, $n = 25$
D. A 95 percent confidence interval, $n = 16$

6. Assume that monthly returns are normally distributed with a mean of 1 percent and a sample standard deviation of 4 percent. The population standard deviation is unknown. Construct a 95 percent confidence interval for the sample mean of monthly returns if the sample size is 24.

7. Ten analysts have given the following fiscal year earnings forecasts for a stock:

Forecast (X_i)	Number of Analysts (n_i)
1.40	1
1.43	1
1.44	3
1.45	2
1.47	1
1.48	1
1.50	1

Because the sample is a small fraction of the number of analysts who follow this stock, assume that we can ignore the finite population correction factor. Assume that the analyst forecasts are normally distributed.

A. What are the mean forecast and standard deviation of forecasts?
B. Provide a 95 percent confidence interval for the population mean of the forecasts.

8. Thirteen analysts have given the following fiscal-year earnings forecasts for a stock:

Forecast (X_i)	Number of Analysts (n_i)
0.70	2
0.72	4
0.74	1
0.75	3
0.76	1
0.77	1
0.82	1

Because the sample is a small fraction of the number of analysts who follow this stock, assume that we can ignore the finite population correction factor.

  A. What are the mean forecast and standard deviation of forecasts?

  B. What aspect of the data makes us uncomfortable about using t-tables to construct confidence intervals for the population mean forecast?

9. Explain the differences between constructing a confidence interval when sampling from a normal population with a known population variance and sampling from a normal population with an unknown variance.

10. An exchange rate has a given expected future value and standard deviation.

  A. Assuming that the exchange rate is normally distributed, what are the probabilities that the exchange rate will be at least 1, 2, or 3 standard deviations away from its mean?

  B. Assume that you do not know the distribution of exchange rates. Use Chebyshev's inequality (that at least $1 - 1/k^2$ proportion of the observations will be within k standard deviations of the mean for any positive integer k greater than 1) to calculate the maximum probabilities that the exchange rate will be at least 1, 2, or 3 standard deviations away from its mean.

11. Although he knows security returns are not independent, a colleague makes the claim that because of the central limit theorem, if we diversify across a large number of investments, the portfolio standard deviation will eventually approach zero as n becomes large. Is he correct?

12. Why is the central limit theorem important?

13. What is wrong with the following statement of the central limit theorem?

> ***Central Limit Theorem.*** "If the random variables $X_1, X_2, X_3, \ldots, X_n$ are a random sample of size n from any distribution with finite mean μ and variance σ^2, then the distribution of $\overline{X}$ will be approximately normal, with a standard deviation of $\sigma/\sqrt{n}$."

14. Suppose we take a random sample of 30 companies in an industry with 200 companies. We calculate the sample mean of the ratio of cash flow to total debt for the prior year. We find that this ratio is 23 percent. Subsequently, we learn that the population cash flow to total debt ratio (taking account of all 200 companies) is 26 percent. What is the explanation for the discrepancy between the sample mean of 23 percent and the population mean of 26 percent?

  A. Sampling error

  B. Bias

  C. A lack of consistency

  D. A lack of efficiency

15. Alcorn Mutual Funds is placing large advertisements in several financial publications. The advertisements prominently display the returns of 5 of Alcorn's 30 funds for the past 1-, 3-, 5-, and 10-year periods. The results are indeed impressive, with all of the funds beating the major market indexes and a few beating them by a large margin. Is the Alcorn family of funds superior to its competitors?

16. A pension plan executive says, "One hundred percent of our portfolio managers are hired because they have above-average performance records relative to their benchmarks. We do not keep portfolio managers who have below-average records. And yet, each year about half of our managers beat their benchmarks and about half do not. What is going on?" Give a possible statistical explanation.

17. Julius Spence has tested several predictive models in order to identify undervalued stocks. Spence used about 30 company-specific variables and 10 market-related variables to predict returns for about 5,000 North American and European stocks. He found that a final model using eight variables applied to telecommunications and computer stocks yields spectacular results. Spence wants you to use the model to select investments. Should you? What steps would you take to evaluate the model?

18. Hand Associates manages two portfolios that are meant to closely track the returns of two stock indexes. One index is a value-weighted index of 500 stocks in which the weight for each stock depends on the stock's total market value. The other index is an equal-weighted index of 500 stocks in which the weight for each stock is 1/500. Hand Associates invests in only about 50 to 100 stocks in each portfolio in order to control transactions costs. Should Hand use simple random sampling or stratified random sampling to choose the stocks in each portfolio?

19. Give an example of each of the following:

    A. Sample-selection bias
    B. Look-ahead bias
    C. Time-period bias

20. What are some of the desirable statistical properties of an estimator, such as a sample mean?

CHAPTER 7

HYPOTHESIS TESTING

LEARNING OUTCOMES

After reading chapter 7, you should be able to do the following:

- Define a hypothesis and describe the steps of hypothesis testing.
- Define and interpret the null hypothesis and alternative hypothesis.
- Distinguish between one-tailed and two-tailed tests of hypotheses.
- Discuss the choice of the null and alternative hypotheses.
- Define and interpret a test statistic.
- Define and interpret a Type I error and a Type II error.
- Define and interpret a significance level and explain how significance levels are used in hypothesis testing.
- Discuss how the choice of significance level affects the probabilities of Type I and Type II errors.
- Define the power of a test.
- Define and interpret a decision rule.
- Explain the relation between confidence intervals and hypothesis tests.
- Distinguish between a statistical decision and an economic decision.
- Discuss the *p*-value approach to hypothesis testing.
- Identify the appropriate test statistic and interpret the results for a hypothesis test concerning the population mean of a normally distributed population with (1) known or (2) unknown variance.
- Formulate a null and an alternative hypothesis about a population mean and determine whether to reject the null hypothesis at a given level of significance.
- Discuss the choice between tests of differences between means and tests of mean differences (paired comparisons test) in relation to the independence of samples.
- Identify the appropriate test statistic and interpret the results for a hypothesis test concerning the equality of two population means of two normally distributed populations, based on independent random samples, with (1) equal or (2) unequal assumed variances.
- Formulate a null and an alternative hypothesis about the equality of two population means (normally distributed populations, independent samples), select the appropriate test statistic, and determine whether to reject the null hypothesis at a given level of significance.
- Identify the appropriate test statistic and interpret the results for a hypothesis test concerning the mean difference between two normally distributed populations (paired comparisons test).

- Formulate a null and an alternative hypothesis about the mean difference between two normally distributed populations (paired comparisons test), select the appropriate test statistic, and determine whether to reject the null hypothesis at a given level of significance.
- Identify the appropriate test statistic and interpret the results for a hypothesis test concerning the variance of a normally distributed population.
- Identify the appropriate test statistic and interpret the results for a hypothesis test concerning the equality of the variance of two normally distributed populations, based on two independent random samples.
- Formulate a null and an alternative hypothesis about the equality of the variances of two populations (normally distributed populations, independent samples), select the appropriate test statistic, and determine whether to reject the null hypothesis at a given level of significance.
- Distinguish between parametric and nonparametric tests and describe the situations in which the use of nonparametric tests may be appropriate.
- Explain the use of the Spearman rank correlation coefficient in a test that the correlation between two variables is zero.

SUMMARY OVERVIEW

In chapter 7, we have presented the concepts and methods of statistical inference and hypothesis testing.

- A hypothesis is a statement about one or more populations.
- The steps in testing a hypothesis are as follows:
  1. Stating the hypotheses.
  2. Identifying the appropriate test statistic and its probability distribution.
  3. Specifying the significance level.
  4. Stating the decision rule.
  5. Collecting the data and calculating the test statistic.
  6. Making the statistical decision.
  7. Making the economic or investment decision.
- We state two hypotheses: The null hypothesis is the hypothesis to be tested; the alternative hypothesis is the hypothesis accepted when the null hypothesis is rejected.
- There are three ways to formulate hypotheses:
  1. $H_0: \theta = \theta_0$ versus $H_a: \theta \neq \theta_0$
  2. $H_0: \theta \leq \theta_0$ versus $H_a: \theta > \theta_0$
  3. $H_0: \theta \geq \theta_0$ versus $H_a: \theta < \theta_0$

  where θ_0 is a hypothesized value of the population parameter and θ is the true value of the population parameter. In the above, Formulation 1 is a two-sided test and Formulations 2 and 3 are one-sided tests.
- When we have a "suspected" or "hoped for" condition for which we want to find supportive evidence, we frequently set up that condition as the alternative hypothesis and use a one-sided test. To emphasize a neutral attitude, however, the researcher may select a "not equal to" alternative hypothesis and conduct a two-sided test.
- A test statistic is a quantity, calculated on the basis of a sample, whose value is the basis for deciding whether to reject or not reject the null hypothesis. To decide whether to reject, or not to reject, the null hypothesis, we compare the computed value of the test statistic to a critical value (rejection point) for the same test statistic.

- In reaching a statistical decision, we can make two possible errors: We may reject a true null hypothesis (a Type I error), or we may fail to reject a false null hypothesis (a Type II error).
- The level of significance of a test is the probability of a Type I error that we accept in conducting a hypothesis test. The probability of a Type I error is denoted by the Greek letter alpha, α. The standard approach to hypothesis testing involves specifying a level of significance (probability of Type I error) only.
- The power of a test is the probability of correctly rejecting the null (rejecting the null when it is false).
- A decision rule consists of determining the rejection points (critical values) with which to compare the test statistic to decide whether to reject or not to reject the null hypothesis. When we reject the null hypothesis, the result is said to be statistically significant.
- The $(1 - \alpha)$ confidence interval represents the range of values of the test statistic for which the null hypothesis will not be rejected at an α significance level.
- The statistical decision consists of rejecting or not rejecting the null hypothesis. The economic decision takes into consideration all economic issues pertinent to the decision.
- The p-value is the smallest level of significance at which the null hypothesis can be rejected. The smaller the p-value, the stronger the evidence against the null hypothesis and in favor of the alternative hypothesis. The p-value approach to hypothesis testing does not involve setting a significance level; rather it involves computing a p-value for the test statistic and allowing the consumer of the research to interpret its significance.
- For hypothesis tests concerning the population mean of a normally distributed population with unknown (known) variance, the theoretically correct test statistic is the t-statistic (z-statistic). In the unknown variance case, given large samples (generally, samples of 30 or more observations), the z-statistic may be used in place of the t-statistic because of the force of the central limit theorem.
- The t-distribution is a symmetrical distribution defined by a single parameter: degrees of freedom. Compared to the standard normal distribution, the t-distribution has fatter tails.
- When we want to test whether the observed difference between two means is statistically significant, we must first decide whether the samples are independent or dependent (related). If the samples are independent, we conduct tests concerning differences between means. If the samples are dependent, we conduct tests of mean differences (paired comparisons tests).
- When we conduct a test of the difference between two population means from normally distributed populations with unknown variances, if we can assume the variances are equal, we use a t-test based on pooling the observations of the two samples to estimate the common (but unknown) variance. This test is based on an assumption of independent samples.
- When we conduct a test of the difference between two population means from normally distributed populations with unknown variances, if we cannot assume that the variances are equal, we use an approximate t-test using modified degrees of freedom given by a formula. This test is based on an assumption of independent samples.
- In tests concerning two means based on two samples that are not independent, we often can arrange the data in paired observations and conduct a test of mean differences (a paired comparisons test). When the samples are from normally distributed populations with unknown variances, the appropriate test statistic is a t-statistic. The denominator of the t-statistic, the standard error of the mean differences, takes account of correlation between the samples.
- In tests concerning the variance of a single, normally distributed population, the test statistic is chi-square (χ^2) with $n - 1$ degrees of freedom, where n is sample size.

- For tests concerning differences between the variances of two normally distributed populations based on two random, independent samples, the appropriate test statistic is based on an F-test (the ratio of the sample variances).
- The F-statistic is defined by the numerator and denominator degrees of freedom. The numerator degrees of freedom (number of observations in the sample minus 1) is the divisor used in calculating the sample variance in the numerator. The denominator degrees of freedom (number of observations in the sample minus 1) is the divisor used in calculating the sample variance in the denominator. In forming an F-test, a convention is to use the larger of the two ratios, s_1^2/s_2^2 or s_2^2/s_1^2, as the actual test statistic.
- A parametric test is a hypothesis test concerning a parameter or a hypothesis test based on specific distributional assumptions. In contrast, a nonparametric test either is not concerned with a parameter or makes minimal assumptions about the population from which the sample comes.
- A nonparametric test is primarily used in three situations: when data do not meet distributional assumptions, when data are given in ranks, or when the hypothesis we are addressing does not concern a parameter.
- The Spearman rank correlation coefficient is calculated on the ranks of two variables within their respective samples.

PROBLEMS

1. Define the following terms:

   A. Null hypothesis
   B. Alternative hypothesis
   C. Test statistic
   D. Type I error
   E. Type II error
   F. Power of a test
   G. Rejection point (critical value)

2. Suppose that, on the basis of a sample, we want to test the hypothesis that the mean debt-to-total-assets ratio of companies that become takeover targets is the same as the mean debt-to-total-assets ratio of companies in the same industry that do not become takeover targets. Explain under what conditions we would commit a Type I error and under what conditions we would commit a Type II error.

3. Suppose we are testing a null hypothesis, H_0, versus an alternative hypothesis, H_a, and the p-value for the test statistic is 0.031. At which of the following levels of significance—$\alpha = 0.10, \alpha = 0.05$, and/or $\alpha = 0.01$—would we reject the null hypothesis?

4. Identify the appropriate test statistic or statistics for conducting the following hypothesis tests. (Clearly identify the test statistic and, if applicable, the number of degrees of freedom. For example, "We conduct the test using an x-statistic with y degrees of freedom.")

   A. $H_0: \mu = 0$ versus $H_a: \mu \neq 0$, where μ is the mean of a normally distributed population with unknown variance. The test is based on a sample of 15 observations.
   B. $H_0: \mu = 0$ versus $H_a: \mu \neq 0$, where μ is the mean of a normally distributed population with unknown variance. The test is based on a sample of 40 observations.

C. $H_0: \mu \leq 0$ versus $H_a: \mu > 0$, where μ is the mean of a normally distributed population with known variance σ^2. The sample size is 45.

D. $H_0: \sigma^2 = 200$ versus $H_a: \sigma^2 \neq 200$, where σ^2 is the variance of a normally distributed population. The sample size is 50.

E. $H_0: \sigma_1^2 = \sigma_2^2$ versus $H_a: \sigma_1^2 \neq \sigma_2^2$, where σ_1^2 is the variance of one normally distributed population and σ_2^2 is the variance of a second normally distributed population. The test is based on two independent random samples.

F. $H_0:$ (Population mean 1) $-$ (Population mean 2) $= 0$ versus $H_a:$ (Population mean 1) $-$ (Population mean 2) $\neq 0$, where the samples are drawn from normally distributed populations with unknown variances. The observations in the two samples are correlated.

G. $H_0:$ (Population mean 1) $-$ (Population mean 2) $= 0$ versus $H_a:$ (Population mean 1) $-$ (Population mean 2) $\neq 0$, where the samples are drawn from normally distributed populations with unknown but assumed equal variances. The observations in the two samples (of size 25 and 30, respectively) are independent.

5. For each of the following hypothesis tests concerning the population mean, μ, state the rejection point condition or conditions for the test statistic (e.g., $t > 1.25$); n denotes sample size.

A. $H_0: \mu = 10$ versus $H_a: \mu \neq 10$, using a t-test with $n = 26$ and $\alpha = 0.05$

B. $H_0: \mu = 10$ versus $H_a: \mu \neq 10$, using a t-test with $n = 40$ and $\alpha = 0.01$

C. $H_0: \mu \leq 10$ versus $H_a: \mu > 10$, using a t-test with $n = 40$ and $\alpha = 0.01$

D. $H_0: \mu \leq 10$ versus $H_a: \mu > 10$, using a t-test with $n = 21$ and $\alpha = 0.05$

E. $H_0: \mu \geq 10$ versus $H_a: \mu < 10$, using a t-test with $n = 19$ and $\alpha = 0.10$

F. $H_0: \mu \geq 10$ versus $H_a: \mu < 10$, using a t-test with $n = 50$ and $\alpha = 0.05$

6. For each of the following hypothesis tests concerning the population mean, μ, state the rejection point condition or conditions for the test statistic (e.g., $z > 1.25$); n denotes sample size.

A. $H_0: \mu = 10$ versus $H_a: \mu \neq 10$, using a z-test with $n = 50$ and $\alpha = 0.01$

B. $H_0: \mu = 10$ versus $H_a: \mu \neq 10$, using a z-test with $n = 50$ and $\alpha = 0.05$

C. $H_0: \mu = 10$ versus $H_a: \mu \neq 10$, using a z-test with $n = 50$ and $\alpha = 0.10$

D. $H_0: \mu \leq 10$ versus $H_a: \mu > 10$, using a z-test with $n = 50$ and $\alpha = 0.05$

7. Identify the theoretically correct test statistic to use for a hypothesis test concerning the mean of a single population under the following conditions:

A. The sample comes from a normally distributed population with known variance.

B. The sample comes from a normally distributed population with unknown variance.

C. The sample comes from a population following a non-normal distribution with unknown variance. The sample size is large.

8. Willco is a manufacturer in a mature cyclical industry. During the most recent industry cycle, its net income averaged $30 million per year with a standard deviation of $10 million ($n = 6$ observations). Management claims that Willco's performance during the most recent cycle results from new approaches and that we can dismiss profitability expectations based on its average or normalized earnings of $24 million per year in prior cycles.

A. With μ as the population value of mean annual net income, formulate null and alternative hypotheses consistent with testing Willco management's claim.
B. Assuming that Willco's net income is at least approximately normally distributed, identify the appropriate test statistic.
C. Identify the rejection point or points at the 0.05 level of significance for the hypothesis tested in Part A.
D. Determine whether or not to reject the null hypothesis at the 0.05 significance level.

Use the following table to answer Problems 9 and 10.

Performance in Forecasting Quarterly Earnings per Share

	Number of Forecasts	Mean Forecast Error (Predicted−Actual)	Standard Deviations of Forecast Errors
Analyst A	101	0.05	0.10
Analyst B	121	0.02	0.09

9. Investment analysts often use earnings per share (EPS) forecasts. One test of forecasting quality is the zero-mean test, which states that optimal forecasts should have a mean forecasting error of 0. (Forecasting error = Predicted value of variable − Actual value of variable.)

   You have collected data (shown in the table above) for two analysts who cover two different industries: Analyst A covers the telecom industry; Analyst B covers automotive parts and suppliers.

   A. With μ as the population mean forecasting error, formulate null and alternative hypotheses for a zero-mean test of forecasting quality.
   B. For Analyst A, using both a t-test and a z-test, determine whether to reject the null at the 0.05 and 0.01 levels of significance.
   C. For Analyst B, using both a t-test and a z-test, determine whether to reject the null at the 0.05 and 0.01 levels of significance.

10. Reviewing the EPS forecasting performance data for Analysts A and B, you want to investigate whether the larger average forecast errors of Analyst A are due to chance or to a higher underlying mean value for Analyst B. Assume that the forecast errors of both analysts are normally distributed and that the samples are independent.

   A. Formulate null and alternative hypotheses consistent with determining whether the population mean value of Analyst A's forecast errors (μ_1) are larger than Analyst B's (μ_2).
   B. Identify the test statistic for conducting a test of the null hypothesis formulated in Part A.
   C. Identify the rejection point or points for the hypothesis tested in Part A, at the 0.05 level of significance.
   D. Determine whether or not to reject the null hypothesis at the 0.05 level of significance.

11. Altman and Kishore (1996), in the course of a study on the recovery rates on defaulted bonds, investigated the recovery of utility bonds versus other bonds, stratified by seniority. The following table excerpts their findings.

Recovery Rates by Seniority

Industry Group/ Seniority	Industry Group			Ex-Utilities Sample		
	Number of Observations	Average Price*	Standard Deviation	Number of Observations	Average Price*	Standard Deviation
Public Utilities						
Senior Unsecured	32	$77.74	$18.06	189	$42.56	$24.89

Source: Altman and Kishore (1996, Table 5).
*This is the average price at default and is a measure of recovery rate.

Assume that the populations (recovery rates of utilities, recovery rates of non-utilities) are normally distributed and that the samples are independent. The population variances are unknown; do not assume they are equal. The test hypotheses are $H_0: \mu_1 - \mu_2 = 0$ versus $H_a: \mu_1 - \mu_2 \neq 0$, where μ_1 is the population mean recovery rate for utilities and μ_2 is the population mean recovery rate for non-utilities.

A. Calculate the test statistic.
B. Determine whether to reject the null hypothesis at the 0.01 significance level without reference to degrees of freedom.
C. Calculate the degrees of freedom.

12. The table below gives data on the monthly returns on the S&P 500 and small-cap stocks for the period January 1960 through December 1999 and provides statistics relating to their mean differences.

Measure	S&P 500 Return (%)	Small-Cap Stock Return (%)	Differences (S&P 500 − Small-Cap Stock)
January 1960–December 1999, 480 months			
Mean	1.0542	1.3117	−0.258
Standard deviation	4.2185	5.9570	3.752
January 1960–December 1979, 240 months			
Mean	0.6345	1.2741	−0.640
Standard deviation	4.0807	6.5829	4.096
January 1980–December 1999, 240 months			
Mean	1.4739	1.3492	0.125
Standard deviation	4.3197	5.2709	3.339

Let μ_d stand for the population mean value of difference between S&P 500 returns and small-cap stock returns. Use a significance level of 0.05 and suppose that mean differences are approximately normally distributed.

A. Formulate null and alternative hypotheses consistent with testing whether any difference exists between the mean returns on the S&P 500 and small-cap stocks.
B. Determine whether or not to reject the null hypothesis at the 0.05 significance level for the January 1960 to December 1999 period.

C. Determine whether or not to reject the null hypothesis at the 0.05 significance level for the January 1960 to December 1979 subperiod.

D. Determine whether or not to reject the null hypothesis at the 0.05 significance level for the January 1980 to December 1999 subperiod.

13. During a 10-year period, the standard deviation of annual returns on a portfolio you are analyzing was 15 percent a year. You want to see whether this record is sufficient evidence to support the conclusion that the portfolio's underlying variance of return was less than 400, the return variance of the portfolio's benchmark.

A. Formulate null and alternative hypotheses consistent with the verbal description of your objective.

B. Identify the test statistic for conducting a test of the hypotheses in Part A.

C. Identify the rejection point or points at the 0.05 significance level for the hypothesis tested in Part A.

D. Determine whether the null hypothesis is rejected or not rejected at the 0.05 level of significance.

14. You are investigating whether the population variance of returns on the S&P 500/BARRA Growth Index changed subsequent to the October 1987 market crash. You gather the following data for 120 months of returns before October 1987 and for 120 months of returns after October 1987. You have specified a 0.05 level of significance.

Time Period	n	Mean Monthly Return (%)	Variance of Returns
Before October 1987	120	1.416	22.367
After October 1987	120	1.436	15.795

A. Formulate null and alternative hypotheses consistent with the verbal description of the research goal.

B. Identify the test statistic for conducting a test of the hypotheses in Part A.

C. Determine whether or not to reject the null hypothesis at the 0.05 level of significance. (Use the F-tables in the back of this book.)

15. You are interested in whether excess risk-adjusted return (alpha) is correlated with mutual fund expense ratios for U.S. large-cap growth funds. The following table presents the sample.

Mutual Fund	1	2	3	4	5	6	7	8	9
Alpha (X)	−0.52	−0.13	−0.60	−1.01	−0.26	−0.89	−0.42	−0.23	−0.60
Expense Ratio (Y)	1.34	0.92	1.02	1.45	1.35	0.50	1.00	1.50	1.45

A. Formulate null and alternative hypotheses consistent with the verbal description of the research goal.
B. Identify the test statistic for conducting a test of the hypotheses in Part A.
C. Justify your selection in Part B.
D. Determine whether or not to reject the null hypothesis at the 0.05 level of significance.

CHAPTER 8

CORRELATION AND REGRESSION

LEARNING OUTCOMES

After reading chapter 8 you should be able to do the following:
- Define and interpret a scatter plot.
- Calculate and interpret a sample covariance.
- Calculate and interpret a sample correlation coefficient.
- Explain how outliers can affect correlations.
- Define and explain the concept of spurious correlation.
- Formulate a test of the hypothesis that the population correlation coefficient equals zero and determine whether the hypothesis is rejected at a given level of significance.
- Differentiate between dependent and independent variables in a linear regression.
- Explain the assumptions underlying linear regression.
- Define and calculate the standard error of estimate.
- Define, calculate, and interpret the coefficient of determination.
- Calculate a confidence interval for a regression coefficient.
- Formulate a null and an alternative hypothesis about a population value of a regression coefficient, select the appropriate test statistic, and determine whether the null hypothesis is rejected at a given level of significance.
- Interpret a regression coefficient.
- Calculate a predicted value for the dependent variable given an estimated regression model and a value for the independent variable.
- Calculate and interpret a confidence interval for the predicted value of a dependent variable.
- Describe the use of analysis of variance (ANOVA) in regression analysis and interpret ANOVA results.
- Discuss the limitations of regression analysis.

SUMMARY OVERVIEW

- A scatter plot shows graphically the relationship between two variables. If the points on the scatter plot cluster together in a straight line, the two variables have a strong linear relation.
- The sample correlation coefficient for two variables X and Y is $r = \dfrac{\text{Cov}(X, Y)}{s_x s_y}$.
- If two variables have a very strong linear relation, then the absolute value of their correlation will be close to 1. If two variables have a weak linear relation, then the absolute value of their correlation will be close to 0.

- The squared value of the correlation coefficient for two variables quantifies the percentage of the variance of one variable that is explained by the other. If the correlation coefficient is positive, the two variables are directly related; if the correlation coefficient is negative, the two variables are inversely related.

- If we have n observations for two variables, we can test whether the population correlation between the two variables is equal to 0 by using a t-test. This test statistic has a t-distribution with $n - 2$ degrees of freedom if the null hypothesis of 0 correlation is true.

- Even one outlier can greatly affect the correlation between two variables. Analysts should examine a scatter plot for the variables to determine whether outliers might affect a particular correlation.

- Correlations can be spurious in the sense of misleadingly pointing toward associations between variables.

- The dependent variable in a linear regression is the variable that the regression model tries to explain. The independent variables are the variables that a regression model uses to explain the dependent variable.

- If there is one independent variable in a linear regression and there are n observations on the dependent and independent variables, the regression model is $Y_i = b_0 + b_1 X_i + \varepsilon_i$, $i = 1, \ldots, n$, where Y_i is the dependent variable, X_i is the independent variable, and ε_i is the error term. In this model, the coefficient b_0 is the intercept. The intercept is the predicted value of the dependent variable when the independent variable has a value of zero. In this model, the coefficient b_1 is the slope of the regression line. If the value of the independent variable increases by one unit, then the model predicts that the value of the dependent variable will increase by b_1 units.

- The assumptions of the classic normal linear regression model are the following:
  A linear relation exists between the dependent variable and the independent variable.
  The independent variable is not random.
  The expected value of the error term is 0.
  The variance of the error term is the same for all observations (homoskedasticity).
  The error term is uncorrelated across observations.
  The error term is normally distributed.

- The estimated parameters in a linear regression model minimize the sum of the squared regression residuals.

- The standard error of estimate measures how well the regression model fits the data. If the SEE is small, the model fits well.

- The coefficient of determination measures the fraction of the total variation in the dependent variable that is explained by the independent variable. In a linear regression with one independent variable, the simplest way to compute the coefficient of determination is to square the correlation of the dependent and independent variables.

- To calculate a confidence interval for an estimated regression coefficient, we must know the standard error of the estimated coefficient and the critical value for the t-distribution at the chosen level of significance, t_c.

- To test whether the population value of a regression coefficient, b_1, is equal to a particular hypothesized value, B_1, we must know the estimated coefficient, $\hat{b}_1$, the standard error of the estimated coefficient, $s_{\hat{b}_1}$, and the critical value for the t-distribution at the chosen level of significance, t_c. The test statistic for this hypothesis is $(\hat{b}_1 - B_1)/s_{\hat{b}_1}$. If the absolute value of this statistic is greater than t_c, then we reject the null hypothesis that $b_1 = B_1$.

- In the regression model $Y_i = b_0 + b_1 X_i + \varepsilon_i$, if we know the estimated parameters, $\hat{b}_0$ and $\hat{b}_1$, for any value of the independent variable, X, then the predicted value of the dependent variable Y is $\hat{Y} = \hat{b}_0 + \hat{b}_1 X$.
- The prediction interval for a regression equation for a particular predicted value of the dependent variable is $\hat{Y} \pm t_c s_f$ where s_f is the square root of the estimated variance of the prediction error and t_c is the critical level for the t-statistic at the chosen significance level. This computation specifies a $(1 - \alpha)$ percent confidence interval. For example, if $\alpha = 0.05$, then this computation yields a 95 percent confidence interval.

PROBLEMS

1. Variable X takes on the values shown in the following table for five observations. The table also shows the values for five other variables, Y_1 through Y_5. Which of the variables Y_1 through Y_5 have a zero correlation with variable X?

X	Y_1	Y_2	Y_3	Y_4	Y_5
1	7	2	4	4	1
2	7	4	2	1	2
3	7	2	0	0	3
4	7	4	2	1	4
5	7	2	4	4	5

2. Use the data sample below to answer the following questions.

$$\sum_{i=1}^{n} X_i = 220 \qquad \sum_{i=1}^{n}(X_i - \overline{X})^2 = 440 \qquad \sum_{i=1}^{n}(X_i - \overline{X})(Y_i - \overline{Y}) = -568$$

$$\sum_{i=1}^{n} Y_i = 385 \qquad \sum_{i=1}^{n}(Y_i - \overline{Y})^2 = 1120 \qquad n = 11$$

A. Calculate the sample mean, variance, and standard deviation for X.
B. Calculate the sample mean, variance, and standard deviation for Y.
C. Calculate the sample covariance between X and Y.
D. Calculate the sample correlation between X and Y.

3. Statistics for three variables are given below. X is the monthly return for a large-stock index, Y is the monthly return for a small-stock index, and Z is the monthly return for a corporate bond index. There are 60 observations.

$$\overline{X} = 0.760 \qquad \sum_{i=1}^{n}(X_i - \overline{X})^2 = 769.081 \qquad \sum_{i=1}^{n}(X_i - \overline{X})(Y_i - \overline{Y}) = 720.535$$

$$\overline{Y} = 1.037 \qquad \sum_{i=1}^{n}(Y_i - \overline{Y})^2 = 1243.309 \qquad \sum_{i=1}^{n}(X_i - \overline{X})(Z_i - \overline{Z}) = 231.007$$

$$\overline{Z} = 0.686 \qquad \sum_{i=1}^{n}(Z_i - \overline{Z})^2 = 183.073 \qquad \sum_{i=1}^{n}(Y_i - \overline{Y})(Z_i - \overline{Z}) = 171.816$$

A. Calculate the sample variance and standard deviation for X, Y, and Z.
B. Calculate the sample covariance between X and Y, X and Z, and Y and Z.
C. Calculate the sample correlation between X and Y, X and Z, and Y and Z.

4. Home sales and interest rates should be negatively related. The following table gives the number of annual unit sales for Packard Homes and mortgage rates for four recent years. Calculate the sample correlation between sales and mortgage rates.

Year	Unit Sales	Interest Rate
2000	50	8.0%
2001	70	7.0%
2002	80	6.0%
2003	60	7.0%

5. The following table shows the sample correlations between the monthly returns for four different mutual funds and the S&P 500. The correlations are based on 36 monthly observations. The funds are as follows:

Fund 1   Large-cap fund
Fund 2   Mid-cap fund
Fund 3   Large-cap value fund
Fund 4   Emerging markets fund
S&P 500   U.S. domestic stock index

	Fund 1	Fund 2	Fund 3	Fund 4	S&P 500
Fund 1	1				
Fund 2	0.9231	1			
Fund 3	0.4771	0.4156	1		
Fund 4	0.7111	0.7238	0.3102	1	
S&P 500	0.8277	0.8223	0.5791	0.7515	1

Test the null hypothesis that each of these correlations, individually, is equal to zero against the alternative hypothesis that it is not equal to zero. Use a 5 percent significance level.

6. Juan Martinez, Dieter Osterburg, and Sara Durbin are discussing the correlations between monthly stock returns. Martinez believes that returns are random and that the correlation between stock returns from one month to the next should be zero. Osterburg believes that high or low returns are followed by strong reversals, causing monthly returns to have a negative month-to-month correlation. Durbin believes that positive or negative returns tend to be followed by returns in the same direction, resulting in positive month-to-month correlation.

They give you a series of 60 monthly returns for the S&P 500 during the 1994–98 time period. You create two variables: X represents the first 59 monthly returns, and Y the last 59 monthly returns. For the first observation, X is the January 1994 return and Y is the February 1994 return; for the second observation, X is the February 1994 return and Y is the March 1994 return, etc. The result is 59 paired, contiguous monthly returns. The calculated sample correlation coefficient between X and Y is -0.0641.

A. Interpret the meaning of the negative correlation.
B. Is this correlation significantly different from 0? Use a two-tailed test and a 5 percent significance level.

7. You have monthly returns for four indexes and want to test for serial correlation. You have 29 years of data, or 348 monthly observations. When you compare monthly returns, your sample is reduced to 347 because Month 1 is compared with Month 2, Month 2 with Month 3, until Month 347 is compared with Month 348. Below are the sample correlations calculated for the indexes:

Index	S&P 500	MSCI Europe	MSCI Pacific	MSCI Far East
Serial correlation	0.0034	0.0335	0.1121	0.1052

For each index, test the hypothesis that its serial correlation is equal to 0. Use a 10 percent significance level.

8. Bouvier Co. is a Canadian company that sells forestry products to several Pacific Rim customers. Bouvier's sales are very sensitive to exchange rates. The following table shows recent annual sales (in millions of Canadian dollars) and the average exchange rate for the year (expressed as the units of foreign currency needed to buy one Canadian dollar).

Year i	Exchange Rate X_i	Sales Y_i
1	0.40	20
2	0.36	25
3	0.42	16
4	0.31	30
5	0.33	35
6	0.34	30

A. Calculate the sample mean and standard deviation for X (the exchange rate) and Y (sales).
B. Calculate the sample covariance between the exchange rate and sales.
C. Calculate the sample correlation between the exchange rate and sales.
D. Calculate the intercept and coefficient for an estimated linear regression with the exchange rate as the independent variable and sales as the dependent variable.

9. Julie Moon is an energy analyst examining electricity, oil, and natural gas consumption in different regions over different seasons. She ran a regression explaining the variation in energy consumption as a function of temperature. The total variation of the dependent variable was 140.58, the explained variation was 60.16, and the unexplained variation was 80.42. She had 60 monthly observations.

A. Compute the coefficient of determination.
B. What was the sample correlation between energy consumption and temperature?
C. Compute the standard error of the estimate of Moon's regression model.
D. Compute the sample standard deviation of monthly energy consumption.

10. You are examining the results of a regression estimation that attempts to explain the unit sales growth of a business you are researching. The analysis of variance output for the regression is given in the table below. The regression was based on five observations ($n = 5$).

ANOVA

	df	SS	MSS	F	Significance F
Regression	1	88.0	88.0	36.667	0.00904
Residual	3	7.2	2.4		
Total	4	95.2			

A. How many independent variables are in the regression to which the ANOVA refers?
B. Define Total SS.
C. Calculate the sample variance of the dependent variable using information in the above table.
D. Define Regression SS and explain how its value of 88 is obtained in terms of other quantities reported in the above table.
E. What hypothesis does the F-statistic test?
F. Explain how the value of the F-statistic of 36.667 is obtained in terms of other quantities reported in the above table.
G. Is the F-test significant at the 5 percent significance level?

11. The first table below contains the regression results for a regression with monthly returns on a large-cap mutual fund as the dependent variable and monthly returns on a market index as the independent variable. The analysis is performed using only 12 monthly returns (in percent). The second table provides summary statistics for the dependent and independent variables.

   A. What is the predicted return on the large-cap mutual fund for a market index return of 8.00 percent?
   B. Find a 95 percent prediction interval for the expected mutual fund return.

Regression Statistics

Multiple R	0.776
R-squared	0.602
Standard error	4.243
Observations	12

	Coefficients	Standard Error	t-Statistic	p-Value
Intercept	−0.287	1.314	−0.219	0.831
Slope coefficient	0.802	0.206	3.890	0.003

Statistic	Market Index Return	Large-Cap Fund Return
Mean	2.30%	1.56%
Standard deviation	6.21%	6.41%
Variance	38.51	41.13
Count	12	12

12. Industry automobile sales should be related to consumer sentiment. The following table provides a regression analysis in which sales of automobiles and light trucks (in millions of vehicles) are estimated as a function of a consumer sentiment index.

Regression Statistics

Multiple R	0.80113
R-squared	0.64181
Standard error	0.81325
Observations	120

	Coefficients	Standard Error	t-Statistic	p-Value
Intercept	6.071	0.58432	10.389	0
Slope coefficient	0.09251	0.00636	14.541	0

For the independent variable and dependent variable, the means, standard deviations, and variances are as follows:

	Sentiment Index X	Automobile Sales (millions of units) Y
Mean	91.0983	14.4981
Standard deviation	11.7178	1.35312
Variance	137.3068	1.83094

A. Find the expected sales and a 95 percent prediction interval for sales if the sentiment index has a value of 90.

B. Find the expected sales and a 95 percent prediction interval for sales if the sentiment index has a value of 100.

13. Use the following information to create a regression model:

$$\sum_{i=1}^{n} X_i = 81 \qquad \sum_{i=1}^{n}(X_i - \overline{X})^2 = 60 \qquad \sum_{i=1}^{n}(X_i - \overline{X})(Y_i - \overline{Y}) = 84$$

$$\sum_{i=1}^{n} X_i^2 = 789$$

$$\sum_{i=1}^{n} Y_i = 144 \qquad \sum_{i=1}^{n}(Y_i - \overline{Y})^2 = 144 \qquad \sum_{i=1}^{n}(Y_i - \hat{b}_0 - \hat{b}_1 X_i)^2 = 26.4$$

$$n = 9$$

A. Calculate the sample mean, variance, and standard deviation for X and for Y.

B. Calculate the sample covariance and the correlation between X and Y.

C. Calculate $\hat{b}_0$ and $\hat{b}_1$ for a regression of the form $Y_i = \hat{b}_0 + \hat{b}_1 X_i$.

For the remaining three parts of this question, assume that the calculations shown above already incorporate the correct values for $\hat{b}_0$ and $\hat{b}_1$.

D. Find the total variation, explained variation, and unexplained variation.

E. Find the coefficient of determination.

F. Find the standard error of the estimate.

14. The bid–ask spread for stocks depends on the market liquidity for stocks. One measure
of liquidity is a stock's trading volume. Below are the results of a regression analysis using
the bid–ask spread at the end of 2002 for a sample of 1,819 Nasdaq-listed stocks as the
independent variable and the natural log of trading volume during December 2002 as
the dependent variable. Several items in the regression output have been intentionally
omitted. Use the reported information to fill in the missing values.

Regression Statistics

Multiple R	**X2**
R-squared	**X1**
Standard error	**X3**
Observations	1819

ANOVA	df	SS	MSS	F	Significance F
Regression	**X5**	14.246	**X7**	**X9**	0
Residual	**X6**	45.893	**X8**		
Total	**X4**	60.139			

	Coefficients	Standard Error	t-Statistic	p-Value	Lower 95%	Upper 95%
Intercept	0.55851	0.018707	29.85540	0	0.52182	0.59520
Slope coefficient	−0.04375	0.001842	**X10**	0	**X11**	**X12**

15. An economist collected the monthly returns for KDL's portfolio and a diversified stock
index. The data collected are shown below:

Month	Portfolio Return	Index Return
1	1.11%	−0.59%
2	72.10%	64.90%
3	5.12%	4.81%
4	1.01%	1.68%
5	−1.72%	−4.97%
6	4.06%	−2.06%

The economist calculated the correlation between the two returns and found it to be
0.996. The regression results with the KDL return as the dependent variable and the
index return as the independent variable are given below:

Regression Statistics

Multiple R	0.996
R-squared	0.992
Standard error	2.861
Observations	6

ANOVA	df	SS	MSS	F	Significance F
Regression	1	4101.62	4101.62	500.79	0
Residual	4	32.76	8.19		
Total	5	4134.38			

(continued)

	Coefficients	Standard Error	*t*-Statistic	*p*-Value
Intercept	2.252	1.274	1.768	0.1518
Slope	1.069	0.0477	22.379	0

When reviewing the results, Andrea Fusilier suspected that they were unreliable. She found that the returns for Month 2 should have been 7.21 percent and 6.49 percent, instead of the large values shown in the first table. Correcting these values resulted in a revised correlation of 0.824 and the revised regression results shown below:

Regression Statistics

Multiple *R*	0.824
R-squared	0.678
Standard error	2.062
Observations	6

ANOVA	df	SS	MSS	F	Significance F
Regression	1	35.89	35.89	8.44	0.044
Residual	4	17.01	4.25		
Total	5	52.91			

	Coefficients	Standard Error	*t*-Statistic	*p*-Value
Intercept	2.242	0.863	2.597	0.060
Slope	0.623	0.214	2.905	0.044

Explain how the bad data affected the results.

16. Diet Partners charges its clients a small management fee plus a percentage of gains whenever portfolio returns are positive. Cleo Smith believes that strong incentives for portfolio managers produce superior returns for clients. In order to demonstrate this, Smith runs a regression with the Diet Partners' portfolio return (in percent) as the dependent variable and its management fee (in percent) as the independent variable. The estimated regression for a 60-month period is

$$\text{RETURN} = -3.021 + 7.062 \, (\text{FEE})$$

$$(-7.28) \quad (14.95)$$

The calculated *t*-values are given in parentheses below the intercept and slope coefficients. The coefficient of determination for the regression model is 0.794.

A. What is the predicted RETURN if FEE is 0 percent? If FEE is 1 percent?
B. Using a two-tailed test, is the relationship between RETURN and FEE significant at the 5 percent level?
C. Would Smith be justified in concluding that high fees are good for clients?

17. Kenneth McCoin, CFA, is a fairly tough interviewer. Last year, he handed each job applicant a sheet of paper with the information in the following table, and he then asked several questions about regression analysis. Some of McCoin's questions, along with a sample of the answers he received to each, are given below. McCoin told the applicants

that the independent variable is the ratio of net income to sales for restaurants with a market cap of more than \$100 million and the dependent variable is the ratio of cash flow from operations to sales for those restaurants. Which of the choices provided is the best answer to each of McCoin's questions?

Regression Statistics

Multiple R	0.8623
R-squared	0.7436
Standard error	0.7320
Observations	24

ANOVA	df	SS	MSS	F	Significance F
Regression	1	0.029	0.029000	63.81	0
Residual	22	0.010	0.000455		
Total	23	0.040			

	Coefficients	Standard Error	t-Statistic	p-Value
Intercept	0.077	0.007	11.328	0
Slope	0.826	0.103	7.988	0

17-1. What is the value of the coefficient of determination?

    A. 0.8261
    B. 0.7436
    C. 0.8623
    D. 7.9883

17-2. Suppose that you deleted several of the observations that had small residual values. If you re-estimated the regression equation using this reduced sample, what would likely happen to the standard error of the estimate and the R-squared?

Standard Error of the Estimate	R-Squared
A. Decrease	Decrease
B. Decrease	Increase
C. Increase	Decrease
D. Increase	Increase

17-3. What is the correlation between X and Y?

    A. −0.8623
    B. −0.7436
    C. 0.7436
    D. 0.8623

17-4. Where did the F-value in the ANOVA table come from?

    A. You look up the F-value in a table. The F depends on the numerator and denominator degrees of freedom.
    B. Divide the "Mean Square" for the regression by the "Mean Square" of the residuals.

    C. The *F*-value is equal to the reciprocal of the *t*-value for the slope coefficient.

    D. Subtract the standard errors of the intercept and the slope from the standard error of the estimate.

17-5. If the ratio of net income to sales for a restaurant is 5 percent, what is the predicted ratio of cash flow from operations to sales?

    A. $0.007 - 0.103(5.0) = -0.510$

    B. $0.007 + 0.103(5.0) = 0.524$

    C. $0.077 - 0.826(5.0) = -4.054$

    D. $0.077 + 0.826(5.0) = 4.207$

17-6. Is the relationship between the ratio of cash flow to operations and the ratio of net income to sales significant at the 5 percent level?

    A. No, because the *R*-squared is greater than 0.05.

    B. No, because the standard error (0.7320) is greater than 0.05.

    C. No, because the *p*-values of the intercept and slope are less than 0.05.

    D. Yes, because the *p*-values for *F* and *t* for the slope coefficient are less than 0.05.

18. Howard Golub, CFA, is preparing to write a research report on Stellar Energy Corp. common stock. One of the world's largest companies, Stellar is in the business of refining and marketing oil. As part of his analysis, Golub wants to evaluate the sensitivity of the stock's returns to various economic factors. For example, a client recently asked Golub whether the price of Stellar Energy Corporation stock has tended to rise following increases in retail energy prices. Golub believes the association between the two variables to be negative, but he does not know the strength of the association.

    Golub directs his assistant, Jill Batten, to study the relationships between Stellar monthly common stock returns versus the previous month's percent change in the U.S. Consumer Price Index for Energy (CPIENG), and Stellar monthly common stock returns versus the previous month's percent change in the U.S. Producer Price Index for Crude Energy Materials (PPICEM). Golub wants Batten to run both a correlation and a linear regression analysis. In response, Batten compiles the summary statistics shown in Exhibit 1 for the 248 months between January 1980 and August 2000. All of the data are in decimal form, where 0.01 indicates a 1 percent return. Batten also runs a regression analysis using Stellar monthly returns as the dependent variable and the monthly change in CPIENG as the independent variable. Exhibit 2 displays the results of this regression model.

EXHIBIT 1   Descriptive Statistics

	Monthly Return Stellar Common Stock	Lagged Monthly Change	
		CPIENG	PPICEM
Mean	0.0123	0.0023	0.0042
Standard Deviation	0.0717	0.0160	0.0534
Covariance, Stellar vs. CPIENG	−0.00017		
Covariance, Stellar vs. PPICEM	−0.00048		
Covariance, CPIENG vs. PPICEM	0.00044		
Correlation, Stellar vs. CPIENG	−0.14524		

EXHIBIT 2   Regression Analysis with CPIENG

Regression Statistics			
Multiple R	0.1452		
R-squared	0.0211		
Standard error of the estimate	0.0710		
Observations	248		
	Coefficients	Standard Error	t-Statistic
Intercept	0.0138	0.0046	3.0275
Slope coefficient	−0.6486	0.2818	−2.3014

18-1. Batten wants to determine whether the sample correlation between the Stellar and CPIENG variables (−0.1452) is statistically significant. The critical value for the test statistic at the 0.05 level of significance is approximately 1.96. Batten should conclude that the statistical relationship between Stellar and CPIENG is

   A. significant, because the calculated test statistic has a lower absolute value than the critical value for the test statistic.
   B. significant, because the calculated test statistic has a higher absolute value than the critical value for the test statistic.
   C. not significant, because the calculated test statistic has a higher absolute value than the critical value for the test statistic.
   D. not significant, because the calculated test statistic has a lower absolute value than the critical value for the test statistic.

18-2. Did Batten's regression analyze cross-sectional or time-series data, and what was the expected value of the error term from that regression?

Data Type	Expected Value of Error Term
A. Time-series	0
B. Time-series	ε_i
C. Cross-sectional	0
D. Cross-sectional	ε_i

18-3. Based on the regression, which used data in decimal form, if the CPIENG *decreases* by 1.0 percent, what is the expected return on Stellar common stock during the next period?

   A. 0.0065 (0.65 percent)
   B. 0.0073 (0.73 percent)
   C. 0.0138 (1.38 percent)
   D. 0.0203 (2.03 percent)

18-4. Based on Batten's regression model, the coefficient of determination indicates that

   A. Stellar's returns explain 2.11 percent of the variability in CPIENG.
   B. Stellar's returns explain 14.52 percent of the variability in CPIENG.

C. Changes in CPIENG explain 2.11 percent of the variability in Stellar's returns.

D. Changes in CPIENG explain 14.52 percent of the variability in Stellar's returns.

18-5. For Batten's regression model, the standard error of the estimate shows that the standard deviation of

A. the residuals from the regression is 0.0710.

B. values estimated from the regression is 0.0710.

C. Stellar's observed common stock returns is 0.0710.

D. the intercept estimate from the regression is 0.0710.

18-6. For the analysis run by Batten, which of the following is an *incorrect* conclusion from the regression output?

A. The estimated intercept coefficient from Batten's regression is statistically significant at the 0.05 level.

B. In the month after the CPIENG declines, Stellar's common stock is expected to exhibit a positive return.

C. Viewed in combination, the slope and intercept coefficients from Batten's regression are not statistically significant at the 0.05 level.

D. In the month after no change occurs in the CPIENG, Stellar's common stock is expected to exhibit a positive return.

CHAPTER 9

MULTIPLE REGRESSION AND ISSUES IN REGRESSION ANALYSIS

LEARNING OUTCOMES

After reading chapter 9, you should be able to do the following:

- Formulate a multiple regression equation to describe the relationship between a dependent variable and several independent variables, determine the statistical significance of each independent variable, and interpret the estimated coefficients.
- Formulate a null and an alternative hypothesis about the population value of a regression coefficient, calculate the value of the test statistic, determine whether the null hypothesis is rejected at a given level of significance using a one-tailed or two-tailed test, and interpret the result of the test.
- Interpret the *p*-values of a multiple regression output.
- Explain the assumptions of a multiple regression model.
- Calculate a predicted value for the dependent variable given an estimated regression model and assumed values for the independent variables.
- Discuss the types of uncertainty involved in regression model predictions.
- Infer how well a regression model explains the dependent variable by analyzing the output of the regression equation and an ANOVA table.
- Define, calculate, and interpret the *F*-statistic and discuss how it is used in regression analysis.
- Define, distinguish between, and interpret R^2 and adjusted R^2 in multiple regression.
- Formulate a multiple regression equation using dummy variables to represent qualitative factors, and interpret the coefficients and regression results.
- Describe conditional and unconditional heteroskedasticity and discuss their effects on statistical inference.
- Describe serial correlation and discuss its effects on statistical inference.
- Explain how to test and correct for heteroskedasticity and serial correlation.
- Calculate and interpret a Durbin–Watson statistic.
- Describe multicollinearity and discuss its effects on statistical inference.
- Explain the principles of model specification.
- Define misspecification and discuss its effects on the results of a regression analysis.
- Explain how to avoid the common forms of misspecification in a regression analysis.

- Discuss models for qualitative dependent variables.
- Interpret the economic meaning of a significant multiple regression.

SUMMARY OVERVIEW

In chapter 9, we have presented the multiple linear regression model and discussed violations of regression assumptions, model specification and misspecification, and models with qualitative variables.

- The general form of a multiple linear regression model is $Y_i = b_0 + b_1X_{1i} + b_2X_{2i} + \cdots + b_kX_{ki} + \epsilon_i$
- We conduct hypothesis tests concerning the population values of regression coefficients using t-tests of the form

$$t = \frac{\hat{b}_j - b_j}{s_{\hat{b}_j}}$$

- The lower the p-value reported for a test, the more significant the result.
- The assumptions of classical normal multiple linear regression model are as follows:

  1. A linear relation exists between the dependent variable and the independent variables.
  2. The independent variables are not random. Also, no exact linear relation exists between two or more of the independent variables.
  3. The expected value of the error term, conditioned on the independent variables, is 0.
  4. The variance of the error term is the same for all observations.
  5. The error term is uncorrelated across observations.
  6. The error term is normally distributed.

- To make a prediction using a multiple linear regression model, we take the following three steps:

  1. Obtain estimates of the regression coefficients.
  2. Determine the assumed values of the independent variables.
  3. Compute the predicted value of the dependent variable.

- When predicting the dependent variable using a linear regression model, we encounter two types of uncertainty: uncertainty in the regression model itself, as reflected in the standard error of estimate, and uncertainty about the estimates of the regression coefficients.
- The F-test is reported in an ANOVA table. The F-statistic is used to test whether at least one of the slope coefficients on the independent variables is significantly different from 0.

$$F = \frac{\text{RSS}/k}{\text{SSE}/[n - (k + 1)]} = \frac{\text{Mean regression sum of squares}}{\text{Mean squared error}}$$

Under the null hypothesis that all the slope coefficients are jointly equal to 0, this test statistic has a distribution of $F_{k, n-(k+1)}$, where the regression has n observations and k independent variables. The F-test measures the overall significance of the regression.

- R^2 is nondecreasing in the number of independent variables, so it is less reliable as a measure of goodness of fit in a regression with more than one independent variable than in a one-independent-variable regression. Analysts often choose to use adjusted R^2 because it does not necessarily increase when one adds an independent variable.

- Dummy variables in a regression model can help analysts determine whether a particular qualitative independent variable explains the model's dependent variable. A dummy variable takes on the value of 0 or 1. If we need to distinguish among n categories, the regression should include $n - 1$ dummy variables. The intercept of the regression measures the average value of the dependent variable of the omitted category, and the coefficient on each dummy variable measures the average incremental effect of that dummy variable on the dependent variable.

- If a regression shows significant conditional heteroskedasticity, the standard errors and test statistics computed by regression programs will be incorrect unless they are adjusted for heteroskedasticity.

- One simple test for conditional heteroskedasticity is the Breusch–Pagan test. Breusch and Pagan showed that, under the null hypothesis of no conditional heteroskedasticity, nR^2 (from the regression of the squared residuals on the independent variables from the original regression) will be a χ^2 random variable with the number of degrees of freedom equal to the number of independent variables in the regression.

- The principal effect of serial correlation in a linear regression is that the standard errors and test statistics computed by regression programs will be incorrect unless adjusted for serial correlation. Positive serial correlation typically inflates the t-statistics of estimated regression coefficients as well as the F-statistic for the overall significance of the regression.

- The most commonly used test for serial correlation is based on the Durbin–Watson statistic. If the Durbin–Watson statistic differs sufficiently from 2, then the regression errors have significant serial correlation.

- Multicollinearity occurs when two or more independent variables (or combinations of independent variables) are highly (but not perfectly) correlated with each other. With multicollinearity, the regression coefficients may not be individually statistically significant even when the overall regression is significant as judged by the F-statistic.

- Model specification refers to the set of variables included in the regression and the regression equation's functional form. The following principles can guide model specification:

  - The model should be grounded in cogent economic reasoning.
  - The functional form chosen for the variables in the regression should be appropriate given the nature of the variables.
  - The model should be parsimonious.
  - The model should be examined for violations of regression assumptions before being accepted.
  - The model should be tested and be found useful out of sample before being accepted.

- If a regression is misspecified, then statistical inference using OLS is invalid and the estimated regression coefficients may be inconsistent.

- Assuming that a model has the correct functional form, when in fact it does not, is one example of misspecification. There are several ways this assumption may be violated:

  - One or more important variables could be omitted from the regression.
  - One or more of the regression variables may need to be transformed before estimating the regression.
  - The regression model pools data from different samples that should not be pooled.

- Another type of misspecification occurs when independent variables are correlated with the error term. This is a violation of Regression Assumption 3, that the error term has a mean of 0, and causes the estimated regression coefficients to be biased and inconsistent. Three common problems that create this type of time-series misspecification are

- including lagged dependent variables as independent variables in regressions with serially correlated errors;
- including a function of dependent variable as an independent variable, sometimes as a result of the incorrect dating of variables; and
- independent variables that are measured with error.

- Probit and logit models estimate the probability of a discrete outcome (the value of a qualitative dependent variable, such as whether a company enters bankruptcy) given the values of the independent variables used to explain that outcome. The probit model, which is based on the normal distribution, estimates the probability that $Y = 1$ (a condition is fulfilled) given the values of the independent variables. The logit model is identical, except that it is based on the logistic distribution rather than the normal distribution.

PROBLEMS

1. With many U.S. companies operating globally, the effect of the U.S. dollar's strength on a U.S. company's returns has become an important investment issue. You would like to determine whether changes in the U.S. dollar's value and overall U.S. equity market returns affect an asset's returns. You decide to use the S&P 500 Index to represent the U.S. equity market.

   A. Write a multiple regression equation to test whether changes in the value of the dollar and equity market returns affect an asset's returns. Use the notations below.

   R_{it} = return on the asset in period t
   R_{Mt} = return on the S&P 500 in period t
   ΔX_t = change in period t in the log of a trade-weighted index of the foreign exchange value of the U.S. dollar against the currencies of a broad group of major U.S. trading partners.

   B. You estimate the regression for Archer Daniels Midland Company (NYSE: ADM). You regress its monthly returns for the period January 1990 to December 2002 on S&P 500 Index returns and changes in the log of the trade-weighted exchange value of the U.S. dollar. The table below shows the coefficient estimates and their standard errors.

   Coefficient Estimates from Regressing ADM's Returns: Monthly Data, January 1990–December 2002

	Coefficient	Standard Error
Intercept	0.0045	0.0062
R_{Mt}	0.5373	0.1332
ΔX_t	−0.5768	0.5121
$n = 156$		

   Source: FactSet, Federal Reserve Bank of Philadelphia.

   Determine whether S&P 500 returns affect ADM's returns. Then determine whether changes in the value of the U.S. dollar affect ADM's returns. Use a 0.05 significance level to make your decisions.

C. Based on the estimated coefficient on R_{Mt}, is it correct to say that "for a 1 percentage point increase in the return on the S&P 500 in period t, we expect a 0.5373 percentage point increase in the return on ADM"?

2. One of the most important questions in financial economics is what factors determine the cross-sectional variation in an asset's returns. Some have argued that book-to-market ratio and size (market value of equity) play an important role.

   A. Write a multiple regression equation to test whether book-to-market ratio and size explain the cross-section of asset returns. Use the notations below.

   $(B/M)_i$ = book-to-market ratio for asset i
   R_i = return on asset i in a particular month
   $Size_i$ = natural log of the market value of equity for asset i

   B. The table below shows the results of the linear regression for a cross-section of 66 companies. The size and book-to-market data for each company are for December 2001. The return data for each company are for January 2002.

   Results from Regressing Returns on the Book-to-Market Ratio and Size

	Coefficient	Standard Error
Intercept	0.0825	0.1644
$(B/M)_i$	−0.0541	0.0588
$Size_i$	−0.0164	0.0350
$n = 66$		

   Source: FactSet.

   Determine whether the book-to-market ratio and size are each useful for explaining the cross-section of asset returns. Use a 0.05 significance level to make your decision.

3. There is substantial cross-sectional variation in the number of financial analysts who follow a company. Suppose you hypothesize that a company's size (market cap) and financial risk (debt-to-equity ratios) influence the number of financial analysts who follow a company. You formulate the following regression model:

$$(\text{Analyst following})_i = b_0 + b_1 Size_i + b_2 (D/E)_i + \epsilon_i$$

where

$(\text{Analyst following})_i$ = the natural log of $(1 + n_i)$, where n_i is the number of analysts following company i
$Size_i$ = the natural log of the market capitalization of company i in millions of dollars
$(D/E)_i$ = the debt-to-equity ratio for company i

In the definition of Analyst following, 1 is added to the number of analysts following a company because some companies are not followed by any analysts, and the natural log of 0 is indeterminate. The following table gives the coefficient estimates of the above regression model for a randomly selected sample of 500 companies. The data are for the year 2002.

Coefficient Estimates from Regressing Analyst Following on Size and Debt-to-Equity Ratio

	Coefficient	Standard Error	t-Statistic
Intercept	−0.2845	0.1080	−2.6343
$Size_i$	0.3199	0.0152	21.0461
$(D/E)_i$	−0.1895	0.0620	−3.0565
$n = 500$			

Source: First Call/Thomson Financial, Compustat.

A. Consider two companies, both of which have a debt-to-equity ratio of 0.75. The first company has a market capitalization of $100 million, and the second company has a market capitalization of $1 billion. Based on the above estimates, how many more analysts will follow the second company than the first company?

B. Suppose the p-value reported for the estimated coefficient on $(D/E)_i$ is 0.00236. State the interpretation of 0.00236.

4. In early 2001, U.S. equity marketplaces started trading all listed shares in minimal increments (ticks) of $0.01 (decimalization). After decimalization, bid–ask spreads of stocks traded on the Nasdaq tended to decline. In response, spreads of Nasdaq stocks cross-listed on the Toronto Stock Exchange (TSE) tended to decline as well. Researchers Oppenheimer and Sabherwal (2003) hypothesized that the percentage decline in TSE spreads of cross-listed stocks was related to company size, the predecimalization ratio of spreads on Nasdaq to those on the TSE, and the percentage decline in Nasdaq spreads. The following table gives the regression coefficient estimates from estimating that relationship for a sample of 74 companies. Company size is measured by the log of book value of company's assets in thousands of Canadian dollars.

Coefficient Estimates from Regressing Percentage Decline in TSE Spreads on Company Size, Predecimalization Ratio of Nasdaq to TSE Spreads, and Percentage Decline in Nasdaq Spreads

	Coefficient	t-Statistic
Intercept	−0.45	−1.86
$Size_i$	0.05	2.56
$(Ratio of spreads)_i$	−0.06	−3.77
$(Decline in Nasdaq spreads)_i$	0.29	2.42
$n = 74$		

Source: Oppenheimer and Sabherwal (2003).

The average company in the sample has a book value of assets of C$900 million and a predecimalization ratio of spreads equal to 1.3. Based on the above model, what is the predicted decline in spread on the TSE for a company with these average characteristics, given a 1 percent decline in Nasdaq spreads?

5. The "neglected-company effect" claims that companies that are followed by fewer analysts will earn higher returns on average than companies that are followed by many analysts. To test the neglected-company effect, you have collected data on 66 companies and the number of analysts providing earnings estimates for each company. You decide to also include size as an independent variable, measuring size as the log of the market value of the company's equity, to try to distinguish any small-company effect from a neglected-company effect. The small-company effect asserts that small-company stocks may earn average higher risk-adjusted returns than large-company stocks.

The table below shows the results from estimating the model $R_i = b_0 + b_1 \text{Size}_i + b_2 (\text{Number of analysts})_i + \epsilon_i$ for a cross-section of 66 companies. The size and number of analysts for each company are for December 2001. The return data are for January 2002.

Results from Regressing Returns on Size and Number of Analysts

	Coefficient	Standard Error	*t*-Statistic
Intercept	0.0388	0.1556	0.2495
Size$_i$	−0.0153	0.0348	−0.4388
(Number of analysts)$_i$	0.0014	0.0015	0.8995
ANOVA	df	SS	MSS
Regression	2	0.0094	0.0047
Residual	63	0.6739	0.0107
Total	65	0.6833	
Residual standard error	0.1034		
R-squared	0.0138		
Observations	66		

Source: First Call/Thomson Financial, FactSet.

A. What test would you conduct to see whether the two independent variables are *jointly* statistically related to returns (H_0: $b_1 = b_2 = 0$)?
B. What information do you need to conduct the appropriate test?
C. Determine whether the two variables jointly are statistically related to returns at the 0.05 significance level.
D. Explain the meaning of adjusted R^2 and state whether adjusted R^2 for the regression would be smaller than, equal to, or larger than 0.0138.

6. Some developing nations are hesitant to open their equity markets to foreign investment because they fear that rapid inflows and outflows of foreign funds will increase volatility. In July 1993, India implemented substantial equity market reforms, one of which allowed foreign institutional investors into the Indian equity markets. You want to test whether the volatility of returns of stocks traded on the Bombay Stock Exchange (BSE) increased after July 1993, when foreign institutional investors were first allowed to invest in India. You have collected monthly return data for the BSE from February 1990 to December 1997. Your dependent variable is a measure of return volatility of stocks traded on the BSE; your independent variable is a dummy variable that is coded 1 if foreign investment was allowed during the month, and 0 otherwise.

You believe that market return volatility actually *decreases* with the opening up of equity markets. The table below shows the results from your regression.

Results from Dummy Regression for Foreign Investment in India with a Volatility Measure as the Dependent Variable

	Coefficient	Standard Error	t-Statistic
Intercept	0.0133	0.0020	6.5351
Dummy	−0.0075	0.0027	−2.7604
$n = 95$			

Source: FactSet.

A. State null and alternative hypotheses for the slope coefficient of the dummy variable that are consistent with testing your stated belief about the effect of opening the equity markets on stock return volatility.

B. Determine whether you can reject the null hypothesis at the 0.05 significance level (in a one-sided test of significance).

C. According to the estimated regression equation, what is the level of return volatility before and after the market-opening event?

7. Both researchers and the popular press have discussed the question as to which of the two leading U.S. political parties, Republicans or Democrats, is better for the stock market.

A. Write a multiple regression equation to test whether overall market returns, as measured by the annual returns on the S&P 500 Index, tend to be higher when the Republicans or the Democrats control the White House. Use the notations below.

R_{Mt} = return on the S & P 500 Index in period t

$Party_t$ = the political party controlling the White House (1 for a Republican president; 0 for a Democratic president) in period t

B. The table below shows the results of the linear regression from Part A using annual data for the S&P 500 and a dummy variable for the party that controlled the White House. The data are from 1926 to 2002.

Results from Regressing S&P 500 Returns on a Dummy Variable for the Party That Controlled the White House, 1926–2002

	Coefficient	Standard Error	t-Statistic
Intercept	0.1494	0.0323	4.6270
$Party_t$	−0.0570	0.0466	−1.2242

ANOVA	df	SS	MSS	F	Significance F
Regression	1	0.0625	0.0625	1.4987	0.2247
Residual	75	3.1287	0.0417		
Total	76	3.1912			

Residual standard error	0.2042
R-squared	0.0196
Observations	77

Source: FactSet.

Based on the coefficient and standard error estimates, verify to two decimal places the *t*-statistic for the coefficient on the dummy variable reported in the table.

C. Determine at the 0.05 significance level whether overall U.S. equity market returns tend to differ depending on the political party controlling the White House.

8. Problem 3 addressed the cross-sectional variation in the number of financial analysts who follow a company. In that problem, company size and debt-to-equity ratios were the independent variables. You receive a suggestion that membership in the S&P 500 Index should be added to the model as a third independent variable; the hypothesis is that there is greater demand for analyst coverage for stocks included in the S&P 500 because of the widespread use of the S&P 500 as a benchmark.

A. Write a multiple regression equation to test whether analyst following is systematically higher for companies included in the S&P 500 Index. Also include company size and debt-to-equity ratio in this equation. Use the notations below.

$$\begin{aligned}
(\text{Analyst following})_i &= \text{natural log of } (1+ \text{Number of analysts following company } i) \\
\text{Size}_i &= \text{natural log of the market capitalization of company } i \text{ in} \\
&\quad \text{millions of dollars} \\
(\text{D/E})_i &= \text{debt-to-equity ratio for company } i \\
\text{S\&P}_i &= \text{inclusion of company } i \text{ in the S \& P 500 Index (1 if included;} \\
&\quad 0 \text{ if not included)}
\end{aligned}$$

In the above specification for analyst following, 1 is added to the number of analysts following a company because some companies are not followed by any analyst, and the natural log of 0 is indeterminate.

B. State the appropriate null hypothesis and alternative hypothesis in a two-sided test of significance of the dummy variable.

C. The following table gives estimates of the coefficients of the above regression model for a randomly selected sample of 500 companies. The data are for the year 2002. Determine whether you can reject the null hypothesis at the 0.05 significance level (in a two-sided test of significance).

Coefficient Estimates from Regressing Analyst Following on Size, Debt-to-Equity Ratio, and S&P 500 Membership, 2002

	Coefficient	Standard Error	*t*-Statistic
Intercept	−0.0075	0.1218	−0.0616
Size$_i$	0.2648	0.0191	13.8639
(D/E)$_i$	−0.1829	0.0608	−3.0082
S&P$_i$	0.4218	0.0919	4.5898
$n = 500$			

Source: First Call/Thomson Financial, Compustat.

D. Consider a company with a debt-to-equity ratio of 2/3 and a market capitalization of $10 billion. According to the estimated regression equation, how many analysts would follow this company if it were not included in the S&P 500 Index, and how many would follow if it were included in the index?

E. In Problem 3, using the sample, we estimated the coefficient on the size variable as 0.3199, versus 0.2648 in the above regression. Discuss whether there is an inconsistency in these results.

9. You believe there is a relationship between book-to-market ratios and subsequent returns. The output from a cross-sectional regression and a graph of the actual and predicted relationship between the book-to-market ratio and return are shown below.

Results from Regressing Returns on the Book-to-Market Ratio

	Coefficient	Standard Error	t-Statistic
Intercept	12.0130	3.5464	3.3874
$\left(\dfrac{\text{Book value}}{\text{Market value}}\right)_i$	−9.2209	8.4454	−1.0918

ANOVA	df	SS	MSS	F	Significance F
Regression	1	154.9866	154.9866	1.1921	0.2831
Residual	32	4162.1895	130.0684		
Total	33	4317.1761			

Residual standard error	11.4048
R-squared	0.0359
Observations	34

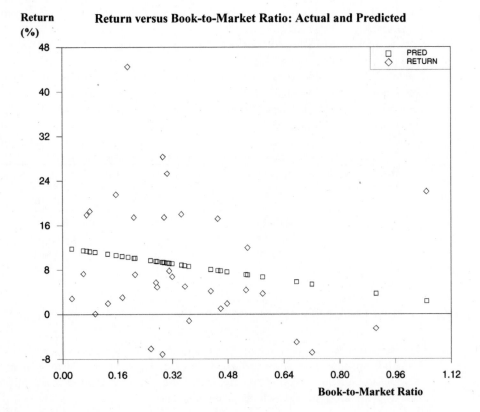

Return versus Book-to-Market Ratio: Actual and Predicted

   A. You are concerned with model specification problems and regression assumption violations. Focusing on assumption violations, discuss symptoms of conditional heteroskedasticity based on the graph of the actual and predicted relationship.

   B. Describe in detail how you could formally test for conditional heteroskedasticity in this regression.

   C. Describe a recommended method for correcting for conditional heteroskedasticity.

10. You are examining the effects of the January 2001 NYSE implementation of the trading of shares in minimal increments (ticks) of $0.01 (decimalization). In particular, you are analyzing a sample of 52 Canadian companies cross-listed on both the NYSE and the Toronto Stock Exchange (TSE). You find that the bid–ask spreads of these shares decline on both exchanges after the NYSE decimalization. You run a linear regression analyzing the decline in spreads on the TSE, and find that the decline on the TSE is related to company size, predecimalization ratio of NYSE to TSE spreads, and decline in the NYSE spreads. The relationships are statistically significant. You want to be sure, however, that the results are not influenced by conditional heteroskedasticity. Therefore, you regress the squared residuals of the regression model on the three independent variables. The R^2 for this regression is 14.1 percent. Perform a statistical test to determine if conditional heteroskedasticity is present.

11. You are analyzing if institutional investors such as mutual funds and pension funds prefer to hold shares of companies with less volatile returns. You have the percentage of shares held by institutional investors at the end of 1998 for a random sample of 750 companies. For these companies, you compute the standard deviation of daily returns during that year. Then you regress the institutional holdings on the standard deviation of returns. You find that the regression is significant at the 0.01 level and the F-statistic is 12.98. The R^2 for this regression is 1.7 percent. As expected, the regression coefficient of the standard deviation of returns is negative. Its t-statistic is -3.60, which is also significant at the 0.01 level. Before concluding that institutions prefer to hold shares of less volatile stocks, however, you want to be sure that the regression results are not influenced by conditional heteroskedasticity. Therefore, you regress the squared residuals of the regression model on the standard deviation of returns. The R^2 for this regression is 0.6 percent.

   A. Perform a statistical test to determine if conditional heteroskedasticity is present.

   B. In view of your answer to Part A, what remedial action, if any, is appropriate?

12. In estimating a regression based on monthly observations from January 1987 to December 2002 inclusive, you find that the coefficient on the independent variable is positive and significant at the 0.05 level. You are concerned, however, that the t-statistic on the independent variable may be inflated because of serial correlation between the error terms. Therefore, you examine the Durbin–Watson statistic, which is 1.8953 for this regression.

   A. Based on the value of the Durbin–Watson statistic, what can you say about the serial correlation between the regression residuals? Are they positively correlated, negatively correlated, or not correlated at all?

   B. Compute the sample correlation between the regression residuals from one period and those from the previous period.

   C. Perform a statistical test to determine if serial correlation is present. Assume that the critical values for 192 observations when there is a single independent variable are about 0.09 above the critical values for 100 observations.

13. The book-to-market ratio and the size of a company's equity are two factors that have been asserted to be useful in explaining the cross-sectional variation in subsequent returns. Based on this assertion, you want to estimate the following regression model:

$$R_i = b_0 + b_1 \left(\frac{Book}{Market} \right)_i + b_2 Size_i + \epsilon_i$$

where

R_i = the return of Company i's shares (in the following period)

$\left(\dfrac{Book}{Market} \right)_i$ = Company i's book-to-market ratio

$Size_i$ = the market value of Company i's equity

A colleague suggests that this regression specification may be erroneous, because he believes that the book-to-market ratio may be strongly related to (correlated with) company size.

A. To what problem is your colleague referring, and what are its consequences for regression analysis?

B. With respect to multicollinearity critique the choice of variables in the regression model above.

Regression of Return on Book-to-Market and Size

	Coefficient	Standard Error	t-Statistic
Intercept	14.1062	4.220	3.3427
$\left(\dfrac{Book}{Market} \right)_i$	−12.1413	9.0406	−1.3430
$Size_i$	−0.00005502	0.00005977	−0.92047
R-squared	0.06156		
Observations	34		

Correlation Matrix

	Book-to-Market Ratio	Size
Book-to-Market Ratio	1.0000	
Size	−0.3509	1.0000

C. State the classic symptom of multicollinearity and comment on that basis whether multicollinearity appears to be present, given the additional fact that the F-test for the above regression is not significant.

14. You are analyzing the variables that explain the returns on the stock of the Boeing Company. Because overall market returns are likely to explain a part of the returns on Boeing, you decide to include the returns on a value-weighted index of all the companies listed on the NYSE, Amex, and Nasdaq as an independent variable. Further, because Boeing is a large company, you also decide to include the returns on the S&P 500 Index, which is a value-weighted index of the larger market-capitalization companies. Finally,

you decide to include the changes in the U.S. dollar's value. To conduct your test, you have collected the following data for the period 1990–2002.

R_t = monthly return on the stock of Boeing in month t

R_{ALLt} = monthly return on a value-weighted index of all the companies listed on the NYSE, AMEX, and Nasdaq in month t

R_{SPt} = monthly return on the S&P 500 Index in month t

ΔX_t = change in month t in the log of a trade-weighted index of the foreign exchange value of the U.S. dollar against the currencies of a broad group of major U.S. trading partners

The table below shows the output from regressing the monthly return on Boeing stock on the three independent variables.

Regression of Boeing Returns on Three Explanatory Variables: Monthly Data, January 1990–December 2002

	Coefficient	Standard Error	t-Statistic
Intercept	0.0026	0.0066	0.3939
R_{ALLt}	−0.1337	0.6219	−0.2150
R_{SPt}	0.8875	0.6357	1.3961
ΔX_t	0.2005	0.5399	0.3714
ANOVA	df	SS	MSS
Regression	3	0.1720	0.0573
Residual	152	0.8947	0.0059
Total	155	1.0667	
Residual standard error	0.0767		
R-squared	0.1610		
Observations	156		

Source: FactSet, Federal Reserve Bank of Philadelphia.

From the t-statistics, we see that none of the explanatory variables is statistically significant at the 5 percent level or better. You wish to test, however, if the three variables *jointly* are statistically related to the returns on Boeing.

A. Your null hypothesis is that all three population slope coefficients equal 0—that the three variables *jointly* are statistically not related to the returns on Boeing. Conduct the appropriate test of that hypothesis.

B. Examining the regression results, state the regression assumption that may be violated in this example. Explain your answer.

C. State a possible way to remedy the violation of the regression assumption identified in Part B.

15. You are analyzing the cross-sectional variation in the number of financial analysts that follow a company (also the subject of Problems 3 and 8). You believe that there is less analyst following for companies with a greater debt-to-equity ratio and greater analyst

following for companies included in the S&P 500 Index. Consistent with these beliefs, you estimate the following regression model.

$$(\text{Analyst following})_i = b_0 + b_1(\text{D/E})_i + b_2(\text{S\&P})_i + \epsilon_i$$

where

$(\text{Analyst following})_i$ = natural log of (1+ Number of analysts following company i)
$(\text{D/E})_i$ = debt-to-equity ratio for company i
$\text{S\&P}_i$ = inclusion of company i in the S & P 500 Index (1 if included; 0 if not included)

In the above specification, 1 is added to the number of analysts following a company because some companies are not followed by any analysts, and the natural log of 0 is indeterminate. The following table gives the coefficient estimates of the above regression model for a randomly selected sample of 500 companies. The data are for the year 2002.

Coefficient Estimates from Regressing Analyst Following on Debt-to-Equity Ratio and S&P 500 Membership, 2002

	Coefficient	Standard Error	t-Statistic
Intercept	1.5367	0.0582	26.4038
$(\text{D/E})_i$	−0.1043	0.0712	−1.4649
$\text{S\&P}_i$	1.2222	0.0841	14.5327
$n = 500$			

Source: First Call/Thomson Financial, Compustat.

You discuss your results with a colleague. She suggests that this regression specification may be erroneous, because analyst following is likely to be also related to the size of the company.

A. What is this problem called, and what are its consequences for regression analysis?
B. To investigate the issue raised by your colleague, you decide to collect data on company size also. You then estimate the model after including an additional variable, Size$_i$, which is the natural log of the market capitalization of company i in millions of dollars. The following table gives the new coefficient estimates.

Coefficient Estimates from Regressing Analyst Following on Size, Debt-to-Equity Ratio, and S&P 500 Membership, 2002

	Coefficient	Standard Error	t-Statistic
Intercept	−0.0075	0.1218	−0.0616
Size$_i$	0.2648	0.0191	13.8639
$(\text{D/E})_i$	−0.1829	0.0608	−3.0082
$\text{S\&P}_i$	0.4218	0.0919	4.5898
$n = 500$			

Source: First Call/Thomson Financial, Compustat.

What do you conclude about the existence of the problem mentioned by your colleague in the original regression model you had estimated?

16. You have noticed that hundreds of non-U.S. companies are listed not only on a stock exchange in their home market but also on one of the exchanges in the United States. You have also noticed that hundreds of non-U.S. companies are listed only in their home market and not in the United States. You are trying to predict whether or not a non-U.S. company will choose to list on a U.S. exchange. One of the factors that you think will affect whether or not a company lists in the United States is its size relative to the size of other companies in its home market.

   A. What kind of a dependent variable do you need to use in the model?
   B. What kind of a model should be used?

CHAPTER 10

TIME-SERIES ANALYSIS

LEARNING OUTCOMES

After reading chapter 10, you should be able to do the following:

- Compute the predicted trend value for a time series modeled as either a linear trend or log-linear trend, given the estimated trend coefficients.
- Discuss the factors affecting the choice between a linear trend and a log-linear trend model for a time series incorporating a trend.
- Discuss a limitation of trend models.
- Discuss the structure of an autoregressive model of order p.
- Explain the requirements for a time series to be covariance stationary, differentiate between stationary and nonstationary time series by visual inspection of time-series plots, and explain the impact of nonstationarity in the context of autoregressive time-series models.
- Explain how autocorrelations of the residuals from an autoregressive model can be used to test whether the model fits the time series.
- Explain mean reversion and determine whether particular time series are mean reverting.
- Compute the one- and two-period-ahead forecasts of a time series using an autoregressive model.
- Explain the difference between in-sample forecasts and out-of-sample forecasts, and contrast the forecasting accuracy of different time-series models based on the root mean squared error criterion.
- Discuss the instability of coefficients of time-series models.
- Define a random walk.
- Explain the relationship between a random walk and unit roots, and discuss the unit root test for nonstationarity.
- Discuss how a time series with a unit root can be transformed so that it can be analyzed with an autoregressive model.
- Compute an n-period moving average of a time series.
- Discuss the structure of a moving-average model of order q.
- Determine the moving-average order of a time series from the autocorrelations of that series.
- Distinguish an autoregressive time series from a moving-average time series.
- Discuss how to test and correct for seasonality in a time-series model.
- Compute a forecast using an autoregressive model with a seasonal lag.
- Discuss the limitations of autoregressive moving-average models.
- Discuss how to test for autoregressive conditional heteroskedasticity.

- Discuss how to predict the variance of a time series using an autoregressive conditional heteroskedasticity model.
- Discuss the effects of cointegration on regression results.
- Select and justify the choice of a particular time-series model from a group of models, given regression output and other information for those models.

SUMMARY OVERVIEW

- The predicted trend value of a time series in period t is $\hat{b}_0 + \hat{b}_1 t$ in a linear trend model; the predicted trend value of a time series in a log-linear trend model is $e^{\hat{b}_0 + \hat{b}_1 t}$.
- Time series that tend to grow by a constant amount from period to period should be modeled by linear trend models, whereas time series that tend to grow at a constant rate should be modeled by log-linear trend models.
- Trend models often do not completely capture the behavior of a time series, as indicated by serial correlation of the error term. If the Durbin–Watson statistic from a trend model differs significantly from 2, indicating serial correlation, we need to build a different kind of model.
- An autoregressive model of order p, denoted AR(p), uses p lags of a time series to predict its current value: $x_t = b_0 + b_1 x_{t-1} + b_2 x_{t-2} + \cdots + b_p x_{t-p} + \epsilon_t$.
- A time series is covariance stationary if the following three conditions are satisfied: First, the expected value of the time series must be constant and finite in all periods. Second, the variance of the time series must be constant and finite in all periods. Third, the covariance of the time series with itself for a fixed number of periods in the past or future must be constant and finite in all periods. Inspection of a nonstationary time-series plot may reveal an upward or downward trend (nonconstant mean) and/or nonconstant variance. The use of linear regression to estimate an autoregressive time-series model is not valid unless the time series is covariance stationary.
- For a specific autoregressive model to be a good fit to the data, the autocorrelations of the error term should be 0 at all lags.
- A time series is mean reverting if it tends to fall when its level is above its long-run mean and rise when its level is below its long-run mean. If a time series is covariance stationary, then it will be mean reverting.
- The one-period-ahead forecast of a variable x_t from an AR(1) model made in period t for period $t + 1$ is $\hat{x}_{t+1} = \hat{b}_0 + \hat{b}_1 x_t$. This forecast can be used to create the two-period ahead forecast from the model made in period t, $\hat{x}_{t+2} = \hat{b}_0 + \hat{b}_1 \hat{x}_{t+1}$. Similar results hold for AR(p) models.
- In-sample forecasts are the in-sample predicted values from the estimated time-series model. Out-of-sample forecasts are the forecasts made from the estimated time-series model for a time period different from the one for which the model was estimated. Out-of-sample forecasts are usually more valuable in evaluating the forecasting performance of a time-series model than are in-sample forecasts. The root mean squared error (RMSE), defined as the square root of the average squared forecast error, is a criterion for comparing the forecast accuracy of different time-series models; a smaller RMSE implies greater forecast accuracy.
- Just as in regression models, the coefficients in time-series models are often unstable across different sample periods. In selecting a sample period for estimating a time-series model, we should seek to assure ourselves that the time series was stationary in the sample period.
- A random walk is a time series in which the value of the series in one period is the value of the series in the previous period plus an unpredictable random error. If the time series is a

random walk, it is not covariance stationary. A random walk with drift is a random walk with a nonzero intercept term. All random walks have unit roots. If a time series has a unit root, then it will not be covariance stationary.

- If a time series has a unit root, we can sometimes transform the time series into one that is covariance stationary by first-differencing the time series; we may then be able to estimate an autoregressive model for the first-differenced series.
- An *n*-period moving average of the current and past $(n-1)$ values of a time series, x_t, is calculated as $[x_t + x_{t-1} + \cdots + x_{t-(n-1)}]/n$.
- A moving-average model of order *q*, denoted MA(*q*), uses *q* lags of a random error term to predict its current value.
- The order *q* of a moving average model can be determined using the fact that if a time series is a moving-average time series of order *q*, its first *q* autocorrelations are nonzero while autocorrelations beyond the first *q* are zero.
- The autocorrelations of most autoregressive time series start large and decline gradually, whereas the autocorrelations of an MA(*q*) time series suddenly drop to 0 after the first *q* autocorrelations. This helps in distinguishing between autoregressive and moving-average time series.
- If the error term of a time-series model shows significant serial correlation at seasonal lags, the time series has significant seasonality. This seasonality can often be modeled by including a seasonal lag in the model, such as adding a term lagged four quarters to an AR(1) model on quarterly observations.
- The forecast made in time *t* for time $t+1$ using a quarterly AR(1) model with a seasonal lag would be $x_{t+1} = \hat{b}_0 + \hat{b}_1 x_t + \hat{b}_2 x_{t-3}$.
- ARMA models have several limitations: the parameters in ARMA models can be very unstable; determining the AR and MA order of the model can be difficult; and even with their additional complexity, ARMA models may not forecast well.
- The variance of the error in a time-series model sometimes depends on the variance of previous errors, representing autoregressive conditional heteroskedasticity (ARCH). Analysts can test for first-order ARCH in a time-series model by regressing the squared residual on the squared residual from the previous period. If the coefficient on the squared residual is statistically significant, the time-series model has ARCH(1) errors.
- If a time-series model has ARCH(1) errors, then the variance of the errors in period $t+1$ can be predicted in period *t* using the formula $\hat{\sigma}_{t+1}^2 = \hat{a}_0 + \hat{a}_1 \hat{\epsilon}_t^2$.
- If linear regression is used to model the relationship between two time series, a test should be performed to determine whether either time series has a unit root:

  - If neither of the time series has a unit root, then we can safely use linear regression.
  - If one of the two time series has a unit root, then we should not use linear regression.
  - If both time series have a unit root and the time series are cointegrated, we may safely use linear regression; however, if they are not cointegrated, we should not use linear regression. The (Engle–Granger) Dickey–Fuller test can be used to determine if time series are cointegrated.

PROBLEMS

Note: In Chapter 10 Problems and Solutions, we use the hat (ˆ) to indicate an estimate if we are trying to differentiate between an estimated and an actual value. However, we suppress the hat when we are clearly showing regression output.

1. The civilian unemployment rate (UER) is an important component of many economic models. The following table gives regression statistics from estimating a linear trend model of the unemployment rate: $UER_t = b_0 + b_1 t + \epsilon_t$.

Estimating a Linear Trend in the Civilian Unemployment Rate
Monthly Observations, January 1996–December 2000

Regression Statistics		
R-squared	0.9314	
Standard error	0.1405	
Observations	60	
Durbin–Watson	0.9099	

	Coefficient	Standard Error	t-Statistic
Intercept	5.5098	0.0367	150.0363
Trend	−0.0294	0.0010	−28.0715

A. Using the regression output in the above table, what is the models prediction of the unemployment rate for July 1996, midway through the first year of the sample period?

B. How should we interpret the Durbin–Watson (DW) statistic for this regression? What does the value of the DW statistic say about the validity of a t-test on the coefficient estimates?

2. The following figure compares the predicted civilian unemployment rate (PRED) with the actual civilian unemployment rate (UER) from January 1996 to December 2000. The predicted results come from estimating the linear time trend model $UER_t = b_0 + b_1 t + \epsilon_t$.

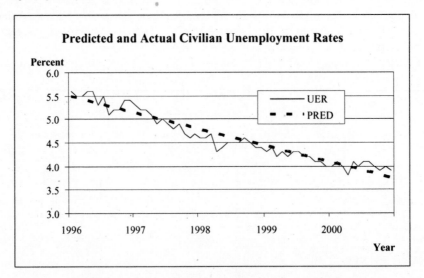

What can we conclude about the appropriateness of this model?

3. You have been assigned to analyze automobile manufacturers and as a first step in your analysis, you decide to model monthly sales of lightweight vehicles to determine

sales growth in that part of the industry. The following figure gives lightweight vehicle monthly sales (annualized) from January 1992 to December 2000.

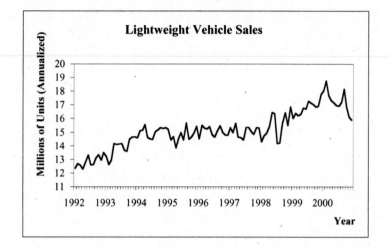

Monthly sales in the lightweight vehicle sector, $Sales_t$, have been increasing over time, but you suspect that the growth rate of monthly sales is relatively constant. Write the simplest time-series model for $Sales_t$ that is consistent with your perception.

4. The figure below shows a plot of the first differences in the civilian unemployment rate (UER) between January 1996 and December 2000, $\Delta UER_t = UER_t - UER_{t-1}$.

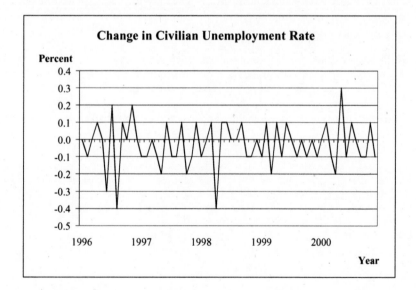

A. Has differencing the data made the new series, ΔUER_t, covariance stationary? Explain your answer.

B. Given the graph of the change in the unemployment rate shown in the figure, describe the steps we should take to determine the appropriate autoregressive time-series model specification for the series ΔUER_t.

5. The following table gives the regression output of an AR(1) model on first differences in the unemployment rate. Describe how to interpret the DW statistic for this regression.

Estimating an AR(1) Model of Changes in the Civilian Unemployment Rate: Monthly Observations, March 1996–December 2000

Regression Statistics		
R-squared		0.2184
Standard error		0.1202
Observations		58
Durbin–Watson		2.1852
	Coefficient	Standard Error	t-Statistic
Intercept	−0.0405	0.0161	−2.5110
ΔUER_{t-1}	−0.4674	0.1181	−3.9562

6. Assume that changes in the civilian unemployment rate are covariance stationary and that an AR(1) model is a good description for the time series of changes in the unemployment rate. Specifically, we have $\Delta UER_t = -0.0405 - 0.4674\Delta UER_{t-1}$ (using the coefficient estimates given in the previous problem). Given this equation, what is the mean-reverting level to which changes in the unemployment rate converge?

7. Suppose the following model describes changes in the civilian unemployment rate: $\Delta UER_t = -0.0405 - 0.4674\Delta UER_{t-1}$. The current change (first difference) in the unemployment rate is 0.0300. Assume that the mean-reverting level for changes in the unemployment rate is −0.0276.

   A. What is the best prediction of the next change?
   B. What is the prediction of the change following the next change?
   C. Explain your answer to Part B in terms of equilibrium.

8. The following table gives the actual sales, log of sales, and changes in the log of sales of Cisco Systems for the period 1Q:2001 to 4Q:2001.

Date Quarter:Year	Actual Sales (millions)	Log of Sales	Changes in Log of Sales $\Delta \ln(Sales_t)$
1Q:2001	$6,519	8.7825	0.1308
2Q:2001	$6,748	8.8170	0.0345
3Q:2001	$4,728	8.4613	−0.3557
4Q:2001	$4,298	8.3659	−0.0954
1Q:2002			
2Q:2002			

Forecast the first- and second-quarter sales of Cisco Systems for 2002 using the regression $\Delta \ln (Sales_t) = 0.0661 + 0.4698\Delta \ln (Sales_{t-1})$.

9. The following table gives the actual change in the log of sales of Cisco Systems from 1Q:2001 to 4Q:2001, along with the forecasts from the regression model $\Delta \ln (Sales_t) = 0.0661 + 0.4698 \Delta \ln (Sales_{t-1})$ estimated using data from 3Q:1991 to 4Q:2000. (Note that the observations after the fourth quarter of 2000 are out of sample.)

Date	Actual Values of Changes in the Log of Sales $\Delta \ln (Sales_t)$	Forecast Values of Changes in the Log of Sales $\Delta \ln (Sales_t)$
1Q:2001	0.1308	0.1357
2Q:2001	0.0345	0.1299
3Q:2001	−0.3557	0.1271
4Q:2001	−0.0954	0.1259

A. Calculate the RMSE for the out-of-sample forecast errors.

B. Compare the forecasting performance of the model given with that of another model having an out-of-sample RMSE of 20 percent.

10. A. The AR(1) model for the civilian unemployment rate, $\Delta UER_t = -0.0405 - 0.4674 \Delta UER_{t-1}$, was developed with five years of data. What would be the drawback to using the AR(1) model to predict changes in the civilian unemployment rate 12 months or more ahead, as compared with 1 month ahead?

B. For purposes of estimating a predictive equation, what would be the drawback to using 30 years of civilian unemployment data rather than only 5 years?

11. The following figure shows monthly observations on the natural log of lightweight vehicle sales, $\ln (Sales_t)$, for the period January 1992 to December 2000.

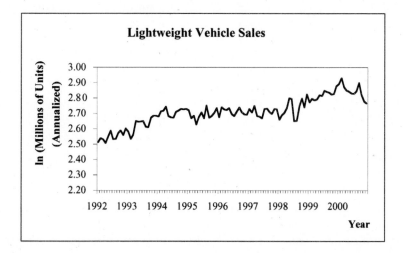

A. Using the figure, comment on whether the specification $\ln (Sales_t) = b_0 + b_1 [\ln (Sales_{t-1})] + \epsilon_t$ is appropriate.

B. State an appropriate transformation of the time series.

12. The following figure shows a plot of first differences in the log of monthly lightweight vehicle sales over the same period as in Problem 11. Has differencing the data made the resulting series, $\Delta \ln (Sales_t) = \ln (Sales_t) - \ln (Sales_{t-1})$, covariance stationary?

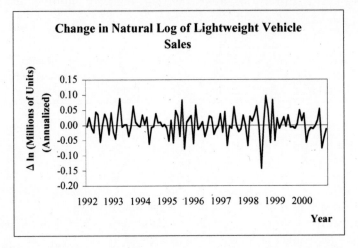

13. Using monthly data from January 1992 to December 2000, we estimate the following equation for lightweight vehicle sales: $\Delta \ln (Sales_t) = 2.7108 + 0.3987 \Delta \ln (Sales_{t-1}) + \epsilon_t$. The table below gives sample autocorrelations of the errors from this model.

Different Order Autocorrelations of Differences in the Logs of Vehicle Sales

Lag	Autocorrelation	Standard Error	t-Statistic
1	0.9358	0.0962	9.7247
2	0.8565	0.0962	8.9005
3	0.8083	0.0962	8.4001
4	0.7723	0.0962	8.0257
5	0.7476	0.0962	7.7696
6	0.7326	0.0962	7.6137
7	0.6941	0.0962	7.2138
8	0.6353	0.0962	6.6025
9	0.5867	0.0962	6.0968
10	0.5378	0.0962	5.5892
11	0.4745	0.0962	4.9315
12	0.4217	0.0962	4.3827

A. Use the information in the table to assess the appropriateness of the specification given by the equation.

B. If the residuals from the AR(1) model above violate a regression assumption, how would you modify the AR(1) specification?

14. The following figure shows the quarterly sales of Cisco Systems from 1Q:1991 to 4Q:2000.

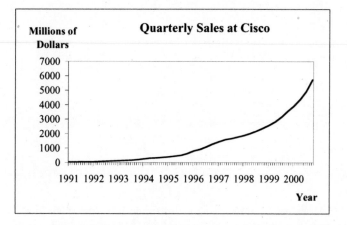

The following table gives the regression statistics from estimating the model $\Delta \ln (\text{Sales}_t) = b_0 + b_1 \Delta \ln (\text{Sales}_{t-1}) + \epsilon_t$.

Change in the Natural Log of Sales for Cisco Systems
Quarterly Observations, 3Q:1991–4Q:2000

Regression Statistics		
R-squared	0.2899	
Standard error	0.0408	
Observations	38	
Durbin–Watson	1.5707	

	Coefficient	Standard Error	t-Statistic
Intercept	0.0661	0.0175	3.7840
$\Delta \ln (\text{Sales}_{t-1})$	0.4698	0.1225	3.8339

A. Describe the salient features of the quarterly sales series.
B. Describe the procedures we should use to determine whether the AR(1) specification is correct.
C. Assuming the model is correctly specified, what is the long-run change in the log of sales toward which the series will tend to converge?

15. The following figure shows the quarterly sales of Avon Products from 1Q:1992 to 2Q:2002. Describe the salient features of the data shown.

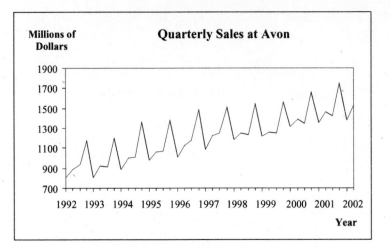

16. The first table below shows the autocorrelations of the residuals from an AR(1) model fit to the changes in the gross profit margin (GPM) of The Home Depot, Inc.

Autocorrelations of the Residuals from Estimating the Regression $\Delta \text{GPM}_t = 0.0006 - 0.3330_1 \Delta\text{GPM}_{t-1} + \epsilon_t$ 1Q:1992–4Q: 2001 (40 observations)

Lag	Autocorrelation
1	−0.1106
2	−0.5981
3	−0.1525
4	0.8496
5	−0.1099

The next table shows the output from a regression on changes in the GPM for Home Depot, where we have changed the specification of the AR regression.

Change in Gross Profit Margin for Home Depot, 1Q:1992–4Q:2001

Regression Statistics			
R-squared	0.9155		
Standard error	0.0057		
Observations	40		
Durbin–Watson	2.6464		

	Coefficient	Standard Error	t-Statistic
Intercept	−0.0001	0.0009	−0.0610
ΔGPM_{t-1}	−0.0608	0.0687	−0.8850
ΔGPM_{t-4}	0.8720	0.0678	12.8683

A. Identify the change that was made to the regression model.

B. Discuss the rationale for changing the regression specification.

17. Suppose we want to predict sales for Johnson & Johnson. Using observations from the first quarter of 1985 to the fourth quarter of 2001, we estimate an AR(1) model using ordinary least squares on the first-differenced data. We estimate the following equation: $(\ln\ \text{Sales}_t - \ln\ \text{Sales}_{t-1}) = b_0 + b_1(\ln\ \text{Sales}_{t-1} - \ln\ \text{Sales}_{t-2}) + \epsilon_t$. The following table shows the results of the regression

Log Differenced Sales: AR(1) Model Johnson & Johnson
Quarterly Observations, January 1985–December 2001

Regression Statistics		
R-squared		0.1957
Standard error		0.0408
Observations		68
Durbin–Watson		2.1226

	Coefficient	Standard Error	t-Statistic
Intercept	0.0297	0.0058	5.1334
Lag 1	−0.1956	0.1207	−1.6210

Autocorrelations of the Residual			
Lag	Autocorrelation	Standard Error	t-Statistic
1	−0.0616	0.1213	−0.5083
2	−0.3634	0.1213	−2.9969
3	−0.1355	0.1213	−1.1170
4	0.6030	0.1213	4.9728

A. Using the regression output in the above table, determine whether the estimates for b_0 and b_1 are valid.

B. If this model is misspecified, describe the steps we should take to determine the appropriate autoregressive time-series model for these data.

18. Suppose we decide to use an autoregressive model with a seasonal lag because of the seasonal autocorrelation in the previous problem. We are modeling quarterly data, so we estimate Equation 10-15: $(\ln\ \text{Sales}_t - \ln\ \text{Sales}_{t-1}) = b_0 + b_1(\ln\ \text{Sales}_{t-1} - \ln\ \text{Sales}_{t-2}) + b_2(\ln\ \text{Sales}_{t-4} - \ln\ \text{Sales}_{t-5}) + \epsilon_t$. The table below shows the regression statistics from this equation.

Log Differenced Sales: AR(1) Model with Seasonal Lag Johnson & Johnson: Quarterly Observations, January 1985–December 2001

Regression Statistics	
R-squared	0.4220
Standard error	0.0318
Observations	68
Durbin–Watson	1.8784

(continued)

	Coefficient	Standard Error	t-Statistic
Intercept	0.0121	0.0053	2.3055
Lag 1	−0.0839	0.0958	−0.8757
Lag 4	0.6292	0.0958	6.5693

Autocorrelations of the Residual			
Lag	Autocorrelation	Standard Error	t-Statistic
1	0.0572	0.1213	0.4720
2	−0.0700	0.1213	−0.5771
3	0.0065	0.1213	−0.0532
4	−0.0368	0.1213	−0.3033

A. Using the above information, determine if the model is correctly specified.

B. If sales grew by 1 percent last quarter and by 2 percent four quarters ago, use the model to predict the sales growth for this quarter.

19. Describe how to test for autoregressive conditional heteroskedasticity (ARCH) in the residuals from the AR(1) regression on first differences in the civilian unemployment rate, $\Delta UER_t = b_0 + b_1 \Delta UER_{t-1} + \epsilon_t$.

20. The following table shows the regression output for testing for ARCH(1) in the residuals from an AR(1) regression on first differences in the civilian unemployment rate: $\Delta UER_t = b_0 + b_1 \Delta UER_{t-1} + \epsilon_t$. Using the information in the table, determine whether we can reject the null hypothesis of no autoregressive conditional heteroskedasticity.

Testing for ARCH(1) Squared Residuals from the Monthly Changes in Civilian Unemployment Rate

Regression Statistics	
R-squared	0.0007
Standard error	0.0208
Observations	57
Durbin−Watson	1.9783

	Coefficient	Standard Error	t-Statistic
Intercept	0.0146	0.0034	4.3468
$\hat{\epsilon}^2_{t-1}$	−0.0265	0.1348	−0.1670

21. Suppose we want to predict the annualized return of the five-year T-bill using the annualized return of the three-month T-bill with monthly observations from January 1993 to December 2002. Our analysis produces the following data.

**Regression with Three-Month T-Bill as the Independent Variable and
Five-Year Treasury Bill as the Dependent Variable
Monthly Observations, January 1993 to December 2002**

Regression Statistics		
R-squared		0.5829
Standard error		0.6598
Observations		120
Durbin–Watson		0.1130

	Coefficient	Standard Error	t-Statistic
Intercept	3.0530	0.2060	14.8181
Three-month	0.5722	0.0446	12.8408

Can we rely on the above regression model to produce meaningful predictions? Specify
what problem might be a concern with this regression.

CHAPTER 11

PORTFOLIO CONCEPTS

LEARNING OUTCOMES

After reading chapter 11, you should be able to do the following:

Mean–Variance Analysis
- Define mean–variance analysis and list its assumptions.
- Explain the concept of an efficient portfolio.
- Calculate the expected return and variance or standard deviation of return for a portfolio of two or three assets, given the assets' expected returns, variances (or standard deviations), and correlation(s) or covariance(s).
- Define the minimum-variance frontier, the global minimum-variance portfolio, and the efficient frontier.
- Explain the usefulness of the efficient frontier for portfolio management.
- Describe how the correlation between two assets affects the diversification benefits achieved when creating a portfolio of the two assets.
- Describe how to solve for the minimum-variance frontier for a set of assets, given expected returns, covariances, and variances with and without a constraint against short sales.
- Calculate the variance of an equally weighted portfolio of n stocks, given the average variance of returns and the average covariance between returns.
- Describe the capital allocation line (CAL), explain its slope coefficient, and calculate the value of one of the variables in the capital allocation line given the values of the remaining variables.
- Describe the capital market line (CML), explain the relationship between the CAL and the CML, and interpret implications of the CML for portfolio choice.
- Describe the capital asset pricing model (CAPM) including its underlying assumptions, resulting conclusions, security market line, beta, and market risk premium.
- Explain the choice between two portfolios given their mean returns and standard deviations, with and without borrowing and lending at the risk-free rate.
- Appraise whether an investor can achieve a mean–variance improvement by adding a particular asset class to his existing portfolio.
- Explain the limitations of using historical estimates of inputs in a mean–variance optimization.
- Define the market model; state the market model's predictions with regard to expected asset returns, variances, and covariances; and contrast the use of market model estimates and historical estimates of the inputs to a mean–variance optimization.
- Calculate the correlation between the returns on two assets implied by the assets' betas, their residual standard deviations from the market model, and the variance of market return.

- Discuss the use of adjusted and unadjusted betas as predictors of future betas.
- Calculate an adjusted beta, given an adjustment model.
- Discuss the reasons for and problems related to instability in the minimum-variance frontier.

Multifactor Models
- Explain a multifactor model (including priced risk and systematic factors) and describe the categories of multifactor models.
- Discuss the main features of a macroeconomic factor model and calculate the expected return on a portfolio of two stocks, given the estimated factor model for each stock.
- Discuss the arbitrage pricing theory (APT), including its underlying assumptions, and explain the relationship between the APT and multifactor models.
- Calculate the expected return on an asset, given the asset's factor sensitivities to a specified set of factors and the factor risk premiums.
- Determine whether an arbitrage opportunity exists, given a set of portfolio expected returns and factor sensitivities, and explain the arbitrage operation if arbitrage is possible.
- Contrast a fundamental factor model with macroeconomic factor models and interpret the factor sensitivities of an asset or portfolio.
- Describe the information ratio and its relationship to tracking risk.
- Calculate and appraise the sources of active return of a portfolio given a multifactor model.
- Calculate active risk (tracking risk), active risk squared, and the marginal contribution of a factor to active risk squared.
- Appraise the sources of active risk of a portfolio given a multifactor model.
- Evaluate the performance of a portfolio given active return and tracking risk objectives, and interpret the information ratio of a portfolio.
- Calculate the weights of a tracking portfolio, given three well-diversified portfolios, their estimated two-factor models, and a target configuration of factor sensitivities.
- Explain why an investor can possibly earn a substantial premium for exposure to dimensions of risk unrelated to market movements.

SUMMARY OVERVIEW

In chapter 11, we have presented a set of concepts, models, and tools that are key ingredients to quantitative portfolio management today.

Mean–Variance Analysis
- Mean–variance analysis is a part of modern portfolio theory that deals with the trade-offs between risk, as represented by variance or standard deviation of return, and expected return.
- Mean–variance analysis assumes the following:
  - Investors are risk averse.
  - Assets' expected returns, variances of returns, and covariances of returns are known.
  - Investors need to know only the expected returns, the variances of returns, and covariances between returns in order to determine which portfolios are optimal.
  - There are no transaction costs or taxes.
- For any portfolio composed of two assets, the expected return to the portfolio, $E(R_p)$, is $E(R_p) = w_1 E(R_1) + w_2 E(R_2)$, where $E(R_1)$ is the expected return to Asset 1 and $E(R_2)$ is

the expected return to Asset 2. In general, the expected return on a portfolio is a weighted average of the expected returns on the individual assets, where the weight applied to each asset's return is the fraction of the portfolio invested in that asset.

- The variance of return on a two-asset portfolio and a three-asset portfolio are, respectively,

$$\sigma_p^2 = w_1^2 \sigma_1^2 + w_2^2 \sigma_2^2 + 2 w_1 w_2 \rho_{1,2} \sigma_1 \sigma_2$$

and

$$\sigma_p^2 = w_1^2 \sigma_1^2 + w_2^2 \sigma_2^2 + w_3^2 \sigma_3^2 + 2 w_1 w_2 \rho_{1,2} \sigma_1 \sigma_2 + 2 w_1 w_3 \rho_{1,3} \sigma_1 \sigma_3 + 2 w_2 w_3 \rho_{2,3} \sigma_2 \sigma_3$$

where

σ_i = the standard deviation of return on asset i, $i = 1, 2, 3$
$\rho_{i,j}$ = the correlation between the returns on asset i and asset j

- In mean–variance analysis, the investment attributes of individual assets and portfolios are represented by points in a figure having standard deviation or variance of return as the x-axis and expected return as the y-axis.
- The minimum-variance frontier graphs the smallest variance of return attainable for each level of expected return.
- The global minimum-variance portfolio is the portfolio of risky assets having the minimum variance.
- An efficient portfolio is one providing the maximum expected return for a given level of variance or standard deviation of return.
- The efficient frontier represents all combinations of mean return and variance or standard deviation of return that can be attained by holding efficient portfolios (portfolios giving maximum expected return for their levels of standard deviation of return). The efficient frontier is the upper portion of the minimum-variance frontier (the global minimum-variance portfolio and points above).
- According to mean–variance analysis, investors optimally select a portfolio from portfolios that lie on the efficient frontier. By restricting attention to the efficient portfolios, the investor's portfolio selection task is greatly simplified.
- When the correlation between the returns on two assets is less than +1, the potential exists for diversification benefits. Diversification benefits occur when portfolio standard deviation of return can be reduced through diversification without decreasing expected return.
- For the two-asset case, the potential benefits from diversifying increase as we lower the correlation between the two portfolios towards −1, holding all else constant. For a correlation of −1, a portfolio of the two assets exists that eliminates risk. As we lower correlation, the efficient frontier improves in the sense of offering a higher expected return for a given feasible level of standard deviation of return, holding all other values constant.
- In general, to determine the minimum-variance frontier for a set of n assets, we first determine the minimum expected return and the maximum expected return among all the expected returns offered by the n assets. We then choose the individual asset weights that minimize portfolio variance of return for different levels of expected return, subject to the constraint that the individual asset weights sum to 1.

- The introduction of a risk-free asset into the portfolio selection problem results in the efficient frontier having a linear portion that is tangent to the efficient frontier defined using only risky assets. This line is called the capital allocation line (CAL). Portfolios on the CAL represent combinations of the risk-free asset and the tangency portfolio.
- When all investors share identical expectations about mean returns, variance of returns, and correlations, the CAL for all investors is the same and is known as the capital market line (CML). The tangency portfolio is the market portfolio of risky assets held in market value weights. The implication of the CML for portfolio choice is that all mean–variance investors, whatever their risk tolerance, can satisfy their investment needs using the risk-free asset and a single risky portfolio, the market portfolio of all risky assets held in market value weights.
- The assumptions of the capital asset pricing model (CAPM) are that investors have identical views about the expected returns, the variances, and the covariances of assets, and only need to know these characteristics to determine which portfolios are optimal for them. Furthermore, investors can buy and sell assets in any quantity without affecting price, and all assets are marketable (can be traded); they can borrow and lend at the risk-free rate without limit and can sell short any asset in any quantity; and they pay no taxes on returns or transaction costs on trades.
- The CAPM equation describes the expected return on an asset or portfolio (whether efficient or not) as a linear function of its beta (a measure of the sensitivity of an asset's returns to the return on the market portfolio). The CAPM equation is

$$E(R_i) = R_F + \beta_i[E(R_M) - R_F]$$

where

$E(R_i)$ = the expected return on asset i

R_F = the risk-free rate of return

$E(R_M)$ = the expected return on the market portfolio

$\beta_i = \text{Cov}(R_i, R_M)/\sigma_M^2$, called beta.

- The CAPM implies that the expected excess rate of return on an asset is directly proportional to its covariance with the market return.
- The Markowitz decision rule states that an investor should prefer Investment A to Investment B if A's expected return is higher than that of B with no more risk than B, or if A has the same expected return as B with strictly less risk.
- Adding a new asset to a portfolio is optimal if the asset's Sharpe ratio is greater than the product (Sharpe ratio of existing portfolio p) × (Correlation of new investment with p).
- To trace out the minimum-variance frontier with n assets, we need n expected returns, n variances, and $n(n-1)/2$ covariances. If we use historical values as inputs to mean–variance optimization, then for realistic values of n, the number of parameters that needs to be estimated is very large, owing mostly to the number of covariances needed. Historical estimates are also critically subject to estimation error.
- The market model explains the return on a risky asset as a linear regression with the return on the market as the independent variable.
- According to the market model,

$$\text{Var}(R_i) = \beta_i^2 \sigma_M^2 + \sigma_{\epsilon_i}^2 \text{ and } \text{Cov}(R_i, R_j) = \beta_i \beta_j \sigma_M^2$$

- We can use the expression for covariance from the market model to greatly simplify the calculational task of estimating the covariances needed to trace out the minimum-variance frontier.
- Using the parameters of the market model, we can express the correlation between the returns on two assets as

$$\text{Corr}(R_1, R_2) = \frac{\beta_1 \beta_2 \sigma_M^2}{(\beta_1^2 \sigma_M^2 + \sigma_{\epsilon_1}^2)^{1/2}(\beta_2^2 \sigma_M^2 + \sigma_{\epsilon_2}^2)^{1/2}}$$

- Adjusted beta is a historical beta adjusted to reflect the tendency of beta to be mean reverting. For example, one common adjustment is

$$\text{Adjusted Beta} = 0.33 + 0.67 \text{ Historical Beta}$$

An adjusted beta tends to predict future beta better than historical beta does.

- A problem with standard mean–variance optimization is that small changes in inputs frequently lead to large changes in the weights of portfolios that appear on the minimum-variance frontier. This is the problem of instability. The problem of instability is practically important because the inputs to mean–variance optimization are often based on sample statistics, which are subject to random variation. Relatedly, the minimum-variance frontier is not stable over time. Besides the estimation error in means, variances, and covariance, shifts in the distribution of asset returns between sample time periods can give rise to this time instability of the minimum-variance frontier.

Multifactor Models

- Multifactor models describe the return on an asset in terms of the risk of the asset with respect to a set of factors. Such models generally include systematic factors, which explain the average returns of a large number of risky assets. Such factors represent priced risk, risk which investors require an additional return for bearing.
- Multifactor models are categorized as macroeconomic factor models, fundamental factor models, and statistical factor models, according to the type of factor used.
- In macroeconomic factor models, the factors are surprises in macroeconomic variables that significantly explain equity returns. Surprise is defined as actual minus forecasted value and has an expected value of zero. The factors can be understood as affecting either the expected future cash flows of companies or the interest rate used to discount these cash flows back to the present.
- In fundamental factor models, the factors are attributes of stocks or companies that are important in explaining cross-sectional differences in stock prices. Among the fundamental factors are book-value-to-price ratio, market capitalization, price–earnings ratio, and financial leverage.
- In statistical factor models, statistical methods are applied to a set of historical returns to determine portfolios that explain historical returns in one of two senses. In factor analysis models, the factors are the portfolios that best explain (reproduce) historical return covariances. In principal-components models, the factors are portfolios that best explain (reproduce) the historical return variances.
- Arbitrage pricing theory (APT) describes the expected return on an asset (or portfolio) as a linear function of the risk of the asset with respect to a set of factors. Like the CAPM, the APT describes a financial market equilibrium, but the APT makes less-strong assumptions.

- The major assumptions of the APT are as follows:

  - Asset returns are described by a factor model.
  - There are many assets, so asset-specific risk can be eliminated.
  - Assets are priced so that there are no arbitrage opportunities.

- APT explains the intercept term in the equation of a multifactor model, in which the factors are surprises, as an expected return.
- In contrast to macroeconomic factor models, in fundamental models the factors are stated as returns rather than surprises. In fundamental factor models, we generally specify the factor sensitivities (attributes) first and then estimate the factor returns through regressions, in contrast to macroeconomic factor models, in which we first develop the factor (surprise) series and then estimate the factor sensitivities through regressions. The factors of most fundamental factor models may be classified as company fundamental factors, company share-related factors, or macroeconomic factors.
- Active return is return in excess of the return on the benchmark.
- Active risk is the standard deviation of active returns. Active risk is also called tracking risk. Active risk squared can be decomposed as the sum of active factor risk and active specific risk.
- The information ratio (IR) is mean active return divided by active risk (tracking risk). The IR measures the increment in mean active return per unit of active risk.
- Factor j's marginal contribution to active risk squared is

$$\text{FMCAR}_j = \frac{b_j^a \sum_{i=1}^{K} b_i^a \text{Cov}(F_j, F_i)}{\text{Active risk squared}}$$

where b_j^a is the portfolio's active exposure to factor j. The numerator is the active factor risk for factor j. The concept explains how factor tilts away from the benchmark explain a portfolio's tracking risk.
- A factor portfolio is a portfolio with unit sensitivity to a factor and zero sensitivity to other factors. A tracking portfolio is a portfolio with factor sensitivities that match those of benchmark portfolio or other portfolio. Factor and tracking portfolios can be constructed using as many assets as there are constraints on the portfolio.
- Multifactor models permit a nuanced view of risk that may contrast with a single-factor perspective. From a CAPM perspective, investors should allocate their money between the risk-free asset and a broad-based index fund. With multiple sources of systematic risk, when an investor's factor risk exposures to other sources of income and risk aversion differ from the average investor's, a tilt away from an indexed investment may be optimal.

PROBLEMS

Mean–Variance Analysis

1. Given the large-cap stock index and the government bond index data in the following table, calculate the expected mean return and standard deviation of return for a portfolio 75 percent invested in the stock index and 25 percent invested in the bond index.

Assumed Returns, Variances, and Correlations

	Large-Cap Stock Index	Government Bond Index
Expected return	15%	5%
Variance	225	100
Standard deviation	15%	10%
Correlation	0.5	

For Problems 2 and 3, assume the following:

- Each stock has the same variance of return, denoted σ^2.
- The correlation between all pairs of stocks is the same, ρ.
- Stocks are equally weighted.

2. Suppose 0.3 is the common correlation of returns between any two stocks in a portfolio containing 100 stocks. Also, suppose the average variance of stocks in the portfolio is 625 (corresponding to a standard deviation of return of 25 percent). Calculate the portfolio standard deviation of return.

3. Suppose the average variance of return of all stocks in a portfolio is 625 and the correlation between the returns of any two stocks is 0.3. Calculate the variance of return of an equally weighted portfolio of 24 stocks. Then state that variance as a percent of the portfolio variance achievable given an unlimited number of stocks, holding stock variance and correlation constant.

4. Suppose a risk-free asset has a 5 percent return and a second asset has an expected return of 13 percent with a standard deviation of 23 percent. Calculate the expected portfolio return and standard deviation of a portfolio consisting 10 percent of the risk-free asset and 90 percent of the second asset.

5. Suppose you have a $100,000 investment in an S&P 500 index fund. You then replace 10 percent of your investment in the index fund with an investment in a stock having a beta of 2 with respect to the index. Why is it impossible for your new portfolio, consisting of the index fund and the stock, to have a lower standard deviation of return than the original portfolio?

6. Suppose that the risk-free rate is 6 percent and the expected return on the investor's tangency portfolio is 14 percent, with a standard deviation of 24 percent.

   A. Calculate the investor's expected risk premium per unit of risk.
   B. Calculate the portfolio's expected return if the portfolio's standard deviation of return is 20 percent.

7. Eduardo Martinez is evaluating the following investments:

   Portfolio A: $E(R_A) = 12$ percent, $\sigma(R_A) = 15$
   Portfolio B: $E(R_B) = 10$ percent, $\sigma(R_B) = 8$
   Portfolio C: $E(R_C) = 10$ percent, $\sigma(R_C) = 9$

   A. Explain the choice among Portfolios A, B, and C using the Markowitz decision rule.

    B. Explain the choice among Portfolios A, B, and C assuming that borrowing and lending at a risk-free rate of $R_F = 2$ percent is possible.

8. Gita Subramaniam is the chief investment officer of an Indian pension scheme invested in Indian equities, Indian government bonds, and U.S. equities. Her current portfolio has a Sharpe ratio of 0.15, and she is considering adding U.S. bonds to this portfolio. The predicted Sharpe ratio of U.S. bonds is 0.10, and their predicted correlation with the existing portfolio is 0.20. Explain whether Subramaniam should add U.S. bonds to the pension fund.

9. Suppose that the risk-free rate is 5 percent and the expected return on the market portfolio of risky assets is 13 percent. An investor with \$1 million to invest wants to achieve a 17 percent rate of return on a portfolio combining a risk-free asset and the market portfolio of risky assets. Calculate how much this investor would need to borrow at the risk-free rate in order to establish this target expected return.

10. Two assets have betas of 1.5 and 1.2, respectively. The residual standard deviation from the market model is 2 for the first asset and 4 for the second. The market standard deviation is 8. What is the correlation between the two assets?

11. Suppose that the best predictor for a stock's future beta is determined to be Expected beta = 0.33 + 0.67(Historical beta). The historical beta is calculated as 1.2. The risk-free rate is 5 percent, and the market risk premium is 8.5 percent. Calculate the expected return on the stock using expected (adjusted) beta in the CAPM.

Multifactor Models

12. Suppose that the expected return on the stock in the following table is 11 percent. Using a two-factor model, calculate the stock's return if the company-specific surprise for the year is 3 percent.

Variable	Actual Value	Expected Value	Stock's Factor Sensitivity
Change in interest rate	2.0%	0.0%	−1.5
Growth in GDP	1.0%	4.0%	2.0

13. A portfolio manager plans to create a portfolio from two stocks, Manumatic (MANM) and Nextech (NXT). The following equations describe the returns for those stocks:

$$R_{MANM} = 0.09 - 1F_{INFL} + 1F_{GDP} + \epsilon_{MANM}$$

$$R_{NXT} = 0.12 + 2F_{INFL} + 4F_{GDP} + \epsilon_{NXT}$$

You form a portfolio with market value weights of 50 percent Manumatic and 50 percent Nextech. Calculate the sensitivity of the portfolio to a 1 percent surprise in inflation.

14. Suppose we have the three portfolios with factor sensitivities given in the table below. Using the information in the following table, create an arbitrage portfolio using a short position in A and B and a long position in C. Calculate the expected cash flow on the arbitrage portfolio for a \$10,000 investment in C.

**Expected Returns and Factor Sensitivities
(One-Factor Model)**

Portfolio	Expected Return	Factor Sensitivity
A	0.1500	2.00
B	0.0700	0.40
C	0.0800	0.45

15. Gayle Tobias has proposals from two investment managers in response to an RFP (request for proposal). She is seeking an active manager for a domestic common stock portfolio that will be benchmarked on a domestic equity benchmark. Both investment managers responding to her RFP have 10-year track records in managing such portfolios. The table below summarizes the information Tobias received.

Active Risk Squared Decomposition

		Active Factor		Active Specific Risk	Active Risk Squared
Manager	Industry	Risk Indexes	Total Factor		
A	10.0	12.0	22.0	14	36
B	2.0	25.0	27.0	13	40

Note: Entries are percent squared.

She further notes that Managers A and B achieved mean returns of 12 and 14 percent, respectively, compared with a mean return of 10.5 percent for the benchmark during the same period.

A. Calculate the tracking risk for Manager A and Manager B.
B. Explain the sources of the differences in tracking risk for Managers A and B.
C. Evaluate the risk-adjusted performance of Managers A and B.

16. Wendy Sherman is analyzing the risk of an actively managed Canadian government bond portfolio using a three-factor model that she has developed. The model incorporates factors related to

- duration
- steepness of the zero-coupon yield curve
- curvature of the zero-coupon yield curve

She has constructed the factor return series such that the factor returns are mutually uncorrelated. The table below details the results of a risk analysis for the most recent fiscal year.

Factor Risk Decomposition

Factor	Sensitivity		Factor Variance
	Portfolio	Benchmark	
Duration	6.00	5.00	121
Steepness of yield curve	0.50	0.35	64
Curvature of yield curve	−0.15	0.30	150
		Active Specific Risk =	25
		Average Active Return =	−0.2%

Use the above table to address the following:

A. For each factor, calculate the

    i. active factor risk

    ii. marginal contribution to active risk squared

B. Identify Sherman's largest bet against the benchmark.

C. Appraise Sherman's risk-adjusted performance.

17. Suppose that an institution holds Portfolio K. The institution wants to use Portfolio L to hedge its exposure to inflation. Specifically, it wants to combine K and L to reduce its inflation exposure to 0. Portfolios K and L are well diversified, so the manager can ignore the risk of individual assets and assume that the only source of uncertainty in the portfolio is the surprises in the two factors. The returns to the two portfolios are

$$R_K = 0.12 + 0.5F_{INFL} + 1.0F_{GDP}$$

$$R_L = 0.11 + 1.5F_{INFL} + 2.5F_{GDP}$$

Calculate the weights that a manager should have on K and L to achieve this goal.

18. Portfolio A has an expected return of 10.25 percent and a factor sensitivity of 0.5. Portfolio B has an expected return of 16.2 percent and a factor sensitivity of 1.2. The risk-free rate is 6 percent, and there is one factor. Determine the factor's price of risk.

19. A portfolio manager uses the multifactor model shown in the following table:

Risk Factor	Portfolio A Factor Sensitivity	Portfolio B Factor Sensitivity	S&P 500 Factor Sensitivity	Portfolio A Excess Factor Sensitivity
Confidence risk	0.27	0.27	0.27	0.00
Time horizon risk	0.56	0.56	0.56	0.00
Inflation risk	−0.12	−0.45	−0.37	0.25
Business cycle risk	2.25	1.00	1.71	0.54
Market timing risk	1.00	1.00	1.00	0.00

The S&P 500 is the benchmark portfolio for Portfolios A and B. Calculate the weights the manager would put on Portfolios A and B to have zero excess business cycle factor sensitivity (relative to the business cycle sensitivity of the S&P 500). Then calculate the inflation factor sensitivity of the resulting portfolio.

20. A wealthy investor has no other source of income beyond her investments. Her investment advisor recommends that she tilt her portfolio to cyclical stocks and high-yield bonds because the average investor holds a job and is recession sensitive. Explain the advisor's advice.

PART I

LEARNING OUTCOMES, SUMMARY OVERVIEW, AND PROBLEMS

CHAPTER 1

THE TIME VALUE OF MONEY

SOLUTIONS

1. A. Investment 2 is identical to Investment 1 except that Investment 2 has low liquidity. The difference between the interest rate on Investment 2 and Investment 1 is 0.5 percentage point. This amount represents the liquidity premium, which represents compensation for the risk of loss relative to an investment's fair value if the investment needs to be converted to cash quickly.

    B. To estimate the default risk premium, find the two investments that have the same maturity but different levels of default risk. Both Investments 4 and 5 have a maturity of eight years. Investment 5, however, has low liquidity and thus bears a liquidity premium. The difference between the interest rates of Investments 5 and 4 is 2.5 percentage points. The liquidity premium is 0.5 percentage point (from Part A). This leaves $2.5 - 0.5 = 2.0$ percentage points that must represent a default risk premium reflecting Investment 5's high default risk.

    C. Investment 3 has liquidity risk and default risk comparable to Investment 2, but with its longer time to maturity, Investment 3 should have a higher maturity premium. The interest rate on Investment 3, r_3, should thus be above 2.5 percent (the interest rate on Investment 2). If the liquidity of Investment 3 were high, Investment 3 would match Investment 4 except for Investment 3's shorter maturity. We would then conclude that Investment 3's interest rate should be less than the interest rate on Investment 4, which is 4 percent. In contrast to Investment 4, however, Investment 3 has low liquidity. It is possible that the interest rate on Investment 3 exceeds that of Investment 4 despite 3's shorter maturity, depending on the relative size of the liquidity and maturity premiums. However, we expect r_3 to be less than 4.5 percent, the expected interest rate on Investment 4 if it had low liquidity. Thus 2.5 percent $< r_3 < 4.5$ percent.

2. i. Draw a time line.

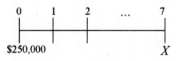

    ii. Identify the problem as the future value of a lump sum.
    iii. Use the formula for the future value of a lump sum.

$$PV = 0.05 \times \$5,000,000 = \$250,000$$
$$FV_N = PV(1 + r)^N$$
$$= \$250,000(1.03)^7$$
$$= \$307,468.47$$

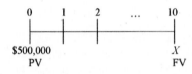

The future value in seven years of $250,000 received today is $307,468.47 if the interest rate is 3 percent compounded annually.

3. i. Draw a time line.

ii. Identify the problem as the future value of a lump sum.
iii. Use the formula for the future value of a lump sum.

$$FV_N = PV(1 + r)^N$$
$$= \$500,000(1.07)^{10}$$
$$= \$983,575.68$$

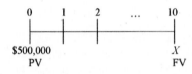

Your client will have $983,575.68 in 10 years if she invests $500,000 today and earns 7 percent annually.

4. A. To solve this problem, take the following steps:

i. Draw a time line and recognize that a year consists of four quarterly periods.

ii. Recognize the problem as the future value of a lump sum with quarterly compounding.
iii. Use the formula for the future value of a lump sum with periodic compounding, where m is the frequency of compounding within a year and N is the number of years.

$$FV_N = PV \left(1 + \frac{r_s}{m}\right)^{mN}$$

$$= \$100,000 \left(1 + \frac{0.07}{4}\right)^{4(1)}$$

$$= \$107,185.90$$

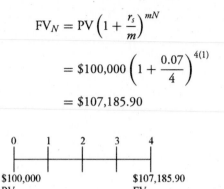

iv. As an alternative to Step iii, use a financial calculator. Most of the equations in this chapter can be solved using a financial calculator. Calculators vary in the exact keystrokes required (see your calculator's manual for the appropriate keystrokes), but the table below illustrates the basic variables and algorithms.

Time Value of Money Variable	Notation Used on Most Calculators	Numerical Value for This Problem
Number of periods or payments	N	4
Interest rate per period	%i	7/4
Present value	PV	$100,000
Future value	FV **compute**	X
Payment size	PMT	n/a (= 0)

Remember, however, that a financial calculator is only a shortcut way of performing the mechanics and is not a substitute for setting up the problem or knowing which equation is appropriate.

In summary, your client will have $107,185.90 in one year if he deposits $100,000 today in a bank account paying a stated interest rate of 7 percent compounded quarterly.

B. To solve this problem, take the following steps:

i. Draw a time line and recognize that with monthly compounding, we need to express all values in monthly terms. Therefore, we have 12 periods.

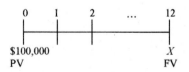

ii. Recognize the problem as the future value of a lump sum with monthly compounding.

iii. Use the formula for the future value of a lump sum with periodic compounding, where m is the frequency of compounding within a year and N is the number of years.

$$FV_N = PV \left(1 + \frac{r_s}{m}\right)^{mN}$$

$$= \$100{,}000 \left(1 + \frac{0.07}{12}\right)^{12(1)}$$

$$= \$107{,}229.01$$

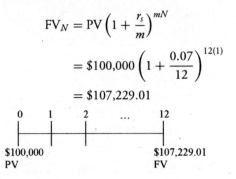

iv. As an alternative to Step iii, use a financial calculator.

Notation Used on Most Calculators	Numerical Value for This Problem
N	12
%i	7/12
PV	$100,000
FV **compute**	X
PMT	n/a ($= 0$)

Using your calculator's financial functions, verify that the future value, X, equals $107,229.01.

In summary, your client will have $107,229.01 at the end of one year if he deposits $100,000 today in his bank account paying a stated interest rate of 7 percent compounded monthly.

C. To solve this problem, take the following steps:

i. Draw a time line and recognize that with continuous compounding, we need to use the formula for the future value with continuous compounding.

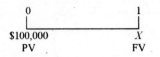

ii. Use the formula for the future value with continuous compounding (N is the number of years in the expression).

$$FV_N = PVe^{r_s N}$$

$$= \$100{,}000 e^{0.07(1)}$$

$$= \$107{,}250.82$$

iii. The notation $e^{0.07(1)}$ is the exponential function, where e is a number approximately equal to 2.718282. On most calculators, this function is on the key marked e^x. First calculate the value of X. In this problem, X is $0.07(1) = 0.07$. Key 0.07 into the calculator. Next press the e^x key. You should get 1.072508. If you cannot get this figure, check your calculator's manual.

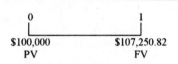

In summary, your client will have $107,250.82 at the end of one year if he deposits $100,000 today in his bank account paying a stated interest rate of 7 percent compounded continuously.

5. Stated annual interest rate = 5.89 percent.
   Effective annual rate on bank deposits = 6.05 percent.

$$1 + \text{EAR} = \left(1 + \frac{\text{Stated interest rate}}{m}\right)^m$$

$$1.0605 = \left(1 + \frac{0.0589}{m}\right)^m$$

For annual compounding, with $m = 1$, $1.0605 \neq 1.0589$.
For quarterly compounding, with $m = 4$, $1.0605 \neq 1.060214$.
For monthly compounding, with $m = 12$, $1.0605 \approx 1.060516$.
Hence, the bank uses monthly compounding.

6. A. Use the formula for the effective annual rate.

$$\text{Effective annual rate} = (1 + \text{Periodic interest rate})^m - 1$$

$$\left(1 + \frac{0.08}{4}\right)^{4(1)} - 1 = 0.0824 \text{ or } 8.24\%$$

   B. Use the formula for the effective annual rate.

$$\text{Effective annual rate} = (1 + \text{Periodic interest rate})^m - 1$$

$$\left(1 + \frac{0.08}{12}\right)^{12(1)} - 1 = 0.0830 \text{ or } 8.30\%$$

   C. Use the formula for the effective annual rate with continuous compounding.

$$\text{Effective annual rate} = e^{r_s} - 1$$

$$e^{0.08} - 1 = 0.0833 \text{ or } 8.33\%$$

7. i. Draw a time line.

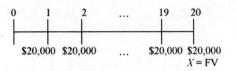

ii. Identify the problem as the future value of an annuity.
iii. Use the formula for the future value of an annuity.

$$FV_N = A\left[\frac{(1+r)^N - 1}{r}\right]$$

$$= \$20,000\left[\frac{(1+0.07)^{20} - 1}{0.07}\right]$$

$$= \$819,909.85$$

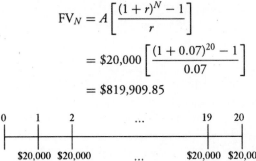

iv. Alternatively, use a financial calculator.

Notation Used on Most Calculators	Numerical Value for This Problem
N	20
%i	7
PV	n/a (= 0)
FV **compute**	X
PMT	$20,000

Enter 20 for N, the number of periods. Enter 7 for the interest rate and 20,000 for the payment size. The present value is not needed, so enter 0. Calculate the future value. Verify that you get $819,909.85 to make sure you have mastered your calculator's keystrokes.

In summary, if the couple sets aside $20,000 each year (starting next year), they will have $819,909.85 in 20 years if they earn 7 percent annually.

8. i. Draw a time line.

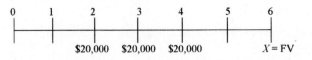

ii. Recognize the problem as the future value of a delayed annuity. Delaying the payments requires two calculations.
iii. Use the formula for the future value of an annuity (Equation 1-7)

$$FV_N = A\left[\frac{(1+r)^N - 1}{r}\right]$$

to bring the three $20,000 payments to an equivalent lump sum of $65,562.00 four years from today.

Notation Used on Most Calculators	Numerical Value for This Problem
N	3
%i	9
PV	n/a (= 0)
FV **compute**	X
PMT	$20,000

iv. Use the formula for the future value of a lump sum (Equation 1-2), $FV_N = PV(1+r)^N$, to bring the single lump sum of $65,562.00 to an equivalent lump sum of $77,894.21 six years from today.

Notation Used on Most Calculators	Numerical Value for This Problem
N	2
%i	9
PV	$65,562.00
FV **compute**	X
PMT	n/a (= 0)

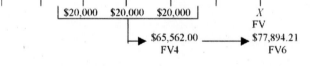

In summary, your client will have $77,894.21 in six years if she receives three yearly payments of $20,000 starting in Year 2 and can earn 9 percent annually on her investments.

9. i. Draw a time line.

ii. Identify the problem as the present value of a lump sum.

iii. Use the formula for the present value of a lump sum.

$$PV = FV_N(1 + r)^{-N}$$
$$= \$75{,}000(1 + 0.06)^{-5}$$
$$= \$56{,}044.36$$

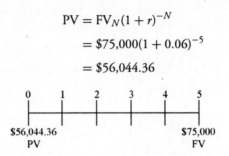

$56,044.36 $75,000
PV   FV

In summary, the father will need to invest $56,044.36 today in order to have $75,000 in five years if his investments earn 6 percent annually.

10. i. Draw a time line and recognize that a year consists of four quarterly periods.

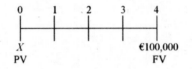

X   €100,000
PV   FV

ii. Recognize the problem as the present value of a lump sum with quarterly compounding.

iii. Use the formula for the present value of a lump sum with periodic compounding, where m is the frequency of compounding within a year and N is the number of years.

$$PV = FV_N \left(1 + \frac{r_s}{m}\right)^{-mN}$$

$$= €100{,}000 \left(1 + \frac{0.07}{4}\right)^{-4(1)}$$

$$= €93{,}295.85$$

€93,295.85   €100,000
PV   FV

iv. Alternatively, use a financial calculator.

Notation Used on Most Calculators	Numerical Value for This Problem
N	4
%i	7/4
PV **compute**	X
FV	€100,000
PMT	n/a (= 0)

Use your calculator's financial functions to verify that the present value, X, equals €93,295.85.

In summary, your client will have to deposit €93,295.85 today to have €100,000 in one year if her bank account pays 7 percent compounded quarterly.

11.   i. Draw a time line for the 10 annual payments.

   ii. Identify the problem as the present value of an annuity.
   iii. Use the formula for the present value of an annuity.

$$PV = A \left[\frac{1 - \dfrac{1}{(1 + r)^N}}{r} \right]$$

$$= \$100{,}000 \left[\frac{1 - \dfrac{1}{(1 + 0.05)^{10}}}{0.05} \right]$$

$$= \$772{,}173.49$$

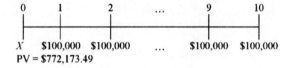

   iv. Alternatively, use a financial calculator.

Notation Used on Most Calculators	Numerical Value for This Problem
N	10
$\%i$	5
PV **compute**	X
FV	n/a ($= 0$)
PMT	$100,000

In summary, the present value of 10 payments of $100,000 is $772,173.49 if the first payment is received in one year and the rate is 5 percent compounded annually. Your client should accept no less than this amount for his lump sum payment.

12.   i. Draw a time line.

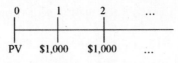

ii. Recognize the problem as the present value of a perpetuity.
iii. Use the formula for the present value of a perpetuity.

$$PV = \left(\frac{A}{r}\right) = \left(\frac{\$1,000}{0.03}\right) = \$33,333.33$$

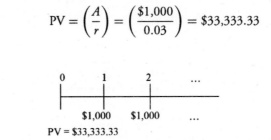

The investor will have to pay $33,333.33 today to receive $1,000 per quarter forever if his required rate of return is 3 percent per quarter (12 percent per year).

13. i. Draw a time line to compare the lump sum and the annuity.

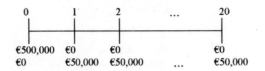

ii. Recognize that we have to compare the present values of a lump sum and an annuity.
iii. Use the formula for the present value of an annuity (Equation 1-11).

$$PV = €50,000 \left[\frac{1 - \dfrac{1}{(1.06)^{20}}}{0.06} \right] = €573,496$$

Notation Used on Most Calculators	Numerical Value for This Problem
N	20
%i	6
PV **compute**	X
FV	n/a (= 0)
PMT	€50,000

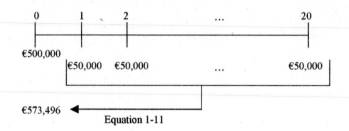

€573,496   Equation 1-11

The annuity plan is better by €73,496 in present value terms (€573,496 − €500,000).

14. A. To evaluate the first instrument, take the following steps:

   i. Draw a time line.

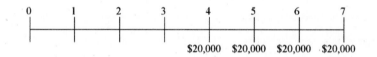

   ii. $PV_3 = A \left[\dfrac{1 - \dfrac{1}{(1 + r)^N}}{r} \right]$

   $= \$20,000 \left[\dfrac{1 - \dfrac{1}{(1 + 0.08)^4}}{0.08} \right]$

   $= \$66,242.54$

   iii. $PV_0 = \dfrac{PV_3}{(1 + r)^N} = \dfrac{\$66,242.54}{1.08^3} = \$52,585.46$

You should be willing to pay $52,585.46 for this instrument.

   B. To evaluate the second instrument, take the following steps:

   i. Draw a time line.

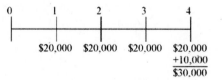

The time line shows that this instrument can be analyzed as an ordinary annuity of $20,000 with four payments (valued in Step ii below) and a $10,000 payment to be received at $t = 4$ (valued in Step iii below).

ii. $$PV = A \left[\frac{1 - \dfrac{1}{(1 + r)^N}}{r} \right]$$

$$= \$20,000 \left[\frac{1 - \dfrac{1}{(1 + 0.08)^4}}{0.08} \right]$$

$$= \$66,242.54$$

iii. $$PV = \frac{FV_4}{(1 + r)^N} = \frac{\$10,000}{(1 + 0.08)^4} = \$7,350.30$$

iv.   Total = $66,242.54 + $7,350.30 = $73,592.84

You should be willing to pay $73,592.84 for this instrument.

15.   i. Draw a time line.

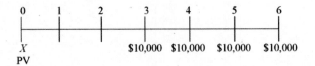

ii. Recognize the problem as a delayed annuity. Delaying the payments requires two calculations.

iii. Use the formula for the present value of an annuity (Equation 1-11)

$$PV = A \left[\frac{1 - \dfrac{1}{(1 + r)^N}}{r} \right]$$

to bring the four payments of $10,000 back to a single equivalent lump sum of $33,121.27 at $t = 2$. Note that we use $t = 2$ because the first annuity payment is then one period away, giving an ordinary annuity.

Notation Used on Most Calculators	Numerical Value for This Problem
N	4
%i	8
PV **compute**	X
PMT	$10,000

iv. Then use the formula for the present value of a lump sum (Equation 1-8), $PV = FV_N(1 + r)^{-N}$, to bring back the single payment of $33,121.27 (at $t = 2$) to an equivalent single payment of $28,396.15 (at $t = 0$).

Notation Used on Most Calculators	Numerical Value for This Problem
N	2
%i	8
PV **compute**	X
FV	$33,121.27
PMT	n/a ($= 0$)

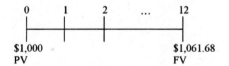

In summary, you should set aside $28,396.15 today to cover four payments of $10,000 starting in three years if your investments earn a rate of 8 percent annually.

16. i. Draw a time line.

ii. Recognize the problem as the future value of a lump sum with monthly compounding.
iii. Use the formula for the future value of a lump sum with periodic compounding

$$FV_N = PV[1 + (r_s/m)]^{mN}$$

and solve for r_s, the stated annual interest rate:

$$\$1,061.68 = \$1,000[1 + (r_s/12)]^{12(1)} \text{ so } r_s = 0.06$$

iv. Alternatively, use a financial calculator to solve for r.

Notation Used on Most Calculators	Numerical Value for This Problem
N	12
%i **compute**	X
PV	$1,000
FV	$1,061.68
PMT	n/a (= 0)

Use your calculator's financial functions to verify that the stated interest rate of the savings account is 6 percent with monthly compounding.

17. i. Draw a time line.

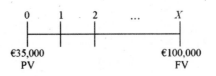

ii. Recognize the problem as the future value of a lump sum with monthly compounding.

iii. Use the formula for the future value of a lump sum, $FV_N = PV[1 + (r_s/m)]^{mN}$, where m is the frequency of compounding within a year and N is the number of years. Solve for mN, the number of months.

$$€100,000 = €35,000[1 + (0.05/12)]^{12N} \text{ so } 12N = 252.48 \text{ months}$$

iv. Alternatively, use a financial calculator.

Notation Used on Most Calculators	Numerical Value for This Problem
N **compute**	X
%i	5/12
PV	€35,000
FV	€100,000
PMT	n/a (= 0)

Use your calculator's financial functions to verify that your client will have to wait 252.48 months to have €100,000 if he deposits €35,000 today in a bank account paying 5 percent compounded monthly. (Some calculators will give 253 months.)

18. i. Draw a time line.

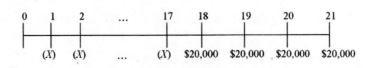

ii. Recognize that you need to equate the values of two annuities.

iii. Equate the value of the four $20,000 payments to a single payment in Period 17 using the formula for the present value of an annuity (Equation 1-11), with $r = 0.05$. The present value of the college costs as of $t = 17$ is $70,919.

$$PV = \$20,000 \left[\frac{1 - \dfrac{1}{(1.05)^4}}{0.05} \right] = \$70,919$$

Notation Used on Most Calculators	Numerical Value for This Problem
N	4
%i	5
PV **compute**	X
FV	n/a (= 0)
PMT	$20,000

iv. Equate the value of the 17 investments of X to the amount calculated in Step iii, college costs as of $t = 17$, using the formula for the future value of an annuity (Equation 1-7). Then solve for X.

$$\$70,919 = X \left[\frac{(1.05)^{17} - 1}{0.05} \right] = 25.840366X$$

$$X = \$2,744.50$$

Notation Used on Most Calculators	Numerical Value for This Problem
N	17
%i	5
PV	n/a (= 0)
FV	$70,919
PMT **compute**	X

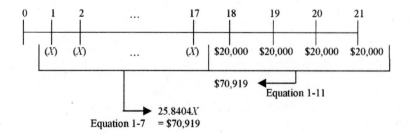

In summary, your client will have to save $2,744.50 each year if she starts next year and makes 17 payments into a savings account paying 5 percent annually.

19. i. Draw a time line.

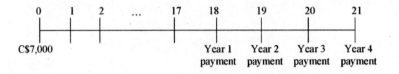

ii. Recognize that the payments in Years 18, 19, 20, and 21 are the future values of a lump sum of C$7,000 in Year 0.

iii. With $r = 5\%$, use the formula for the future value of a lump sum (Equation 1-2), $FV_N = PV(1 + r)^N$, four times to find the payments. These future values are shown on the time line below.

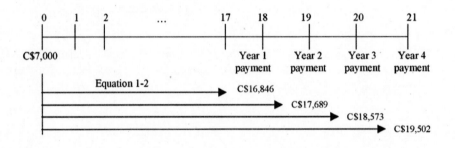

iv. Using the formula for the present value of a lump sum ($r = 6\%$), equate the four college payments to single payments as of $t = 17$ and add them together.
C$16,846(1.06)^{-1} + C\$17,689(1.06)^{-2} + C\$18,573(1.06)^{-3}$
$+ C\$19,502(1.06)^{-4} = C\$62,677$

v. Equate the sum of C$62,677 at $t = 17$ to the 17 payments of X, using the formula for the future value of an annuity (Equation 1-7). Then solve for X.

$$C\$62{,}677 = X\left[\frac{(1.06)^{17} - 1}{0.06}\right] = 28.21288X$$

$$X = C\$2{,}221.58$$

Notation Used on Most Calculators	Numerical Value for This Problem
N	17
$\%i$	6
PV	n/a ($= 0$)
FV	C$62,677
PMT **compute**	X

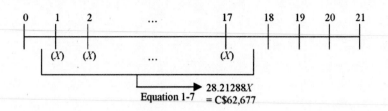

In summary, the couple will need to put aside C\$2,221.58 each year if they start next year and make 17 equal payments.

20. To compute the compound growth rate, we only need the beginning and ending EPS values of \$4.00 and \$7.00 respectively, and use the following equation:.

$$FV_N = PV(1 + r)^N$$

$$7 = 4(1 + r)^4$$

$$1 + r = (7/4)^{1/4}$$

$$r = (7/4)^{1/4} - 1$$

$$= 0.1502 = 15.02\%$$

EPS grew at an annual rate of 15.02 percent during the four years.

CHAPTER 2

DISCOUNTED CASH FLOW APPLICATIONS

SOLUTIONS

1. We can calculate the present value of the cash inflows in several ways. We can discount each cash inflow separately at the required rate of return of 12 percent and then sum the present values. We can also find the present value of a four-year annuity of C$3 million, add to it the present value of the $t = 5$ cash flow of C$10 million, and subtract the $t = 0$ outflow of C$13 million. Or we can compute the present value of a five-year annuity of C$3 million, add to it the present value of a cash inflow of C$7 million = C$10 million − C$3 million dated $t = 5$, and subtract the $t = 0$ outflow of C$13 million. For this last approach, we illustrate the keystrokes for many financial calculators.

Notation Used on Most Calculators	Numerical Value for This Problem
N	5
%i	12
PV **compute**	X
PMT	3,000,000
FV	7,000,000

We find that the PV of the inflows is C$14,786,317.
   A. Therefore, NPV = C$14,786,317 − C$13,000,000 = C$1,786,317.
   B. Waldrup should undertake this project because it has a positive NPV.
2. A. The internal rate of return is the discount rate that makes the NPV equal zero:

$$\text{NPV} = \text{CF}_0 + \frac{\text{CF}_1}{(1 + \text{IRR})^1} + \frac{\text{CF}_2}{(1 + \text{IRR})^2} + \cdots + \frac{\text{CF}_N}{(1 + \text{IRR})^N} = 0$$

To show that the investment project has an IRR of 13.51 percent we need to show that its NPV equals zero, ignoring rounding errors. Substituting the project's cash flows and IRR = 0.1351 into the above equation,

$$NPV = -C\$5,500,000 + \frac{C\$1,000,000}{(1.1351)^1} + \frac{C\$1,500,000}{(1.1351)^4} + \frac{C\$7,000,000}{(1.1351)^5}$$

$$= -C\$5,500,000 + C\$5,499,266 = -C\$734$$

Given that the cash flows were of the magnitude of millions, the amount C$734 differs negligibly from 0.

B. The internal rate of return is unaffected by any change in any external rate, including the increase in Waldrup's opportunity cost of capital.

3. A. NPV is the sum of the present values of all the cash flows associated with the investment, where inflows are signed positive and outflows are signed negative. This problem has only one outflow, an initial expenditure of $10 million at $t = 0$. The projected cash inflows from this advertising project form a perpetuity. We calculate the present value of a perpetuity as $\overline{CF}/r$, where $\overline{CF}$ is the level annual cash flow and r is the discount rate. Using the opportunity cost of capital of 12.5 percent as the discount rate, we have

$$NPV = -\$10,000,000 + 1,600,000/0.125 = -\$10,000,000 + 12,800,000$$

$$= \$2,800,000$$

B. In this case, the cash inflows are a perpetuity. Therefore, we can solve for the internal rate of return as follows:

$$\text{Initial investment} = (\text{Annual cash inflow})/\text{IRR}$$

$$10,000,000 = 1,600,000/\text{IRR}$$

$$\text{IRR} = 16 \text{ percent}$$

C. Yes, Bestfoods should spend $10 million on advertising. The NPV of $2.8 million is positive. The IRR of 16 percent is also in excess of the 12.5 percent opportunity cost of capital.

4. Using the IRR function in a spreadsheet or an IRR-enabled financial calculator, we enter the individual cash flows and apply the IRR function. We illustrate how we can solve for IRR in this particular problem using a financial calculator without a dedicated IRR function. The cash flows from $t = 1$ through $t = 6$ can be treated as a six-year, $4 million annuity with $7 million − $4 million = $3 million, entered as a future amount at $t = 6$.

Notation Used on Most Calculators	Numerical Value for This Problem
N	6
%i **compute**	X
PV	−15,000,000
PMT	4,000,000
FV	3,000,000

    A. The IRR of the project is 18.25 percent.

    B. Because the project's IRR is less than the hurdle rate of 19 percent, the company should not undertake the project.

5. A. *Company A.* Let $\overline{CF} = £300,000$ be the amount of the perpetuity. Then with $r = 0.12$, the NPV in acquiring Company A would be

$$NPV = CF_0 + \overline{CF}/r = -£2,000,000 + £300,000/0.12 = £500,000$$

Company B. Let $\overline{CF} = £435,000$ be the amount of the perpetuity. Then with $r = 0.12$, the NPV in acquiring Company B would be

$$NPV = CF_0 + \overline{CF}/r = -£3,000,000 + £435,000/0.12 = £625,000$$

Both Company A and Company B would be positive NPV acquisitions, but Westcott–Smith cannot purchase both because the total purchase price of £5 million exceeds its budgeted amount of £4 million. Because Company B's NPV of £625,000 is higher than Company A's NPV of £500,000, Westcott–Smith should purchase Company B according to the NPV rule.

    B. *Company A.* Using the notation from Part A, IRR is defined by the expression $NPV = -\text{Investment} + \overline{CF}/\text{IRR} = 0$. Thus $-£2,000,000 + £300,000/\text{IRR} = 0$ and solving for IRR,

$$\text{IRR} = £300,000/£2,000,000 = 0.15 \text{ or } 15 \text{ percent}$$

Company B.

$$\text{IRR} = £435,000/£3,000,000 = 0.145 \text{ or } 14.5 \text{ percent}$$

Both Company A and Company B have IRRs that exceed Westcott–Smith's opportunity cost of 12 percent, but Westcott–Smith cannot purchase both because of its budget constraint. According to the IRR rule, Westcott–Smith should purchase Company A because its IRR of 15 percent is higher than Company B's IRR of 14.5 percent.

    C. Westcott–Smith should purchase Company B. When the NPV and IRR rules conflict in ranking mutually exclusive investments, we should follow the NPV rule because it directly relates to shareholder wealth maximization.

6. A. The money-weighted rate of return is the discount rate that equates the present value of inflows to the present value of outflows.
    Outflows:
    At $t = 0$ (1 January 2002):

$$150 \text{ shares purchased} \times \$156.30 \text{ per share} = \$23,445$$

    Inflows:
    At $t = 1$ (1 January 2003):

$$150 \text{ shares} \times \$10 \text{ dividend per share} = \$1,500$$

$$100 \text{ shares sold} \times \$165 \text{ per share} = \$16,500$$

At $t = 2$ (1 January 2004):

$$50 \text{ shares remaining} \times \$15 \text{ dividend per share} = \$750$$

$$50 \text{ shares sold} \times \$170 \text{ per share} = \$8,500$$

$$PV(\text{Outflows}) = PV(\text{Inflows})$$

$$23,445 = \frac{1,500 + 16,500}{1 + r} + \frac{750 + 8,500}{(1 + r)^2}$$

$$= \frac{18,000}{1 + r} + \frac{9,250}{(1 + r)^2}$$

The last line is the equation for calculating the money-weighted rate of return on Wilson's portfolio.

B. We can solve for the money-weighted return by entering $-23,445$, 18,000, and 9,250 in a spreadsheet or calculator with an IRR function. In this case, we can also solve for money-weighted rate of return as the real root of the quadratic equation $18,000x + 9,250x^2 - 23,445 = 0$, where $x = 1/(1 + r)$. By any method, the solution is $r = 0.120017$ or approximately 12 percent.

C. The time-weighted rate of return is the solution to $(1 + \text{Time-weighted rate of return})^2 = (1 + r_1)(1 + r_2)$, where r_1 and r_2 are the holding period returns in the first and second years, respectively. The value of the portfolio at $t = 0$ is \$23,445. At $t = 1$, there are inflows of sale proceeds of \$16,500 and \$1,500 in dividends, or \$18,000 in total. The balance of 50 shares is worth $\$8,250 = 50 \text{ shares} \times \$165 \text{ per share}$. So at $t = 1$ the valuation is $\$26,250 = \$18,000 + \$8,250$. Thus

$$r_1 = (\$26,250 - \$23,445)/\$23,445 = 0.119642 \text{ for the first year}$$

The amount invested at $t = 1$ is $\$8,250 = (50 \text{ shares})(\$165 \text{ per share})$. At $t = 2$, \$750 in dividends are received, as well as sale proceeds of \$8,500 (50 shares sold $\times$ \$170 per share). So at $t = 2$, the valuation is $\$9,250 = \$750 + \$8,500$. Thus

$$r_2 = (\$9,250 - \$8,250)/\$8,250 = 0.121212 \text{ for the second year}$$

Time-weighted rate of return $= \sqrt{(1.119642)(1.121212)} - 1 = 0.1204$ or approximately 12 percent.

D. If Wilson is a private investor with full discretionary control over the timing and amount of withdrawals and additions to his portfolios, then the money-weighted rate of return is an appropriate measure of portfolio returns.

E. If Wilson is an investment manager whose clients exercise discretionary control over the timing and amount of withdrawals and additions to the portfolio, then the time-weighted rate of return is the appropriate measure of portfolio returns. Time-weighted rate of return is standard in the investment management industry.

7. *Similarities.* The time-weighted returns for Luongo's and Weaver's investments will be equal, because the time-weighted return is not sensitive to additions or withdrawals of funds. Even though Weaver purchased another share at €110, the return earned by Luongo and Weaver each year for the time-weighted return calculation is the same.

Differences. The money-weighted returns for Luongo and Weaver will differ because they take into account the timing of additions and withdrawals. During the two-year period, Weaver owned more shares of the stock during the year that it did poorly (the stock return for Year 1 is $(110 + 5 - 100)/100 = 15$ percent and for Year 2 it is $(100 + 5 - 110)/110 = -4.55$ percent). As a consequence, the money-weighted return for Weaver (1.63 percent) is less than that of Luongo (5.00 percent). The money-weighted return reflects the timing of additions and withdrawals. Note, the cash flows for the money-weighted returns for Luongo and Weaver are (for $t = 0$, 1, and 2) Luongo: $-100, +5, +105$; Weaver: $-100, -105, +210$.

8. In this solution, F stands for face value, P stands for price, and D stands for the discount from face value $(D = F - P)$.

A. Use the discount yield formula (Equation 2-3), $r_{BD} = D/F \times 360/t$:

$$r_{BD} = (\$1,500/\$100,000) \times (360/120) = 0.0150 \times 3 = 0.045$$

The T-bill's bank discount yield is 4.5 percent a year.

B. Use your answer from Part A and the money market yield formula (Equation 2-6), $r_{MM} = (360 \times r_{BD})/(360 - t \times r_{BD})$:

$$r_{MM} = (360 \times 0.045)/(360 - 120 \times 0.045) = 0.04568$$

The T-bill's bank discount yield is 4.57 percent a year.

C. Calculate the holding period yield (using Equation 2-4), then compound it forward to one year. First, the holding period yield (HPY) is

$$HPY = \frac{P_1 - P + D_1}{P_0} = (100,000 - 98,500)/98,500 = 0.015228$$

Next, compound the 120-day holding period yield, a periodic rate, forward to one year using Equation 2-5:

$$\text{Effective annual yield} = (1 + HPY)^{365/t} - 1$$

$$\text{Effective annual yield} = (1.015228)^{365/120} - 1 = 0.047044$$

The T-bill's effective annual yield is 4.7 percent a year.

9. A. In the United States, T-bill yields are quoted on a bank discount basis. The bank discount yield is not a meaningful measure of the return for three reasons: First, the yield is based on the face value of the bond, not on its purchase price. Returns from investments should be evaluated relative to the amount that is invested. Second, the yield is annualized based on a 360-day year rather than a 365-day year. Third, the bank discount yield annualizes with simple interest, which ignores the opportunity to earn interest on interest (compound interest).

B. The money market yield is superior to the bank discount yield because the money market yield is computed relative to the purchase price (not the face value).

C. The T-bill yield can be restated on a money market basis by multiplying the bank discount yield by the ratio of the face value to the purchase price. Cavell could divide the annualized yield by 4 to compute the 90-day holding period yield. This is a more meaningful measure of the return that she will actually earn over 90 days (assuming that she holds the T-bill until it matures).

CHAPTER 3

STATISTICAL CONCEPTS AND MARKET RETURNS

SOLUTIONS

1. A. The S&P MidCap 400 Index represents a sample of all U.S. stocks in the mid-cap or medium capitalization range. The related population is "all U.S. mid-cap stocks."
   B. The statement tells us to enumerate all members of a group and is sufficiently precise to allow us to do that. The statement defines a population.
   C. The two companies constitute a sample of U.S. insurance brokers. The related population is "U.S. insurance brokers."
   D. The statement defines a population. The 31 estimates for Microsoft EPS are the population of publicly available U.S. analyst estimates of Microsoft's FY2003 EPS, as of the report's date.

2. A. Sales in euros are measured on a ratio scale.
   B. Mutual fund investment styles are measured on a nominal scale. We can count the number of funds following a particular style, but whatever classification scheme we use, we cannot order styles into "greater than" or "less than" relationships.
   C. The ratings are measured on an ordinal scale. An analyst's rating of a stock as underweight, market weight, or overweight orders the rated securities in terms of levels of expected investment performance.
   D. The risk measurements are measured on an interval scale because not only do the measurements involve a ranking, but differences between adjacent values represent equal differences in risk. Because the measurement scale does not have a true zero, they are not measured on a ratio scale.

3. A. The entries in the table are as follows.

Return Interval	Frequency	Cumulative Frequency	Relative Frequency	Cumulative Relative Frequency
$-9.19\% \leq A < -4.55\%$	3	3	25.00%	25.00%
$-4.55\% \leq B < 0.09\%$	4	7	33.33%	58.33%
$0.09\% \leq C < 4.73\%$	3	10	25.00%	83.33%
$4.73\% \leq D \leq 9.37\%$	2	12	16.67%	100.00%

The frequency column provides the count of the observations falling in each return interval. The cumulative frequency adds up (cumulates) the frequencies. For example, the cumulative frequency of 7 for Interval B is the sum of the frequency of 3 for Interval A and the frequency of 4 for Interval B. The cumulative frequency for the last interval, D, equals the total number of observations, 12. The relative frequency column gives the frequency of an interval as a percentage of the total number of observations. The relative frequency for Interval B, for example, is $4/12 = 33.33$ percent. The cumulative relative frequency column cumulates the relative frequencies. After reaching the last interval, the cumulative relative frequency should be 100 percent, ignoring rounding errors.

B. The histogram for these data is shown below.

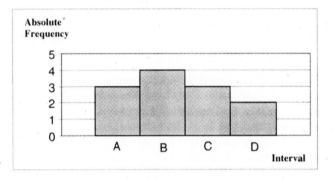

C. From the frequency distribution in Part A or the histogram in Part B, we can see that Interval B (-4.55 to 0.09) has the most members, 4. Interval B is thus the modal interval.

4. To calculate tracking risk of the portfolio, we use the sample standard deviation of the data in the table. We use the expression for sample standard deviation rather than population standard deviation because we are estimating the portfolio's tracking risk based on a sample. We use Equation 3-14,

$$s = \sqrt{\dfrac{\displaystyle\sum_{i=1}^{n}(X_i - \overline{X})^2}{n-1}}$$

where X_i is the ith entry in the table of return deviations. The calculation in detail is as follows:

i. $\overline{X} = (-7.14 + 1.62 + 2.48 - 2.59 + 9.37 - 0.55 - 0.89 - 9.19 - 5.11 - 0.49 + 6.84 + 3.04)/12 = -2.61/12 = -0.2175$ percent.

ii. Having established that the mean deviation from the benchmark was $\overline{X} = -0.2175$, we calculate the squared deviations from the mean as follows:
$[-7.14 - (-0.2175)]^2 = (-6.9225)^2 = 47.921006$
$[1.62 - (-0.2175)]^2 = (1.8375)^2 = 3.376406$
$[2.48 - (-0.2175)]^2 = (2.6975)^2 = 7.276506$
$[-2.59 - (-0.2175)]^2 = (-2.3725)^2 = 5.628756$

$$[9.37 - (-0.2175)]^2 = (9.5875)^2 = 91.920156$$
$$[-0.55 - (-0.2175)]^2 = (-0.3325)^2 = 0.110556$$
$$[-0.89 - (-0.2175)]^2 = (-0.6725)^2 = 0.452256$$
$$[-9.19 - (-0.2175)]^2 = (-8.9725)^2 = 80.505756$$
$$[-5.11 - (-0.2175)]^2 = (-4.8925)^2 = 23.936556$$
$$[-0.49 - (-0.2175)]^2 = (-0.2725)^2 = 0.074256$$
$$[6.84 - (-0.2175)]^2 = (7.0575)^2 = 49.808306$$
$$[3.04 - (-0.2175)]^2 = (3.2575)^2 = 10.611306$$

iii. The sum of the squared deviations from the mean is

$$\sum_{i=1}^{12}(X_i - \overline{X})^2 = 321.621825$$

Note that the sum is given with full precision. You may also get 321.621822, adding the terms rounded at the sixth decimal place. The solution is not affected.

iv. Divide the sum of the squared deviations from the mean by $n - 1$:

$$321.621825/(12 - 1) = 321.621825/11 = 29.238347$$

v. Take the square root: $s = \sqrt{29.238347} = 5.41$ percent. Thus the portfolio's tracking risk was 5.41 percent a year.

5. A. A frequency distribution is a tabular display of data summarized into a relatively small number of equally sized intervals. In this example, we want five equally sized intervals. To make the frequency distribution table, we take the following seven steps.

i. Sort the data in ascending order.

−43.06%
−17.75%
−9.53%
−6.18%
8.04%
20.32%
22.87%
41.20%
45.90%
46.21%

ii. Calculate the range. Recall that the range formula is

$$\text{Range} = \text{Maximum value} - \text{Minimum value}$$

In this case, the range is $46.21 - (-43.06) = 89.27$.

iii. Decide on the number of intervals in the frequency distribution, k. This number was specified as $k = 5$ in the statement of the problem.

    iv. Determine the interval width as Range/k = 89.27/5 = 17.854 or 17.86, rounding up at the second decimal place as instructed in the statement of the problem. Note that if we rounded down to 17.85, the final class would terminate at 46.19 and not capture the largest return, 46.21.

    v. Determine the intervals by successively adding the interval width to the minimum value, to determine the ending points of intervals, stopping after we reach an interval that includes the maximum value.

$$
\begin{aligned}
-43.06 + 17.86 &= -25.20 \\
-25.20 + 17.86 &= -7.34 \\
-7.34 + 17.86 &= 10.52 \\
10.52 + 17.86 &= 28.38 \\
28.38 + 17.86 &= 46.24
\end{aligned}
$$

Thus the intervals are from −43.06 up to (but not including) −25.20, −25.20 to −7.34, −7.34 to 10.52, 10.52 to 28.38, and 28.38 to (including) 46.24.

    vi. Count the number of observations falling in each interval. The count is one observation in −43.06 to −25.20, two observations in −25.20 to −7.34, two observations in −7.34 to 10.52, two observations in 10.52 to 28.38, and three observations in 28.38 to 46.24.

    vii. Construct a table of the intervals listed from smallest to largest that shows the number of observations falling in each interval. The heading of the last column may be "frequency" or "absolute frequency."

Interval		Frequency
A	−43.06 ≤ observation < −25.20	1
B	−25.20 ≤ observation < −7.34	2
C	−7.34 ≤ observation < 10.52	2
D	10.52 ≤ observation < 28.38	2
E	28.38 ≤ observation ≤ 46.24	3

B. We find the cumulative frequencies by adding the absolute frequencies as we move from the first interval to the last interval.

Interval		Absolute Frequency	Calculations for Cumulative Frequency	Cumulative Frequency
A	−43.06 ≤ observation < −25.20	1		1
B	−25.20 ≤ observation < −7.34	2	1 + 2 =	3
C	−7.34 ≤ observation < 10.52	2	3 + 2 =	5
D	10.52 ≤ observation < 28.38	2	5 + 2 =	7
E	28.38 ≤ observation ≤ 46.24	3	7 + 3 =	10

The cumulative frequency is a running total of the absolute frequency, and the cumulative frequency for the last interval equals the total number of observations, 10.

C. The relative frequency of an interval is the frequency of the interval divided by the total number of observations. The cumulative relative frequency sums the relative frequencies. The cumulative relative frequency for the last interval is 100 percent.

Intervals	Absolute Frequency	Relative Frequency	Calculations for Cumulative Frequency	Cumulative Relative Frequency
A. $-43.06 \leq$ observation < -25.20	1	$1/10 = 10\%$		10%
B. $-25.20 \leq$ observation < -7.34	2	$2/10 = 20\%$	$10\% + 20\% =$	30%
C. $-7.34 \leq$ observation < 10.52	2	$2/10 = 20\%$	$30\% + 20\% =$	50%
D. $10.52 \leq$ observation < 28.38	2	$2/10 = 20\%$	$50\% + 20\% =$	70%
E. $28.38 \leq$ observation ≤ 46.24	3	$3/10 = 30\%$	$70\% + 30\% =$	100%
	10			

D. The last interval in the frequency distribution contains 30 percent of the observations, whereas the first interval contains 10 percent of the observations. The middle three intervals each contain 20 percent of the observations. The last two intervals thus contain 50 percent of the observations. The distribution is asymmetric. With most observations somewhat concentrated to the right but with one extreme negative observation (in the first interval), we conclude that the distribution is negatively skewed.

6. A. We calculate the sample mean by finding the sum of the 10 values in the table and then dividing by 10. According to Equation 3-3, the sample mean return, $\overline{R}$, is

$$\overline{R} = \frac{\sum_{i=1}^{10} R_i}{10}$$

using a common notation for returns, R_i. Thus $\overline{R} = (46.21 - 6.18 + 8.04 + 22.87 + 45.90 + 20.32 + 41.20 - 9.53 - 17.75 - 43.06)/10 = 108.02/10 = 10.802$ or 10.80 percent.

B. The median is defined as the value of the middle item of a group that has been sorted into ascending or descending order. In a sample of n items, where n is an odd number, the median is the value of the item in the sorted data set occupying the $(n + 1)/2$ position. When the data set has an even number of observations (as in this example), the median is the mean of the values of the items occupying the $n/2$ and $(n + 2)/2$ positions (the two middle items). With $n = 10$, these are the fifth and sixth positions.

To find the median, the first step is to rank the data. We previously sorted the returns in ascending order in Solution 5A(i).

Returns	Position
−43.06%	1
−17.75%	2
−9.53%	3
−6.18%	4
8.04%	5
20.32%	6
22.87%	7
41.20%	8
45.90%	9
46.21%	10

The value of the item in the fifth position is 8.04, and the value of the item in the sixth position is 20.32. The median return is then $(8.04 + 20.32)/2 = 28.36/2 = 14.18$ percent.

C. The modal return interval, as noted in Solution 5A, is Interval E, running from 28.38 percent to 46.24 percent.

7. The geometric mean requires that all the numbers be greater than or equal to 0. To ensure that the returns satisfy this requirement, after converting the returns to decimal form we add 1 to each return. We then use Equation 3-6 for the geometric mean return, R_G:

$$R_G = \left[\prod_{t=1}^{10} (1 + R_t) \right]^{(1/10)} - 1$$

which can also be written as

$$R_G = \sqrt[10]{(1 + R_1)(1 + R_2)\ldots(1 + R_{10})} - 1$$

To find the geometric mean in this example, we take the following five steps:

i. Divide each figure in the table by 100 to put the returns into decimal representation.
ii. Add 1 to each return to obtain the terms $1 + R_t$.

Return	Return in Decimal Form	1 + Return
46.21%	0.4621	1.4621
−6.18%	−0.0618	0.9382
8.04%	0.0804	1.0804
22.87%	0.2287	1.2287
45.90%	0.4590	1.4590
20.32%	0.2032	1.2032
41.20%	0.4120	1.4120
−9.53%	−0.0953	0.9047
−17.75%	−0.1775	0.8225
−43.06%	−0.4306	0.5694

iii. Multiply together all the numbers in the third column to get 1.9124.
iv. Take the 10th root of 1.9124 to get $\sqrt[10]{1.9124} = 1.0670$. On most calculators, we evaluate $\sqrt[10]{1.9124}$ using the y^x key. Enter 1.9124 with the y^x key. Next, enter $1/10 = 0.10$. Then press the = key to get 1.0670.
v. Subtract 1 to get 0.0670, or 6.70 percent a year. The geometric mean return is 6.70 percent. This result means that the compound annual rate of growth of the MSCI Germany Index was 6.7 percent annually during the 1993–2002 period. Note that this value is much less than the arithmetic mean of 10.80 percent that we calculated in the solution to Problem 6A.

8. Recall the formula for the location of the percentile (Equation 3-8):

$$L_y = (n+1)\frac{y}{100}$$

where L_y is the location or position of the yth percentile, P_y, and y is the percentage point at which we want to divide the distribution.

If we apply the percentile location formula, we find $L_{30} = (10+1)\frac{30}{100} = 3.3$, which is not a whole number. To find the 30th percentile from the sorted data, we interpolate by taking the value in the third position, -9.53, and adding 30 percent of the difference between the items in fourth and third position. The estimate of the 30th percentile is $P_{30} \approx -9.53 + 0.3[-6.18 - (-9.53)] = -9.53 + 0.3(3.35) = -9.53 + 1.005 = -8.53$.

Therefore, the 30th percentile is -8.53. By definition, the 30th percentile is that value at or below which 30 percent of the observations lie. In this problem, 3 observations out of 10 lie below -8.53.

9. A. In the solution to Problem 5A, we calculated the range as Maximum value − Minimum value = $46.21 - (-43.06) = 89.27$.

Original Data R_i	Deviation from Mean $R_i - \bar{R}$	Absolute Value of Deviation from Mean $|R_i - \bar{R}|$
46.21	35.41	35.41
−6.18	−16.98	16.98
8.04	−2.76	2.76
22.87	12.07	12.07
45.90	35.10	35.10
20.32	9.52	9.52
41.20	30.40	30.40
−9.53	−20.33	20.33
−17.75	−28.55	28.55
−43.06	−53.86	53.86
$\bar{R} = 10.8$		

$$\sum_{i=1}^{10} |R_i - \bar{R}| = 244.98$$

$$MAD = \frac{\sum_{i=1}^{10} |R_i - \bar{R}|}{10} = 24.50$$

B. The mean absolute deviation is defined in Equation 3-10 as

$$MAD = \frac{\sum_{i=1}^{10} |R_i - \bar{R}|}{10}$$

To find the MAD for this example, we take the following four steps (results shown on the previous page):

i. Calculate the arithmetic mean of the original values.
ii. Subtract the arithmetic mean from each value.
iii. Take the absolute value of each deviation from the mean.
iv. Sum the absolute values of the deviations and divide by the total number of observations. The mean absolute deviation in this case is 24.50 percent.

C. Variance is defined as the mean of the squared deviations around the mean. We find the sample variance with Equation 3-13:

$$s^2 = \frac{\sum_{i=1}^{10} (R_i - \bar{R})^2}{10 - 1}$$

To calculate the variance, we take the following four steps:

i. Calculate the arithmetic mean of the original values.
ii. Subtract the arithmetic mean from each value.
iii. Square each deviation from the mean.
iv. Sum the squared deviations and divide by the total number of observations minus 1. The variance, in this case, is 896.844711.

The following table summarizes the calculation.

Original Data R_i	Deviation from Mean $R_i - \bar{R}$	Squared Value of Deviation from Mean $(R_i - \bar{R})^2$
46.21	35.41	1253.8681
−6.18	−16.98	288.3204
8.04	−2.76	7.6176
22.87	12.07	145.6849
45.90	35.10	1232.0100
20.32	9.52	90.6304
41.20	30.40	924.1600
−9.53	−20.33	413.3089
−17.75	−28.55	815.1025
−43.06	−53.86	2900.8996
$\bar{R} = 10.8$		

$$\sum_{i=1}^{10} (R_i - \bar{R})^2 = 8{,}071.6024$$

$$s^2 = \frac{\sum_{i=1}^{10} (R_i - \bar{R})^2}{9} = 896.844711$$

Recall that the units of variance are the squared units of the underlying variable, so to be precise we say that the sample variance is 896.844711 percent squared. To have a result in the original units of measurement, we calculate the standard deviation.

D. The standard deviation is the positive square root of the variance. We calculate the standard deviation with Equation 3-14:

$$s = \sqrt{896.844711} = 29.9474 \text{ or } 29.95\%$$

The standard deviation is thus 29.95 percent.

E. Semivariance is the average squared deviation below the mean. Five observations (−43.06, −17.75, −9.53, −6.18, and 8.04) lie below the mean return of 10.8. We compute the sum of the squared deviations from the mean as $(−43.06 − 10.8)^2 + (−17.75 − 10.8)^2 + (−9.53 − 10.8)^2 + (−6.18 − 10.8)^2 + (8.04 − 10.8)^2 = 4,425.2490$. Semivariance equals $4,425.2490/(5 − 1) = 1,106.3123$.

F. Semideviation equals $\sqrt{1,106.3123} = 33.2613$ or 33.26%.

10. A. According to Equation 3-17, (sample) skewness S_K is

$$S_k = \left[\frac{n}{(n-1)(n-2)} \right] \frac{\sum\limits_{i=1}^{n}(R_i - \overline{R})^3}{s^3}$$

The sample size, n, is 10. We previously calculated $\overline{R} = 10.8$ and deviations from the mean (see the tables in the solution to Problems 9B and 9C). We also calculated $s = 29.9474$ (showing four decimal places) in the solution to 9D. Thus $s^3 = 26,858.2289$. Using these results, we calculate the sum of the cubed deviations from the mean as follows:

$$\sum_{i=1}^{10}(R_i - \overline{R})^3 = \sum_{i=1}^{10}(R_i - 10.8)^3 = 35.41^3 + (−16.98)^3 + (−2.76)^3 + 12.07^3$$

$$+ 35.1^3 + 9.52^3 + 30.4^3 + (−20.33)^3 + (−28.55)^3 + (−53.86)^3$$

$$= 44,399.4694 − 4,895.6804 − 21.0246 + 1,758.4167$$

$$+ 43,243.551 + 862.8014 + 28,094.464 − 8,402.5699$$

$$− 23,271.1764 − 156,242.4525$$

$$= −74,474.2012$$

So finally we have

$$S_K = \frac{10}{(9)(8)} \frac{−74,474.2012}{26,858.2289} = −0.39$$

In the sample period, the returns on the MSCI Germany Index were slightly negatively skewed.

B. For a negatively skewed distribution, the median is greater than the arithmetic mean. In our sample, the median return of 14.18 percent is greater than the mean return of 10.80.

C. According to Equation 3-18 sample excess kurtosis, K_E, is

$$K_E = \left\{ \left[\frac{n(n+1)}{(n-1)(n-2)(n-3)} \right] \frac{\sum_{i=1}^{n}(R_i - \overline{R})^4}{s^4} \right\} - \frac{3(n-1)^2}{(n-2)(n-3)}$$

The sample size, n, is 10. We previously calculated $\overline{R} = 10.8$ and deviations from the mean (see the tables in the solution to Problems 9B and 9C). We also calculated $s = 29.9474$ (showing four decimal places) in the answer to 9D. Thus $s^4 = 804,334.1230$. Using these results, we calculate the sum of the deviations from the mean raised to the fourth power as follows:

$$\sum_{i=1}^{10}(R_i - \overline{R})^4 = \sum_{i=1}^{10}(R_i - 10.8)^4 = 35.41^4 + (-16.98)^4 + (-2.76)^4 + 12.07^4$$

$$+ 35.1^4 + 9.52^4 + 30.4^4 + (-20.33)^4 + (-28.55)^4 + (-53.86)^4$$

$$= 1,572,185.212 + 83,128.6531 + 58.0278 + 21,224.0901$$

$$+ 1,517,848.64 + 8,213.8694 + 854,071.7056 + 170,824.2468$$

$$+ 664,392.0855 + 8,415,218.489$$

$$= 13,307,165.02$$

Thus we have

$$\left\{ \left[\frac{10(11)}{(9)(8)(7)} \right] \frac{13,307,165.02}{804,334.123} \right\} - \frac{3(9)^2}{(8)(7)} = 3.6109 - 4.3393 = -0.73$$

In the sample period, the returns on the MSCI Germany Index were slightly platykurtic. This means that there were fewer observations in the tails of the distribution than we would expect based on a normal distribution model for returns.

D. In contrast to a normal distribution, the distribution of returns on the MSCI Germany Index is somewhat asymmetric in direction of negative skew and is somewhat platykurtic (less peaked).

11. A. So long as a return series has any variability, the geometric mean return must be less than the arithmetic mean return. As one illustration of this relationship, in the solution to Problem 6A, we computed the arithmetic mean annual return on the MSCI Germany Index as 10.80 percent. In the solution to Problem 7, we computed the geometric mean annual return as 6.7 percent. In general, the difference between the geometric and arithmetic means increases with the variability of the period-by-period observations.

B. The geometric mean return is more meaningful than the arithmetic mean return for an investor concerned with the terminal value of an investment. The geometric mean return is the compound rate of growth, so it directly relates to the terminal value of an investment. By contrast, a higher arithmetic mean return does not necessarily imply a higher terminal value for an investment.

C. The arithmetic mean return is more meaningful than the geometric mean return for an investor concerned with the average one-period performance of an investment. The arithmetic mean return is a direct representation of the average one-period return. In contrast, the geometric mean return, as a compound rate of growth, aims to summarize what a return series means for the growth rate of an investment over many periods.

12. The following table shows the calculation of the portfolio's annual returns, and the mean annual return.

Year	Weighted Mean Calculation	Portfolio Return
1993	$0.60(46.21) + 0.40(15.74) =$	34.02%
1994	$0.60(-6.18) + 0.40(-3.40) =$	-5.07%
1995	$0.60(8.04) + 0.40(18.30) =$	12.14%
1996	$0.60(22.87) + 0.40(8.35) =$	17.06%
1997	$0.60(45.90) + 0.40(6.65) =$	30.20%
1998	$0.60(20.32) + 0.40(12.45) =$	17.17%
1999	$0.60(41.20) + 0.40(-2.19) =$	23.84%
2000	$0.60(-9.53) + 0.40(7.44) =$	-2.74%
2001	$0.60(-17.75) + 0.40(5.55) =$	-8.43%
2002	$0.60(-43.06) + 0.40(10.27) =$	-21.73%
	Sum =	96.46%
	Mean Annual Return =	9.65%

Note: The sum of the portfolio returns carried without rounding is 96.48.

13. A. i. For the 60/40 equity/bond portfolio, the mean return (as computed in Problem 12) was 9.65 percent. We can compute the sample standard deviation of returns as $s = 18.31$ percent using Equation 3-14. The coefficient of variation for the 60/40 portfolio was $CV = s/\overline{R} = 18.31/9.65 = 1.90$.
   ii. For the MSCI Germany Index, $CV = s/\overline{R} = 29.95/10.80 = 2.77$.
   iii. For the JPM Germany 5–7 Year GBI, $CV = s/\overline{R} = 6.94/7.92 = 0.88$.
   B. The coefficient of variation is a measure of relative dispersion. For returns, it measures the amount of risk per unit of mean return. The MSCI Germany Index portfolio, the JPM Germany GBI, and the 60/40 equity/bond portfolio, were respectively most risky, least risky, and intermediate in risk, based on their values of CV.

Portfolio	CV	Risk
MSCI Germany Index	2.77	Highest
60/40 Equity/bond portfolio	1.90	
JPM Germany GBI	0.88	Lowest

14. A. i. For the 60/40 equity/bond portfolio, we earlier computed a mean return and standard deviation of return of 9.65 percent and 18.31, respectively. The statement of the problem gave the mean annual return on the proxy for the risk-free rate, the IMF Germany MMI, as 4.33 percent. We compute the Sharpe ratio as

$$S_h = \frac{\overline{R}_p - \overline{R}_F}{s_p} = \frac{9.65 - 4.33}{18.31} = 0.29$$

ii. For the MSCI Germany Index,

$$S_h = \frac{\overline{R}_p - \overline{R}_F}{s_p} = \frac{10.80 - 4.33}{29.95} = 0.22$$

iii. For the JPM Germany 5–7 Year GBI,

$$S_h = \frac{\overline{R}_p - \overline{R}_F}{s_p} = \frac{7.92 - 4.33}{6.94} = 0.52$$

B. The Sharpe ratio measures excess return per unit of risk as measured by standard deviation. Because we are comparing positive Sharpe ratios, a larger Sharpe ratio reflects better risk-adjusted performance. During the period, the JPM Germany GBI had the best risk-adjusted performance and the MSCI Germany Index had the worst risk-adjusted performance, as measured by the Sharpe ratio. The 60/40 equity/bond portfolio was intermediate in risk-adjusted performance.

Portfolio	Sharpe Ratio	Performance
JPM Germany GBI	0.52	Best
60/40 Equity/bond portfolio	0.29	
MSCI Germany Index	0.22	Worst

15. A. i. The arithmetic mean P/E is $(13.67 + 14.43 + 28.06 + 18.46 + 11.91 + 15.80 + 14.24 + 6.44)/8 = 15.38$.

   ii. Because the portfolio has an even number of stocks (eight), the median P/E is the mean of the P/Es in the $n/2 = 8/2 = 4$th and $(n + 2)/2 = 10/2 = 5$th positions in the data sorted in ascending order. (These are the middle two P/Es.) The fourth position P/E is 14.24, and the fifth position P/E is 14.43. The median P/E is $(14.24 + 14.43)/2 = 14.34$.

   B. i. The arithmetic mean P/S is $(1.66 + 1.13 + 2.45 + 2.39 + 1.34 + 1.04 + 0.40 + 0.07)/8 = 1.31$.

   ii. The median P/S is the mean of the P/Ss in the fourth and fifth positions in the data sorted in ascending order. The fourth position P/S is 1.13, and the fifth position P/S is 1.34. The median P/S is $(1.13 + 1.34)/2 = 1.24$.

   C. i. The arithmetic mean P/B is $(3.43 + 1.96 + 382.72 + 1.65 + 1.30 + 1.70 + 2.13 + 41.31)/8 = 54.53$.

   ii. The median P/B is the mean of the P/Bs in the fourth and fifth positions in the data sorted in ascending order. The fourth position P/B is 1.96, and the fifth position P/B is 2.13. The median P/B is $(1.96 + 2.13)/2 = 2.05$.

   D. i. The distribution of P/Es is not characterized by outliers (extreme values) and the mean P/E and median P/E at 15.38 and 14.34, respectively, are similar in magnitude. Both the mean P/E and the median P/E are appropriate measures of central tendency. Because the mean P/E uses all the information in the sample and is mathematically simpler than the median, however, we might give it preference.

ii. Both the mean P/S and the median P/S are appropriate measures of central tendency. The mean P/S and median P/S at 1.31 and 1.24, respectively, are similar in magnitude. The P/S of 0.07 for Tenneco Automotive, Inc., is very small, yet it has only a moderate influence on the mean. As price is bounded from below at zero and sales is non-negative, the lowest possible P/S is 0. By contrast, there is no upper limit in theory on any price ratio. It is extremely high rather than extremely low P/Ss that would be the greater concern in using an arithmetic mean P/S. Note, too, that the P/E of about 6.4 for Tenneco, the lowest P/E observation, is not inconsistent with the P/S of 0.07 as long as the P/S is a valid observation (rather than a recording error).

iii. The median P/B, but not the mean P/B, is an appropriate measure of central tendency. The mean P/B of 54.53 is unduly influenced by the extreme P/Bs of roughly 383 for Avon Products and roughly 41 for Tenneco Automotive. The case of Tenneco is interesting. The P/E and the P/S in particular appear to indicate that the stock is cheap in terms of the earnings and sales that a dollar buys; the P/B appears to indicate the reverse. Because book value is an accounting number subject to such decisions as write-downs, we might investigate whether book value per share for Tenneco and Avon reflect such actions.

16. A. With identical means, the two return distributions are similarly centered. Portfolio B's distribution has somewhat less dispersion, as measured by standard deviation. Both return distributions are asymmetric but in different ways. The return distribution for Portfolio A is negatively skewed; Portfolio B's distribution is positively skewed.

B. Most investors would prefer the return distribution of Portfolio B, which has the same mean return as Portfolio A but less risk as measured by standard deviation of return. Furthermore, Portfolio B's returns are positively skewed, indicating a higher frequency of very large positive returns relative to Portfolio A. In contrast, Portfolio A's returns are negatively skewed.

17. A. With identical means, the two return distributions are similarly centered. Portfolio B's distribution has somewhat more dispersion, as measured by standard deviation. Both return distributions are negatively skewed to the same degree. Both portfolios have very large excess kurtosis, indicating much more frequent returns at the extremes, both positive and negative, than for a normal distribution.

B. With identical mean returns and skewness, the comparison reduces to risk. Portfolio B is riskier as measured by standard deviation. Furthermore, risk–averse investors might view Portfolio B's more frequent extreme returns (both negative and positive), as indicated by greater kurtosis, as an additional risk element. Consequently, Portfolio A has the better risk–reward profile.

18. A. Portfolio B's returns are centered to the right of Portfolio A's, as indicated by mean return. Portfolio B's distribution has somewhat more dispersion than A's. Both return distributions are asymmetric but in different ways. The return distribution for Portfolio A is slightly negatively skewed. Portfolio B's distribution is moderately positively skewed. Portfolio A's return distribution is mesokurtic, and Portfolio B's return distribution is slightly platykurtic.

B. We cannot know which portfolio particular investors would prefer without knowing their exact preferences for risk and return. Portfolio B has a higher mean return and moderately positive skewness, but it also has more risk as measured by standard deviation of return.

19. To determine which evaluation criterion is the most difficult to achieve, we need to (i) calculate the mean return of the nine funds, (ii) calculate the median return of the nine funds, (iii) calculate two-thirds of the return of the best-performing fund, and (iv) compare the results.

i. Calculate the mean return of the nine funds.
Find the sum of the values in the table and divide by 9.

$$\overline{X} = (17.8 + 21.0 + 38.0 + 19.2 + 2.5 + 24.3 + 18.7 + 16.9 + 12.6)/9$$

$$= 171/9 = 19.0$$

ii. Calculate the median return of the nine funds. The first step is to sort the returns from largest to smallest.

Return	Ranking
38.0%	9
24.3%	8
21.0%	7
19.2%	6
18.7%	5
17.8%	4
16.9%	3
12.6%	2
2.5%	1

The median is the middle item, which occupies the $(n + 1)/2 = 5$th position in this odd-numbered sample. We conclude that the median is 18.7.

iii. Calculate two-thirds of the return of the best-performing fund. The top return is 38.0; therefore, two-thirds of the top return is $(2/3)38.0 = 25.33$.

iv. The following table summarizes what we have learned about these funds.

Criterion 1	Criterion 2	Criterion 3
19.0	18.7	25.3

Criterion 3, two-thirds of the return on the top fund, is the most difficult to meet.

In analyzing this problem, note that Criterion 3 is very sensitive to the value of the maximum observation. For example, if we were to subtract 10 from the maximum (to make it 28) and add 10 to the minimum (to make it 12.5), the mean and median would be unchanged. Criterion 3 would fall to two-thirds of 28, or 18.67. In this case, the mean, at 19.0, would be the most difficult criterion to achieve.

CHAPTER 4

PROBABILITY CONCEPTS

SOLUTIONS

1. A. Probability is defined by the following two properties: (1) the probability of any event is a number between 0 and 1 inclusive, and (2) the sum of the probabilities of any set of mutually exclusive and exhaustive events equals 1.
   B. Conditional probability is the probability of a stated event, given that another event has occurred. For example $P(A \mid B)$ is the probability of A, given that B has occurred.
   C. An event is any specified outcome or set of outcomes of a random variable.
   D. Two events are independent if the occurrence of one event does not affect the probability of occurrence of the other event. In symbols, two events A and B are independent if and only if $P(A \mid B) = P(A)$ or, equivalently, $P(B \mid A) = P(B)$.
   E. The variance of a random variable is the expected value (the probability-weighted average) of squared deviations from the random variable's expected value. In symbols, $\sigma^2(X) = E\{[X - E(X)]^2\}$.

2. One logical set of three mutually exclusive and exhaustive events for the reaction of a company's stock price on the day of a corporate earnings announcement is as follows (wording may vary):

   - Stock price increases on the day of the announcement.
   - Stock price does not change on the day of the announcement.
   - Stock price decreases on the day of the announcement.

   In fact, there is an unlimited number of ways to split up the possible outcomes into three mutually exclusive and exhaustive events. For example, the following list also answers this question satisfactorily:

   - Stock price increases by more than 4 percent on the day of the announcement.
   - Stock price increases by 0 percent to 4 percent on the day of the announcement.
   - Stock price decreases on the day of the announcement.

3. A. The probability is an empirical probability.
   B. The probability is a subjective probability.
   C. The probability is an a priori probability.
   D. The probability is a subjective probability.

4. The implied probabilities of 0.90 and 0.50 are inconsistent in that they create a potential profit opportunity. Compared with Relaxin shares, the shares of BestRest are relatively overvalued because their price incorporates a much higher probability of the favorable event (lifting of the trade restriction) than the shares of Relaxin.

5. The probability that at least one of the two orders executes is given by the addition rule for probabilities. Let A stand for the event that *the first limit order executes before the close of trading* $[P(A) = 0.45]$ and let B stand for the event that *the second limit order executes before the close of trading* $[P(B) = 0.20]$. $P(AB)$ is given as 0.10. Therefore, $P(A \text{ or } B) = P(A) + P(B) - P(AB) = 0.45 + 0.20 - 0.10 = 0.55$. The probability that at least one of the two orders executes before the close of trading is 0.55.

6. Use Equation 4-1 to find this conditional probability: P(*stock is dividend paying* | *telecom stock that meets criteria*) = P(*stock is dividend paying and telecom stock that meets criteria*)/P(*telecom stock that meets criteria*) = 0.01/0.05 = 0.20.

7. According to the multiplication rule for independent events, the probability of a company meeting all three criteria is the product of the three probabilities. Labeling the event that a company passes the first, second, and third criteria, A, B, and C, respectively $P(ABC) = P(A)P(B)P(C) = (0.20)(0.45)(0.78) = 0.0702$. As a consequence, $(0.0702)(500) = 35.10$, so 35 companies pass the screen.

8. Use Equation 4-2, the multiplication rule for probabilities $P(AB) = P(A \mid B)P(B)$, defining A as the event that *a stock meets the financial strength criteria* and defining B as the event that *a stock meets the valuation criteria*. Then $P(AB) = P(A \mid B)P(B) = 0.40 \times 0.25 = 0.10$. The probability that a stock meets both the financial and valuation criteria is 0.10.

9. A. The default rate was ($109.8 billion)/($669.5 billion) = 0.164 or 16.4 percent. This result can be interpreted as the probability that $1 invested in a market-value-weighted portfolio of U.S. high-yield bonds was subject to default in 2002.

   B. The odds against an event are denoted $E = [1 - P(E)]/P(E)$. In this case, the odds against default are $(1 - 0.164)/0.164 = 5.098$, or "5.1 to 1."

   C. First, note that E(*loss* | *bond defaults*) = 1 - $0.22 = $0.78. According to the total probability rule for expected value, E(*loss*) = E(*loss* | *bond defaults*)P(*bond defaults*) + E(*loss* | *bond does not default*)P(*bond does not default*) = ($0.78)(0.164) + ($0.0)(0.836) = 0.128, or $0.128. Thus, the institution's expected loss was approximately 13 cents per dollar of principal value invested.

10. A. Using Equation 4-7 for the expected value of a random variable (dollar amounts are in millions),

$$E(\text{Sales}) = 0.20(\$275) + 0.40(\$250) + 0.25(\$200) + 0.10(\$190)$$
$$+ \, 0.05(\$180) = \$233$$

   B. Using Equation 4-9 for variance,

$$\sigma^2(\text{Sales}) = P(\$275)[\$275 - E(\text{Sales})]^2 + P(\$250)[\$250 - E(\text{Sales})]^2$$
$$+ \, P(\$200)[\$200 - E(\text{Sales})]^2 + P(\$190)[\$190 - E(\text{Sales})]^2$$
$$+ \, P(\$180)[\$180 - E(\text{Sales})]^2$$
$$= 0.20(\$275 - \$233)^2 + 0.40(\$250 - \$233)^2 +$$
$$0.25(\$200 - \$233)^2 + 0.10(\$190 - \$233)^2 +$$
$$0.05(\$180 - \$233)^2$$
$$= \$352.80 + \$115.60 + \$272.25 + \$184.90 + \$140.45$$
$$= \$1,066 \text{ (million)}^2$$

C. The standard deviation of annual sales is $[\$1,066 \ (\text{million})^2]^{1/2} = \$32.649655$ million, or $32.65 million.

11. A. *Outcomes associated with Scenario 1:* With a 0.45 probability of a $0.90 recovery per $1 principal value, given Scenario 1, and with the probability of Scenario 1 equal to 0.75, the probability of recovering $0.90 is $0.45(0.75) = 0.3375$. By a similar calculation, the probability of recovering $0.80 is $0.55(0.75) = 0.4125$.

Outcomes associated with Scenario 2: With a 0.85 probability of a $0.50 recovery per $1 principal value, given Scenario 2, and with the probability of Scenario 2 equal to 0.25, the probability of recovering $0.50 is $0.85(0.25) = 0.2125$. By a similar calculation, the probability of recovering $0.40 is $0.15(0.25) = 0.0375$.

B. $E(recovery \mid Scenario\ 1) = 0.45(\$0.90) + 0.55(\$0.80) = \$0.845$

C. $E(recovery \mid Scenario\ 2) = 0.85(\$0.50) + 0.15(\$0.40) = \$0.485$

D. $E(recovery) = 0.75(\$0.845) + 0.25(\$0.485) = \$0.755$

E.

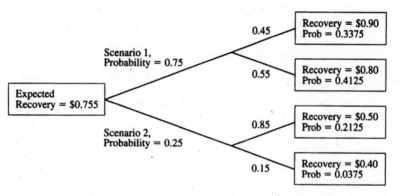

12. A. The diagonal entries in the covariance matrix are the variances, found by squaring the standard deviations.

$$\text{Var(U.S. bond returns)} = 0.409^2 = 0.167281$$

$$\text{Var(German bond returns)} = 0.606^2 = 0.367236$$

$$\text{Var(Italian bond returns)} = 0.635^2 = 0.403225$$

The covariances are found using the relationship $\text{Cov}(R_i, R_j) = \rho(R_i, R_j)\sigma(R_i)\sigma(R_j)$. There are three distinct covariances:

- Cov(U.S. bond returns, German bond returns) = ρ (U.S. bond returns, German bond returns)σ (U.S. bond returns)σ(German bond returns) = $0.09 \times 0.409 \times 0.606 = 0.022307$
- Cov(U.S. bond returns, Italian bond returns) = ρ (U.S. bond returns, Italian bond returns)σ (U.S. bond returns)σ(Italian bond returns) = $0.10 \times 0.409 \times 0.635 = 0.025972$
- Cov(German bond returns, Italian bond returns) = ρ (German bond returns, Italian bond returns)σ (German bond returns)σ(Italian bond returns) = $0.70 \times 0.606 \times 0.635 = 0.269367$

Covariance Matrix of Returns

	U.S. Bonds	German Bonds	Italian Bonds
U.S. Bonds	0.167281	0.022307	0.025972
German Bonds	0.022307	0.367236	0.269367
Italian Bonds	0.025972	0.269367	0.403225

B. Using Equations 4-13 and 4-16, we find

$$E(R_P) = 0.70 \times 0.029 + 0.20 \times 0.021 + 0.10 \times 0.073 = 0.0318, \text{ or } 3.2 \text{ percent}$$

$$\sigma^2(R_P) = w_1^2\sigma^2(R_1) + w_2^2\sigma^2(R_2) + w_3^2\sigma^2(R_3) + 2w_1w_2\text{Cov}(R_1, R_2)$$
$$+ 2w_1w_3\text{Cov}(R_1, R_3) + 2w_2w_3\text{Cov}(R_2, R_3)$$
$$= (0.70)^2(0.167281) + (0.20)^2(0.367236) + (0.10)^2(0.403225)$$
$$+ 2(0.70)(0.20)(0.022307) + 2(0.70)(0.10)(0.025972)$$
$$+ 2(0.20)(0.10)(0.269367)$$
$$= (0.081968 + 0.014689 + 0.004032 + 0.006246 + 0.003636$$
$$+ 0.010775$$
$$= 0.121346$$

C. The standard deviation of this portfolio is $\sqrt{\sigma^2(R_p)} = (0.121346)^{1/2} = 0.348348$, or 34.8 percent.

13. A covariance matrix for five assets has $5 \times 5 = 25$ entries. Subtracting the five diagonal variance terms, we have $25 - 5 = 20$ off-diagonal entries. Because the covariance matrix is symmetric, only 10 entries are unique ($10 = 20/2$). Hence, you must use 10 unique covariances in your five-stock portfolio variance calculation.

14. The covariance is 25, computed as follows. First, we calculate expected values:

$$E(R_B) = (0.25 \times 30\%) + (0.50 \times 15\%) + (0.25 \times 10\%) = 17.5\%$$
$$E(R_Z) = (0.25 \times 15\%) + (0.50 \times 10\%) + (0.25 \times 5\%) = 10\%$$

Then we find the covariance as follows:

$$\text{Cov}(R_B, R_Z) = P(30, 15) \times [(30 - 17.5) \times (15 - 10)] + P(15, 10)$$
$$\times [(15 - 17.5) \times (10 - 10)] + P(10, 5) \times [(10 - 17.5)$$
$$\times (5 - 10)]$$
$$= (0.25 \times 12.5 \times 5) + [0.50 \times (-2.5) \times 0] + [0.25$$
$$\times (-7.5) \times (-5)]$$
$$= 15.625 + 0 + 9.375 = 25$$

15. A. We can set up the equation using the total probability rule:

$$P(pass\ test) = P(pass\ test\ |\ survivor)P(survivor)$$

$$+ P(pass\ test\ |\ nonsurvivor)P(nonsurvivor)$$

We know that $P(survivor) = 1 - P(nonsurvivor) = 1 - 0.40 = 0.60$. Therefore, $P(pass\ test) = 0.55 = 0.85(0.60) + P(pass\ test\ |\ nonsurvivor)(0.40)$. Thus $P(pass\ test\ |\ nonsurvivor) = [0.55 - 0.85(0.60)]/0.40 = 0.10$.

B.

$$P(survivor\ |\ pass\ test) = [P(pass\ test\ |\ survivor)/P(pass\ test)]P(survivor)$$

$$= (0.85/0.55)0.60 = 0.927273$$

The information that a company passes the test causes you to update your probability that it is a survivor from 0.60 to approximately 0.927.

C. According to Bayes' formula, $P(nonsurvivor\ |\ fail\ test) = [P(fail\ test\ |\ nonsurvivor)/P(fail\ test)]P(nonsurvivor) = [P(fail\ test\ |\ nonsurvivor)/0.45]0.40$.
We can set up the following equation to obtain $P(fail\ test\ |\ nonsurvivor)$:

$$P(fail\ test) = P(fail\ test\ |\ nonsurvivor)P(nonsurvivor)$$

$$+ P(fail\ test\ |\ survivor)P(survivor)$$

$$0.45 = P(fail\ test\ |\ nonsurvivor)0.40 + 0.15(0.60)$$

where $P(fail\ test\ |\ survivor) = 1 - P(pass\ test\ |\ survivor) = 1 - 0.85 = 0.15$. So $P(fail\ test\ |\ nonsurvivor) = [0.45 - 0.15(0.60)]/0.40 = 0.90$. Using this result with the formula above, we find $P(nonsurvivor\ |\ fail\ test) = (0.90/0.45)0.40 = 0.80$. Seeing that a company fails the test causes us to update the probability that it is a nonsurvivor from 0.40 to 0.80.

D. A company passing the test greatly increases our confidence that it is a survivor. A company failing the test doubles the probability that it is a nonsurvivor. Therefore, the test appears to be useful.

16. This is a labeling problem in which we assign each NYSE issue a label: advanced, declined, or unchanged. The expression to count the number of ways 3,292 issues can be assigned to these three categories such that 1,303 advanced, 1,764 declined, and 225 remained unchanged is $3,292!/(1,303!)(1,764!)(225!)$.

17. We find the answer using the combination formula $\binom{n}{r} = n!/[(n-r)!r!]$. Here, $n = 10$ and $r = 4$, so the answer is $10!/[(10-4)!4!] = 3,628,800/(720)(24) = 210$.

18. A. The two events that affect a bondholder's returns are *the bond defaults* and *the bond does not default*. First, compute the value of the bond for the two events per $1 invested.

	The Bond Defaults	The Bond Does Not Default
Bond value	$\theta \times \$(1 + R)$	$\$(1 + R)$

Second, find the expected value of the bond (per $1 invested):

$$E(bond) = \theta \times \$(1 + R) \times P(the\ bond\ defaults) + \$(1 + R)$$

$$\times [1 - P(the\ bond\ defaults)]$$

On the other hand, the expected value of the T-bill is the certain value $(1 + R_F)$. Setting the expected value of the bond to the expected value of the T-bill permits us to find the promised return on the bond such that bondholders expect to break even.

$$\theta \times \$(1 + R) \times P(the\ bond\ defaults) + \$(1 + R)$$
$$\times\ [1 - P(the\ bond\ defaults)] = \$(1 + R_F)$$

Rearranging the left-hand side,

$$(1 + R) \times \{\theta \times P(the\ bond\ defaults) + [1 - P(the\ bond\ defaults)]\}$$
$$= (1 + R_F)$$

$$R = (1 + R_F)/\{\theta \times P(the\ bond\ defaults)$$
$$+\ [1 - P(the\ bond\ defaults)]\} - 1$$

B. For this problem, $R_F = 0.058$, $P(the\ bond\ defaults) = 0.06$, $1 - P(the\ bond\ defaults) = 0.94$, and $\theta = 0.35$.

$$R = [1.058/(0.35(0.06) + 0.94)] - 1 = 0.100937,\ \text{or } 10.1 \text{ percent}$$

With a recovery rate of 35 cents on the dollar, a minimum default risk premium of about 430 basis points is required, calculated as $4.3\% = 10.1\% - 5.8\%$.

CHAPTER 5

COMMON PROBABILITY DISTRIBUTIONS

SOLUTIONS

1. A. The put's minimum value is $0. The put's value is $0 when the stock price is at or above $100 at the maturity date of the option. The put's maximum value is $100 = $100 (the exercise price) −$0 (the lowest possible stock price). The put's value is $100 when the stock is worthless at the option's maturity date. The put's minimum price increments are $0.01. The possible outcomes of terminal put value are thus $0.00, $0.01, $0.02, . . . , $100.

   B. The price of the underlying has minimum price fluctuations of $0.01: These are the minimum price fluctuations for terminal put value. For example, if the stock finishes at $98.20, the payoff on the put is $100 − $98.20 = $1.80. We can specify that the nearest values to $1.80 are $1.79 and $1.81. With a continuous random variable, we cannot specify the nearest values. So, we must characterize terminal put value as a discrete random variable.

   C. The probability that terminal put value is less than or equal to $24 is $P(Y \leq 24)$ or $F(24)$, in standard notation, where F is the cumulative distribution function for terminal put value.

2. A. Because $f(2) = -0.01$ is negative, $f(X)$ cannot be a probability function. Probabilities are numbers between 0 and 1.

   B. The function $g(Y)$ does satisfy the conditions of a probability function: All the values of $g(Y)$ are between 0 and 1, and the values of $g(Y)$ sum to 1.

   C. The function $h(Z)$ cannot be a probability function: The values of $h(Z)$ sum to 1.02, which is more than 1.

3. A binomial random variable is defined as the number of successes in n Bernoulli trials (a trial that produces one of two outcomes). The binomial distribution is used to make probability statements about a record of successes and failures or about anything with binary (twofold) outcomes.

4. A. The probability of an earnings increase (success) in a year is estimated as $7/10 = 0.70$ or 70 percent, based on the record of the past 10 years.

   B. The probability that earnings will increase in 5 out of the next 10 years is about 10.3 percent. Define a binomial random variable X, counting the number of earnings increases over the next 10 years. From Part A, the probability of an earnings increase in a given year is $p = 0.70$ and the number of trials (years) is $n = 10$. Equation 5-1 gives the probability that a binomial random variable has x successes in n trials, with the probability of success on a trial equal to p.

$$P(X = x) = \binom{n}{x} p^x (1 - p)^{n-x} = \frac{n!}{(n-x)!x!} p^x (1-p)^{n-x}$$

For this example,

$$\binom{10}{5} 0.7^5 0.3^{10-5} = \frac{10!}{(10-5)!5!} 0.7^5 0.3^{10-5}$$

$$= 252 \times 0.16807 \times 0.00243 = 0.102919$$

We conclude that the probability that earnings will increase in exactly 5 of the next 10 years is 0.1029, or approximately 10.3 percent.

C. The expected number of yearly increases is $E(X) = np = 10 \times 0.70 = 7$.

D. The variance of the number of yearly increases over the next 10 years is $\sigma^2 = np(1 - p) = 10 \times 0.70 \times 0.30 = 2.1$. The standard deviation is 1.449 (the positive square root of 2.1).

E. You must assume that (1) the probability of an earnings increase (success) is constant from year to year and (2) earnings increases are independent trials. If current and past earnings help forecast next year's earnings, Assumption 2 is violated. If the company's business is subject to economic or industry cycles, neither assumption is likely to hold.

5. The observed success rate is $4/7 = 0.571$, or 57.1 percent. The probability of four or fewer successes is $F(4) = p(4) + p(3) + p(2) + p(1) + p(0)$, where $p(4)$, $p(3)$, $p(2)$, $p(1)$, and $p(0)$ are respectively the probabilities of 4, 3, 2, 1, and 0 successes, according to the binomial distribution with $n = 7$ and $p = 0.70$. We have

$$p(4) = (7!/4!3!)(0.70^4)(0.30^3) = 35(0.006483) = 0.226895$$

$$p(3) = (7!/3!4!)(0.70^3)(0.30^4) = 35(0.002778) = 0.097241$$

$$p(2) = (7!/2!5!)(0.70^2)(0.30^5) = 21(0.001191) = 0.025005$$

$$p(1) = (7!/1!6!)(0.70^1)(0.30^6) = 7(0.000510) = 0.003572$$

$$p(0) = (7!/0!7!)(0.70^0)(0.30^7) = 1(0.000219) = 0.003572$$

Summing all these probabilities, you conclude that $F(4) = 0.226895 + 0.097241 + 0.025005 + 0.003572 + 0.000219 = 0.352931$, or 35.3 percent.

6. At each node of a binomial tree, we can test the condition that stock price is at or below the prespecified level. As in Figure 5-2, we calculate stock price at all nodes of the tree. We calculate the value of the call at the terminal nodes as a function of the terminal price of the stock. Using a model for discounting values by one period, we calculate call value one period earlier, and so forth, to reach $t = 0$. But at any node at which stock price is at or below the prespecified level, we automatically set call value to $0.

7. A. The expected value of fourth-quarter sales is €14, 500, 000, calculated as (€ 14,000,000 + € 15,000,000)/2. With a continuous uniform random variable, the mean or expected value is the midpoint between the smallest and largest values. (See Example 5-7.)

   B. The probability that fourth-quarter sales will be less than €14, 125, 000 is 0.125 or 12.5 percent, calculated as (€14, 125, 000 − €14, 000, 000)/(€15, 000, 000 − €14, 000, 000).

8. A. Approximately 68 percent of all outcomes of a normal random variable fall within plus or minus one standard deviation of the mean.

   B. Approximately 95 percent of all outcomes of a normal random variable fall within plus or minus two standard deviations of the mean.

   C. Approximately 99 percent of all outcomes of a normal random variable fall within plus or minus three standard deviations of the mean.

9. A. The lower limit of a one standard deviation confidence interval is the sample mean return (0.56 percent) minus the sample standard deviation (8.86 percent): $0.56\% - 8.86\% = -8.30\%$. The upper limit is the sample mean return (0.56 percent) plus the sample standard deviation (8.86 percent): $0.56\% + 8.86\% = 9.42\%$. Summarizing, the one standard deviation confidence interval runs from -8.30 percent to 9.42 percent, written as $[-8.30\%, 9.42\%]$. If the portfolio return is normally distributed, approximately 68 percent (precisely 68.27 percent) of monthly returns will fall in this interval.

   B. The lower limit of a 95 percent confidence interval is the sample mean return minus 1.96 standard deviations: $0.56\% - 1.96 \times 8.86\% = -16.81\%$. The upper limit is the sample mean return plus 1.96 standard deviations: $0.56\% + 1.96 \times 8.86\% = 17.93\%$. Summarizing, an exact 95 percent confidence interval runs from -16.81 percent to 17.93 percent, written as $[-16.81\%, 17.93\%]$. Only 5 percent of a large number of returns should fall outside of this interval, under the normality assumption. In that sense, we have 95 percent confidence in this interval.

   C. The lower limit of a 99 percent confidence interval is the sample mean return minus 2.58 standard deviations: $0.56\% - 2.58 \times 8.86\% = -22.30\%$. The upper limit is the sample mean return plus 2.58 standard deviations: $0.56\% + 2.58 \times 8.86\% = 23.42\%$. Summarizing, an exact 99 percent confidence interval runs from -22.30 percent to 23.42 percent, written as $[-22.30\%, 23.42\%]$. Only 1 percent of a large number of returns should fall outside of this interval, under the normality assumption. In that sense, we have 99 percent confidence in this interval.

10. The area under the normal curve for $z = 0.36$ is 0.6406 or 64.06 percent. The table below presents an excerpt from the tables of the standard normal cumulative distribution function in the back of this book. To locate $z = 0.36$, find 0.30 in the fourth row of numbers, then look at the column for 0.06 (the second decimal place of 0.36). The entry is 0.6406.

$P(Z \leq x) = N(x)$ for $x \geq 0$ or $P(Z \leq z) = N(z)$ for $z \geq 0$

x or z	0	0.01	0.02	0.03	0.04	0.05	0.06	0.07	0.08	0.09
0.00	0.5000	0.5040	0.5080	0.5120	0.5160	0.5199	0.5239	0.5279	0.5319	0.5359
0.10	0.5398	0.5438	0.5478	0.5517	0.5557	0.5596	0.5636	0.5675	0.5714	0.5753
0.20	0.5793	0.5832	0.5871	0.5910	0.5948	0.5987	0.6026	0.6064	0.6103	0.6141
0.30	0.6179	0.6217	0.6255	0.6293	0.6331	0.6368	**0.6406**	0.6443	0.6480	0.6517
0.40	0.6554	0.6591	0.6628	0.6664	0.6700	0.6736	0.6772	0.6808	0.6844	0.6879
0.50	0.6915	0.6950	0.6985	0.7019	0.7054	0.7088	0.7123	0.7157	0.7190	0.7224

The interpretation of 64.06 percent for $z = 0.36$ is that 64.06 percent of observations on a standard normal random variable are smaller than or equal to the value 0.36. (So $100\% - 64.06\% = 35.94\%$ of the values are greater than 0.36.)

11. A. The probability of exhausting the liquidity pool is 4.7 percent. First calculate $x = \lambda/(\sigma\sqrt{T}) = \$2,000/(\$450\sqrt{5}) = 1.987616$. We can round this value to 1.99 to use the standard normal tables in the back of this book. Using those tables, we find

that $N(1.99) = 0.9767$. Thus, the probability of exhausting the liquidity pool is $2[1 - N(1.99)] = 2(1 - 0.9767) = 0.0466$ or about 4.7 percent.

B. The probability of exhausting the liquidity pool is now 32.2 percent. The calculation follows the same steps as those in Part A. We calculate $x = \lambda/(\sigma\sqrt{T}) = \$2,000/(\$450\sqrt{20}) = 0.993808$. We can round this value to 0.99 to use the standard normal tables in the back of this book. Using those tables, we find that $N(0.99) = 0.8389$. Thus, the probability of exhausting the liquidity pool is $2[1 - N(0.99)] = 2(1 - 0.8389) = 0.3222$ or about 32.2 percent. This is a substantial probability that you will run out of funds to meet mark to market.

In their paper, Kolb et al. call the probability of exhausting the liquidity pool the probability of ruin, a traditional name for this type of calculation.

12. A 90 percent confidence interval for returns on large-cap blend funds is the interval $[-2.857\%, 4.997\%]$. An exact 90 percent confidence interval is equal to the mean plus and minus 1.65 standard deviations. The lower limit is $1.07\% - 1.65(2.38\%) = -2.857\%$. The upper limit is $1.07\% + 1.65(2.38\%) = 4.997\%$.

13. Under a normality assumption, the probability that the average large-cap growth fund will earn a negative monthly return is 34.5 percent. We calculate the standardized value as $(0\% - 1.15\%)/2.89\% = -0.397924$. Rounding this value to -0.40 to use the standard normal tables in the back of the book, we find that $N(-0.40) = 0.3446$. If you use a spreadsheet function on -0.397924, you will find $N(-0.397924) = 0.345343$.

14. The large-cap value fund category minimized the probability of earning a return less than the risk-free rate of return for the period. Large-cap value funds achieved the highest Sharpe ratio during the period. Recall from our discussion of Roy's safety-first criterion that the Sharpe ratio is equivalent to using the risk-free rate as the shortfall level in SFRatio, and the alternative with the largest SFRatio minimizes the probability of earning a return less than the shortfall level (under a normality assumption). Therefore, to answer the question, we select the alternative with the highest Sharpe ratio, the large-cap value fund.

15. A. Because £50,000/£1,350,000 is 3.7 percent, for any return less than 3.7 percent the client will need to invade principal if she takes out £50,000. So $R_L = 3.7$ percent.

B. To decide which of the three allocations is safety-first optimal, select the alternative with the highest ratio $[E(R_P) - R_L]/\sigma_P$:

Allocation A: $0.5125 = (16 - 3.7)/24$

Allocation B: $0.488235 = (12 - 3.7)/17$

Allocation C: $0.525 = (10 - 3.7)/12$

Allocation D: $0.481818 = (9 - 3.7)/11$

Allocation C, with the largest ratio (0.525), is the best alternative according to the safety-first criterion.

C. To answer this question, note that $P(R_C < 3.7) = N(-0.525)$. We can round 0.525 to 0.53 for use with tables of the standard normal cdf. First, we calculate $N(-0.53) = 1 - N(0.53) = 1 - 0.7019 = 0.2981$ or about 30 percent. The safety-first optimal portfolio has a roughly 30 percent chance of not meeting a 3.7 percent return threshold.

16. A. Two important features of the lognormal distribution are that it is bounded below by 0 and it is right-skewed.

   B. Normal random variables can be negative (the bell curve extends to the left without limit). In contrast, lognormal random variables cannot be negative. Asset prices also cannot be negative. So the lognormal distribution is superior to the normal as a probability model for asset prices.

   C. The two parameters of a lognormal distribution are the mean and variance (or standard deviation) of the associated normal distribution. If Y is lognormal and $Y = \ln X$, the two parameters of the distribution of Y are the mean and variance (or standard deviation) of X.

17. To compute volatility for Dollar General Corporation, we begin by calculating the continuously compounded daily returns using Equation 5-5:

$$r_{t,t+1} = \ln(S_{t+1}/S_t) = \ln(1 + R_{t,t+1})$$

Then we find the variance of those continuously compounded returns, the sum of the squared deviations from the mean divided by 8 (the sample size of 9 continuously compounded returns minus 1). We take the square root of the variance to find the standard deviation. Finally, we multiply the standard deviation by $\sqrt{250}$ to annualize it. The continuously compounded daily returns are (reading across the line, then down):

$\ln(10.87/10.68) = 0.017634, \ln(11.00/10.87) = 0.011889,$
$\ln(10.95/11.00) = -0.004556, \ln(11.26/10.95) = 0.027917,$
$\ln(11.31/11.26) = 0.004431, \ln(11.23/11.31) = -0.007099,$
$\ln(10.91/11.23) = -0.028909, \ln(10.80/10.91) = -0.010134,$
$\ln(10.47/10.80) = -0.031032.$
Sum $= -0.019859,$ Mean $= -0.002207,$ Variance $= 0.000398,$ Standard deviation $= 0.019937$

The standard deviation of continuously compounded daily returns is 0.019937. Then $\sigma\sqrt{T} = 0.019937\sqrt{250} = 0.315232$ or 31.5 percent.

18. A. Elements that should appear in a definition of Monte Carlo simulation are that it makes use of a computer; that it is used to represent the operation of a complex system, or in some applications, to find an approximate solution to a problem; and that it involves the generation of a large number of random samples from a specified probability distribution. The exact wording can vary, but one definition follows:

   Monte Carlo simulation in finance involves the use of a computer to represent the operation of a complex financial system. In some important applications, Monte Carlo simulation is used to find an approximate solution to a complex financial problem. An integral part of Monte Carlo simulation is the generation of a large number of random samples from a probability distribution.

   B. *Strengths.* Monte Carlo simulation can be used to price complex securities for which no analytic expression is available, particularly European-style options.
   Weaknesses. Monte Carlo simulation provides only statistical estimates, not exact results. Analytic methods, when available, provide more insight into cause-and-effect relationships than does Monte Carlo simulation.

19. In the text, we described how we could use Monte Carlo simulation to value an Asian option, a complex European-style option. Just as we can calculate the average value of the

stock over a simulation trial to value an Asian option, we can also calculate the minimum value of the stock over a simulation trial. Then, for a given simulation trial, we can calculate the terminal value of the call, given the minimum value of the stock for the simulation trial. We can then discount back this terminal value to the present to get the value of the call today ($t = 0$). The average of these $t = 0$ values over all simulation trials is the Monte Carlo simulated value of the lookback call option.

CHAPTER 6

SAMPLING AND ESTIMATION

SOLUTIONS

1. A. The standard deviation or standard error of the sample mean is $\sigma_{\overline{X}} = \sigma/\sqrt{n}$. Substituting in the values for $\sigma_{\overline{X}}$ and σ, we have $1\% = 6\%/\sqrt{n}$, or $\sqrt{n} = 6$. Squaring this value, we get a random sample of $n = 36$.

   B. As in Part A, the standard deviation of sample mean is $\sigma_{\overline{X}} = \sigma/\sqrt{n}$. Substituting in the values for $\sigma_{\overline{X}}$ and σ, we have $0.25\% = 6\%/\sqrt{n}$, or $\sqrt{n} = 24$. Squaring this value, we get a random sample of $n = 576$, which is substantially larger than for Part A of this question.

2. A. Assume the sample size will be large and thus the 95 percent confidence interval for the mean of a sample of manager returns is $\overline{X} \pm 1.96 s_{\overline{X}}$, where $s_{\overline{X}} = s/\sqrt{n}$. Munzi wants the distance between the upper limit and lower limit in the confidence interval to be 1 percent, which is

$$(\overline{X} + 1.96 s_{\overline{X}}) - (\overline{X} - 1.96 s_{\overline{X}}) = 1\%$$

   Simplifying this equation, we get $2(1.96 s_{\overline{X}}) = 1\%$. Finally, we have $3.92 s_{\overline{X}} = 1\%$, which gives us the standard deviation of the sample mean, $s_{\overline{X}} = 0.255\%$. The distribution of sample means is $s_{\overline{X}} = s/\sqrt{n}$. Substituting in the values for $s_{\overline{X}}$ and s, we have $0.255\% = 4\%/\sqrt{n}$, or $\sqrt{n} = 15.69$. Squaring this value, we get a random sample of $n = 246$.

   B. With her budget, Munzi can pay for a sample of up to 100 observations, which is far short of the 246 observations needed. Munzi can either proceed with her current budget and settle for a wider confidence interval or she can raise her budget (to around $2,460) to get the sample size for a 1 percent width in her confidence interval.

3. A. This is a small-sample problem in which the sample comes from a normal population with a known standard deviation; thus we use the z-distribution in the solution. For a 95 percent confidence interval (and 2.5 percent in each tail), the critical z-value is 1.96. For returns that are normally distributed, a 95 percent confidence interval is of the form

$$\mu + 1.96 \frac{\sigma}{\sqrt{n}}$$

The lower limit is $X_1 = \mu - 1.96\dfrac{\sigma}{\sqrt{n}} = 6\% - 1.96\dfrac{18\%}{\sqrt{4}} = 6\% - 1.96(9\%) = -11.64\%$.

The upper limit is $X_u = \mu + 1.96\dfrac{\sigma}{\sqrt{n}} = 6\% + 1.96\dfrac{18\%}{\sqrt{4}} = 6\% + 1.96(9\%) = 23.64\%$.

There is a 95 percent probability that four-year average returns will be between -11.64 percent and $+23.64$ percent.

B. The critical z-value associated with the -2.0 percent return is

$$Z = \frac{\overline{X} - \mu}{\sigma/\sqrt{n}} = \frac{-2\% - 6\%}{18\%/\sqrt{4}} = \frac{-8\%}{9\%} = -0.89$$

Using a normal table, the probability of a z-value less than -0.89 is $P(Z < -0.89) = 0.1867$. Unfortunately, although your client is unhappy with the investment result, four-year returns of -2.0 percent or lower should occur 18.67 percent of the time.

4. (Refer to Figure 6-1 to help visualize the answer to this question.) Basically, only one standard normal distribution exists, but many t-distributions exist—one for every different number of degrees of freedom. The normal distribution and the t-distribution for a large number of degrees of freedom are practically the same. The lower the degrees of freedom, the flatter the t-distribution becomes. The t-distribution has less mass (lower probabilities) in the center of the distribution and more mass (higher probabilities) out in both tails. Therefore, the confidence intervals based on t-values will be wider than those based on the normal distribution. Stated differently, the probability of being within a given number of standard deviations (such as within ± 1 standard deviation or ± 2 standard deviations) is lower for the t-distribution than for the normal distribution.

5. A. For a 99 percent confidence interval, the reliability factor we use is $t_{0.005}$; for df $= 20$, this factor is 2.845.

   B. For a 90 percent confidence interval, the reliability factor we use is $t_{0.05}$; for df $= 20$, this factor is 1.725.

   C. Degrees of freedom equals $n - 1$, or in this case $25 - 1 = 24$. For a 95 percent confidence interval, the reliability factor we use is $t_{0.025}$; for df $= 24$, this factor is 2.064.

   D. Degrees of freedom equals $16 - 1 = 15$. For a 95 percent confidence interval, the reliability factor we use is $t_{0.025}$; for df $= 15$, this factor is 2.131.

6. Because this is a small sample from a normal population and we have only the sample standard deviation, we use the following model to solve for the confidence interval of the population mean:

$$\overline{X} \pm t_{\alpha/2}\frac{s}{\sqrt{n}}$$

where we find $t_{0.025}$ (for a 95 percent confidence interval) for df $= n - 1 = 24 - 1 = 23$; this value is 2.069. Our solution is $1\% \pm 2.069(4\%)/\sqrt{24} = 1\% \pm 2.069(0.8165) = 1\% \pm 1.69$. The 95 percent confidence interval spans the range from -0.69 percent to $+2.69$ percent.

7. The following table summarizes the calculations used in the answers.

Forecast (X_i)	Number of Analysts (n_i)	$X_i n_i$	$(X_i - \overline{X})$	$(X_i - \overline{X})^2$	$(X_i - \overline{X})^2 n_i$
1.40	1	1.40	−0.05	0.0025	0.0025
1.43	1	1.43	−0.02	0.0004	0.0004
1.44	3	4.32	−0.01	0.0001	0.0003
1.45	2	2.90	0.00	0.0000	0.0000
1.47	1	1.47	0.02	0.0004	0.0004
1.48	1	1.48	0.03	0.0009	0.0009
1.50	1	1.50	0.05	0.0025	0.0025
Sums	10	14.50			0.0070

A. With $n = 10$, $\overline{X} = \sum_{i=1}^{10} X_i/n = 14.50/10 = 1.45$. The variance is $s^2 = \left[\sum_{i=1}^{10} (X_i - \overline{X})^2 \right]/(n-1) = 0.0070/9 = 0.0007778$. The sample standard deviation is $s = \sqrt{0.0007778} = 0.02789$.

B. The confidence interval for the mean can be estimated by using $\overline{X} \pm t_{\alpha/2}(s/\sqrt{n})$. For 9 degrees of freedom, the reliability factor, $t_{0.025}$, equals 2.262 and the confidence interval is $1.45 \pm 2.262 \times 0.02789/\sqrt{10} = 1.45 \pm 2.262(0.00882) = 1.45 \pm 0.02$. The confidence interval for the population mean ranges from 1.43 to 1.47.

8. The following table summarizes the calculations used in the answers.

Forecast (X_i)	Number of Analysts (n_i)	$X_i n_i$	$(X_i - \overline{X})$	$(X_i - \overline{X})^2$	$(X_i - \overline{X})^2 n_i$
0.70	2	1.40	−0.04	0.0016	0.0032
0.72	4	2.88	−0.02	0.0004	0.0016
0.74	1	0.74	0.00	0.0000	0.0000
0.75	3	2.25	0.01	0.0001	0.0003
0.76	1	0.76	0.02	0.0004	0.0004
0.77	1	0.77	0.03	0.0009	0.0009
0.82	1	0.82	0.08	0.0064	0.0064
Sums	13	9.62			0.0128

A. With $n = 13$, $\overline{X} = \sum_{i=1}^{13} X_i/n = 9.62/13 = 0.74$. The variance is $s^2 = \left[\sum_{i=1}^{13} (X_i - \overline{X})^2 \right]/(n-1) = 0.0128/12 = 0.001067$. The sample standard deviation is $s^2 = \sqrt{0.001067} = 0.03266$.

B. The sample is small, and the distribution appears to be bimodal. We cannot compute a confidence interval for the population mean because we have probably sampled from a distribution that is not normal.

9. If the population variance is known, the confidence interval is

$$\overline{X} \pm z_{\alpha/2} \frac{\sigma}{\sqrt{n}}$$

The confidence interval for the population mean is centered at the sample mean, $\overline{X}$. The population standard deviation is σ, and the sample size is n. The population standard deviation divided by the square root of n is the standard error of the estimate of the mean. The value of z depends on the desired degree of confidence. For a 95 percent confidence interval, $z_{0.025} = 1.96$ and the confidence interval estimate is

$$\overline{X} \pm 1.96 \frac{\sigma}{\sqrt{n}}$$

If the population variance is not known, we make two changes to the technique used when the population variance is known. First, we must use the sample standard deviation instead of the population standard deviation. Second, we use the t-distribution instead of the normal distribution. The critical t-value will depend on degrees of freedom $n - 1$. If the sample size is large, we have the alternative of using the z-distribution with the sample standard deviation.

10. A. The probabilities can be taken from a normal table, in which the critical z-values are 1.00, 2.00, or 3.00 and we are including the probabilities in both tails. The probabilities that the exchange rate will be at least 1, 2, or 3 standard deviations away from the mean are

$$P(|X - \mu| \geq 1\sigma) = 0.3174$$
$$P(|X - \mu| \geq 2\sigma) = 0.0456$$
$$P(|X - \mu| \geq 3\sigma) = 0.0026$$

B. With Chebyshev's inequality, the maximum probability of the exchange rate being at least k standard deviations from the mean is $P(|X - \mu| \geq k\sigma) \leq (1/k)^2$. The maximum probabilities of the rate being at least 1, 2, or 3 standard deviations away from the mean are

$$P(|X - \mu| \geq 1\sigma) \leq (1/1)^2 = 1.0000$$
$$P(|X - \mu| \geq 2\sigma) \leq (1/2)^2 = 0.2500$$
$$P(|X - \mu| \geq 3\sigma) \leq (1/3)^2 = 0.1111$$

The probability of the rate being outside 1, 2, or 3 standard deviations of the mean is much smaller with a known normal distribution than when the distribution is unknown and we are relying on Chebyshev's inequality.

11. No. If security returns were independent of each other, your colleague would be correct. We could diversify across a large number of investments and make the portfolio standard deviation very small, approaching zero. The returns of investments, however, are not independent; they are correlated with each other and with common market factors. Diversifying across many investments reduces *unsystematic* (stock-specific) risk, but it does not remove *systematic* (market) risk.

12. In many instances, the distribution that describes the underlying population is not normal or the distribution is not known. The central limit theorem states that if the sample size is

large, regardless of the shape of the underlying population, the distribution of the sample mean is approximately normal. Therefore, even in these instances, we can still construct confidence intervals (and conduct tests of inference) as long as the sample size is large (generally $n \geq 30$).

13. The statement makes the following mistakes:

   - Given the conditions in the statement, the distribution of $\overline{X}$ will be approximately normal only for large sample sizes.
   - The statement omits the important element of the central limit theorem that the distribution of $\overline{X}$ will have mean μ.

14. The discrepancy arises from sampling error. Sampling error exists whenever one fails to observe every element of the population, because a sample statistic can vary from sample to sample. As stated in the text, the sample mean is an unbiased estimator, a consistent estimator, and an efficient estimator of the population mean. Although the sample mean is an unbiased estimator of the population mean—the expected value of the sample mean equals the population mean—because of sampling error, we do not expect the sample mean to exactly equal the population mean in any one sample we may take.

15. No, we cannot say that Alcorn Mutual Funds as a group is superior to competitors. Alcorn Mutual Funds' advertisement may easily mislead readers because the advertisement does not show the performance of all its funds. In particular, Alcorn Mutual Funds is engaging in sample selection bias by presenting the investment results from its best-performing funds only.

16. The question raises the issue of whether above-average money management performance is the result of skill or luck. Assembling a group of above-average portfolio managers can be an attempt to exploit survivorship bias. We attempt it by hiring only managers with above-average records and by firing any managers that have below-average records. If past successful performance is a function of skill that can be repeated, then managers with above-average records will perform better than average in the future. An explanation for what is going on in the statement may be that past superior performance has resulted not from skill but from luck.

   Say we assume that performance is a matter of luck. Suppose there is a 0.5 -chance for a manager to beat his or her benchmark. If we start out with 100 managers and define success as two benchmark-beating years in a row, we will have about 25 successful managers. Their successful track records will not predict future success if performance is random. If performance is random, no matter how we pick our managers, future performance will be above average about half the time and below average about half the time. If we wish to appraise skill, we must discount results that would happen by chance.

17. Spence may be guilty of data mining. He has used so many possible combinations of variables on so many stocks, it is not surprising that he found some instances in which a model worked. In fact, it would have been more surprising if he had not found any. To decide whether to use his model, you should do two things: First, ask that the model be tested on out-of-sample data—that is, data that were not used in building the model. The model may not be successful with out-of-sample data. Second, examine his model to make sure that the relationships in the model make economic sense, have a story, and have a future.

18. Hand Associates should use stratified random sampling for its portfolio that tracks the value-weighted index. Using 50–100 stocks to track 500 means that Hand will invest in all or almost all of the largest stocks in the index and few of the smallest. In addition to size, the stocks may be grouped by industry, riskiness, and other traits, and Hand Associates

may select stocks to represent each of these groups or strata. For the equal-weighted index, Hand can use simple random sampling, in which each stock is equally likely to be chosen. Even in this case, however, Hand could use stratified random sampling to make sure it is choosing stocks that represent the various factors underlying stock performance.

19. A. An example of sample-selection bias is the failure to include the returns of delisted stocks in reporting portfolio returns. Because delisted stocks frequently are troubled stocks with poor returns, ignoring their returns will bias upwards the returns of portfolios that do not include them.

    B. An example of look-ahead bias is a statistician using data that were not yet available at the time a decision was being made. If you are building portfolios on January 1 of each year, you do not yet have the financial results for fiscal years ending on December 31. So, you do not know this information when you make investment decisions. Suppose a statistician is studying historical portfolio returns and has used annual accounting results to make portfolio selections at the beginning of each year. She is using a statistical model that assumes information is available several weeks before it is actually available. The results of such a model are biased.

    C. One kind of time-period bias is an investment manager reporting the results from a short time period that give an inaccurate picture of the investment performance that might be expected over a longer time period. Time-period bias exists when a test is carried out for a time period that may make the results time-period specific. Another type of time-period bias arises with long time series. Long time series may give a more accurate picture of true investment performance than short time series, but they have the potential of including structural changes that would result in two different return distributions within the long period.

20. An estimator should have several desirable properties, including the following.

    • Unbiasedness: The expected value of the estimator is equal to the population parameter.
    • Efficiency: An efficient estimator is unbiased and has a smaller variance than all other unbiased estimators.
    • Consistency: A consistent estimator tends to produce more accurate estimates of the population parameter as sample size increases.

CHAPTER 7

HYPOTHESIS TESTING

SOLUTIONS

1. A. The null hypothesis is the hypothesis to be tested.
   B. The alternative hypothesis is the hypothesis accepted when the null hypothesis is rejected.
   C. A test statistic is a quantity, calculated on the basis of a sample, whose value is the basis for deciding whether to reject or not reject the null hypothesis.
   D. A Type I error, also called alpha, occurs when we reject a true null hypothesis.
   E. A Type II error, also called beta, occurs when we do not reject a false null hypothesis.
   F. The power of a test is the probability of correctly rejecting the null hypothesis (rejecting the null hypothesis when it is false).
   G. The rejection point (critical value) is a value against which a computed test statistic is compared to decide whether to reject or not reject the null hypothesis.

2. If we rejected the hypothesis of the equality of the mean debt-to-total-assets ratios of takeover target companies and non-takeover-target companies when, in fact, the means were equal, we would be committing a Type I error.

   On the other hand, if we failed to reject the equality of the mean debt-to-total-assets ratios of takeover target companies and non-takeover-target companies when the means were different, we would be committing a Type II error.

3. By the definition of p-value, 0.031 is the smallest level of significance at which we can reject the null hypothesis. Because 0.031 is smaller than 0.10 and 0.05, we can reject the null hypothesis at the 0.10 and 0.05 significance levels. Because 0.031 is larger than 0.01, however, we cannot reject the null hypothesis at the 0.01 significance level.

4. A. The appropriate test statistic is a t-statistic with $n - 1 = 15 - 1 = 14$ degrees of freedom. A t-statistic is theoretically correct when the sample comes from a normally distributed population with unknown variance. When the sample size is also small, there is no practical alternative.
   B. The appropriate test statistic is a t-statistic with $40 - 1 = 39$ degrees of freedom. A t-statistic is theoretically correct when the sample comes from a normally distributed population with unknown variance.

   When the sample size is large (generally, 30 or more is a "large" sample), it is also possible to use a z-statistic, whether the population is normally distributed or not. A test based on a t-statistic is more conservative than a z-statistic test.
   C. The appropriate test statistic is a z-statistic because the sample comes from a normally distributed population with known variance. (The known population standard deviation is used to compute the standard error of the mean using Equation 7-2 in the text.)

D. The appropriate test statistic is chi-square (χ^2) with $50 - 1 = 49$ degrees of freedom.

E. The appropriate test statistic is the F-statistic (the ratio of the sample variances).

F. The appropriate test statistic is a t-statistic for a paired observations test (a paired comparisons test), because the samples are correlated.

G. The appropriate test statistic is a t-statistic using a pooled estimate of the population variance. The t-statistic has $25 + 30 - 2 = 53$ degrees of freedom. This statistic is appropriate because the populations are normally distributed with unknown variances; because the variances are assumed equal, the observations can be pooled to estimate the common variance. The requirement of independent samples for using this statistic has been met.

5. A. With degrees of freedom (df) $n - 1 = 26 - 1 = 25$, the rejection point conditions for this two-sided test are $t > 2.060$ and $t < -2.060$. Because the significance level is 0.05, $0.05/2 = 0.025$ of the probability is in each tail. The tables give one-sided (one-tailed) probabilities, so we used the 0.025 column. Read across df $= 25$ to the $\alpha = 0.025$ column to find 2.060, the rejection point for the right tail. By symmetry, -2.060 is the rejection point for the left tail.

B. With df $= 39$, the rejection point conditions for this two-sided test are $t > 2.708$ and $t < -2.708$. This is a two-sided test, so we use the $0.01/2 = 0.005$ column. Read across df $= 39$ to the $\alpha = 0.005$ column to find 2.708, the rejection point for the right tail. By symmetry, -2.708 is the rejection point for the left tail.

C. With df $= 39$, the rejection point condition for this one-sided test is $t > 2.426$. Read across df $= 39$ to the $\alpha = 0.01$ column to find 2.426, the rejection point for the right tail. Because we have a "greater than" alternative, we are concerned with only the right tail.

D. With df $= 20$, the rejection point condition for this one-sided test is $t > 1.725$. Read across df $= 20$ to the $\alpha = 0.05$ column to find 1.725, the rejection point for the right tail. Because we have a "greater than" alternative, we are concerned with only the right tail.

E. With df $= 18$, the rejection point condition for this one-sided test is $t < -1.330$. Read across df $= 18$ to the $\alpha = 0.10$ column to find 1.330, the rejection point for the right tail. By symmetry, the rejection point for the left tail is -1.330.

F. With df $= 49$, the rejection point condition for this one-sided test is $t < -1.677$. Read across df $= 49$ to the $\alpha = 0.05$ column to find 1.677, the rejection point for the right tail. By symmetry, the rejection point for the left tail is -1.677.

6. Recall that with a z-test (in contrast to the t-test), we do not employ degrees of freedom. The standard normal distribution is a single distribution applicable to all z-tests. You should refer to "Rejection Points for a z-Test" in Section 3.1 to answer these questions.

A. This is a two-sided test at a 0.01 significance level. In Part C of "Rejection Points for a z-Test," we find that the rejection point conditions are $z > 2.575$ and $z < -2.575$.

B. This is a two-sided test at a 0.05 significance level. In Part B of "Rejection Points for a z-Test," we find that the rejection point conditions are $z > 1.96$ and $z < -1.96$.

C. This is a two-sided test at a 0.10 significance level. In Part A of "Rejection Points for a z-Test," we find that the rejection point conditions are $z > 1.645$ and $z < -1.645$.

D. This is a one-sided test at a 0.05 significance level. In Part B of "Rejection Points for a z-Test," we find that the rejection point condition for a test with a "greater than" alternative hypothesis is $z > 1.645$.

7. A. When sampling from a normally distributed population with known variance, the correct test statistic for hypothesis tests concerning the mean is the z-statistic.

   B. When sampling from a normally distributed population with unknown variance, the theoretically correct test statistic for hypothesis tests concerning the mean is the t-statistic.

   C. When the sample size is large, the central limit theorem applies. Consequently, the sample mean will be approximately normally distributed. When the population variance is not known, a test using the t-statistic is theoretically preferred. A test using the z-statistic is also sufficient when the sample size is large, as in this case.

8. A. As stated in the text, we often set up the "hoped for" or "suspected" condition as the alternative hypothesis. Here, that condition is that the population value of Willco's mean annual net income exceeds \$24 million. Thus we have H_0: $\mu \leq 24$ versus H_a: $\mu > 24$.

   B. Given that net income is normally distributed with unknown variance, the appropriate test statistic is t with $n - 1 = 6 - 1 = 5$ degrees of freedom.

   C. In the t-distribution table in the back of the book, in the row for df $= 5$ under $\alpha = 0.05$, we read the rejection point (critical value) of 2.015. We will reject the null if $t > 2.015$.

   D. The t-test is given by Equation 7-4:

$$t_5 = \frac{\overline{X} - \mu_0}{s/\sqrt{n}} = \frac{30 - 24}{10/\sqrt{6}} = \frac{6}{4.082483} = 1.469694$$

   or 1.47. Because 1.47 does not exceed 2.015, we do not reject the null hypothesis. The difference between the sample mean of \$30 million and the hypothesized value of \$24 million under the null is not statistically significant.

9. A. H_0: $\mu = 0$ versus H_a: $\mu \neq 0$.

   B. The t-test is based on $t = \dfrac{\overline{X} - \mu_0}{s/\sqrt{n}}$ with $n - 1 = 101 - 1 = 100$ degrees of freedom. At the 0.05 significance level, we reject the null if $t > 1.984$ or if $t < -1.984$. At the 0.01 significance level, we reject the null if $t > 2.626$ or if $t < -2.626$. For Analyst A, we have $t = (0.05 - 0)/(0.10/\sqrt{101}) = 0.05/0.00995 = 5.024938$ or 5.025. We clearly reject the null hypothesis at both the 0.05 and 0.01 levels.

   The calculation of the z-statistic with unknown variance, as in this case, is the same as the calculation of the t-statistic. The rejection point conditions for a two-tailed test are as follows: $z > 1.96$ and $z < -1.96$ at the 0.05 level; and $z > 2.575$ and $z < -2.575$ at the 0.01 level. Note that the z-test is a less conservative test than the t-test, so when the z-test is used, the null is easier to reject. Because $z = 5.025$ is greater than 2.575, we reject the null at the 0.01 level; we also reject the null at the 0.05 level.

   In summary, Analyst A's EPS forecasts appear to be biased upward—they tend to be too high.

   C. For Analyst B, the t-test is based on t with $121 - 1 = 120$ degrees of freedom. At the 0.05 significance level, we reject the null if $t > 1.980$ or if $t < -1.980$. At the 0.01 significance level, we reject the null if $t > 2.617$ or if $t < -2.617$. We calculate $t = (0.02 - 0)/(0.09/\sqrt{121}) = 0.02/0.008182 = 2.444444$ or 2.44. Because $2.44 > 1.98$, we reject the null at the 0.05 level. However, 2.44 is not larger than 2.617, so we do not reject the null at the 0.01 level.

For a z-test, the rejection point conditions are the same as given in Part B, and we come to the same conclusions as with the t-test. Because 2.44 > 1.96, we reject the null at the 0.05 significance level; however, because 2.44 is not greater than 2.575, we do not reject the null at the 0.01 level.

The mean forecast error of Analyst B is only $0.02; but because the test is based on a large number of observations, it is sufficient evidence to reject the null of mean zero forecast errors at the 0.05 level.

10. A. Stating the suspected condition as the alternative hypothesis, we have

$$H_0: \mu_1 - \mu_2 \leq 0 \text{ versus } H_a: \mu_1 - \mu_2 > 0$$

where

$\mu_1 =$ the population mean value of Analyst A's forecast errors

$\mu_2 =$ the population mean value of Analyst B's forecast errors

B. We have two normally distributed populations with unknown variances. Based on the samples, it is reasonable to assume that the population variances are equal. The samples are assumed to be independent; this assumption is reasonable because the analysts cover quite different industries. The appropriate test statistic is t using a pooled estimate of the common variance. The number of degrees of freedom is $n_1 + n_2 - 2 = 101 + 121 - 2 = 222 - 2 = 220$.

C. For df $= 200$ (the closest value to 220), the rejection point for a one-sided test at the 0.05 significance level is 1.653.

D. We first calculate the pooled estimate of variance:

$$s_p^2 = \frac{(n_1 - 1)s_1^2 + (n_2 - 1)s_2^2}{n_1 + n_2 - 2} = \frac{(101 - 1)(0.10)^2 + (121 - 1)(0.09)^2}{101 + 121 - 2}$$

$$= \frac{1.972}{220} = 0.008964$$

Then

$$t = \frac{(\overline{X}_1 - \overline{X}_2) - (\mu_1 - \mu_2)}{\left(\dfrac{s_p^2}{n_1} + \dfrac{s_p^2}{n_2}\right)^{1/2}} = \frac{(0.05 - 0.02) - 0}{\left(\dfrac{0.008964}{101} + \dfrac{0.008964}{121}\right)^{1/2}}$$

$$= \frac{0.03}{0.01276} = 2.351018$$

or 2.35. Because 2.35 > 1.653, we reject the null hypothesis in favor of the alternative hypothesis that the population mean forecast error of Analyst A is greater than that of Analyst B.

11. A. The test statistic is

$$t = \frac{\overline{X}_1 - \overline{X}_2}{\left(\dfrac{s_1^2}{n_1} + \dfrac{s_2^2}{n_2}\right)^{1/2}}$$

where

$\overline{X}_1$ = sample mean recovery rate for utilities = 77.74

$\overline{X}_2$ = sample mean recovery rate for non-utility sectors = 42.56

s_1^2 = sample variance for utilities = 18.06^2 = 326.1636

s_2^2 = sample variance for non-utilities = 24.89^2 = 619.5121

n_1 = sample size of the utility sample = 32

n_2 = sample size of the non-utility sample = 189

Therefore, $t = (77.74 - 42.56)/[(326.1636/32) + (619.5121/189)]^{1/2} = 35.18/(10.192613 + 3.277842)^{1/2} = 35.18/3.670212 = 9.585$. The calculated t-statistic is thus 9.585.

B. Usually, we need to know degrees of freedom to determine whether a t-statistic is significant. The magnitude of the t-statistic is so large that in this case, there is actually no doubt about its significance even at the 0.01 level. For a two-sided test at the 0.01 level of significance, we look under the 0.005 column ($0.01/2 = 0.005$). For all but the very first two entries, for 1 and 2 degrees of freedom, the calculated test statistic is larger than the indicated rejection point (critical value). Clearly, with samples of size 32 and 189, there are more than 2 degrees of freedom.

C. This question confirms that we can calculate the degrees of freedom for the test, if needed:

$$\mathrm{df} = \frac{\left(\dfrac{s_1^2}{n_1} + \dfrac{s_2^2}{n_2}\right)^2}{\dfrac{(s_1^2/n_1)^2}{n_1} + \dfrac{(s_2^2/n_2)^2}{n_2}} = \frac{\left(\dfrac{326.1636}{32} + \dfrac{619.5121}{189}\right)^2}{\dfrac{(326.1636/32)^2}{32} + \dfrac{(619.5121/189)^2}{189}}$$

$$= \frac{181.453139}{3.30339} = 54.93 \text{ or } 55 \text{ degrees of freedom.}$$

12. A. We test H_0: $\mu_d = 0$ versus H_a: $\mu_d \neq 0$.

B. This is a paired comparisons t-test with $n - 1 = 480 - 1 = 479$ degrees of freedom. At the 0.05 significance level, we reject the null hypothesis if either $t > 1.96$ or $t < -1.96$. We use df = ∞ in the t-distribution table under $\alpha = 0.025$ because we have a very large sample and a two-sided test.

$$t = \frac{\overline{d} - \mu_{d0}}{s_{\overline{d}}} = \frac{-0.258 - 0}{3.752/\sqrt{480}} = \frac{-0.258}{0.171255} = -1.506529 \text{ or } -1.51$$

At the 0.05 significance level, because neither rejection point condition is met, we do not reject the null hypothesis that the mean difference between the returns on the S&P 500 and small-cap stocks during the entire sample period was 0.

C. This t-test now has $n - 1 = 240 - 1 = 239$ degrees of freedom. At the 0.05 significance level, we reject the null hypothesis if either if $t > 1.972$ or $t < -1.972$, using df = 200 in the t-distribution tables.

$$t = \frac{\overline{d} - \mu_{d0}}{s_{\overline{d}}} = \frac{-0.640 - 0}{4.096/\sqrt{240}} = \frac{-0.640}{0.264396} = -2.420615 \text{ or } -2.42$$

Because $-2.42 < -1.972$, we reject the null hypothesis at the 0.05 significance level. During this subperiod, small-cap stocks significantly outperformed the S&P 500.

D. This t-test has $n - 1 = 240 - 1 = 239$ degrees of freedom. At the 0.05 significance level, we reject the null hypothesis if either if $t > 1.972$ or $t < -1.972$, using df $= 200$ in the t-distribution tables.

$$t = \frac{\bar{d} - \mu_{d0}}{s_{\bar{d}}} = \frac{0.125 - 0}{3.339/\sqrt{240}} = \frac{0.125}{0.215532} = 0.579962 \text{ or } 0.58$$

At the 0.05 significance level, because neither rejection point condition is met, we do not reject the null hypothesis that for the January 1980–December 1999 period, the mean difference between the returns on the S&P 500 and small-cap stocks was zero.

13. A. We have a "less than" alternative hypothesis, where σ^2 is the variance of return on the portfolio. The hypotheses are $H_0: \sigma^2 \geq 400$ versus $H_a: \sigma^2 < 400$, where 400 is the hypothesized value of variance, σ_0^2.

B. The test statistic is chi-square with $10 - 1 = 9$ degrees of freedom.

C. The rejection point is found across degrees of freedom of 9, under the 0.95 column (95 percent of probability above the value). It is 3.325. We will reject the null hypothesis if we find that $\chi^2 < 3.325$.

D. The test statistic is calculated as

$$\chi^2 = \frac{(n - 1)s^2}{\sigma_0^2} = \frac{9 \times 15^2}{400} = \frac{2,025}{400} = 5.0625 \text{ or } 5.06$$

Because 5.06 is not less than 3.325, we do not reject the null hypothesis.

14. A. We have a "not equal to" alternative hypothesis:

$$H_0: \sigma^2{}_{\text{Before}} = \sigma^2{}_{\text{After}} \text{ versus } H_a: \sigma^2{}_{\text{Before}} \neq \sigma^2{}_{\text{After}}$$

B. To test a null hypothesis of the equality of two variances, we use an F-test:

$$F = \frac{s_1^2}{s_2^2}$$

C. The "before" sample variance is larger, so following a convention for calculating F-statistics, the "before" sample variance goes in the numerator. $F = 22.367/15.795 = 1.416$, with $120 - 1 = 119$ numerator and denominator degrees of freedom. Because this is a two-tailed test, we use F-tables for the 0.025 level (df $= 0.05/2$). Using the tables in the back of the book, the closest value to 119 is 120 degrees of freedom. At the 0.05 level, the rejection point is 1.43. (Using the Insert/Function/Statistical feature on a Microsoft Excel spreadsheet, we would find FINV(0.025, 119, 119) $= 1.434859$ as the critical F-value.) Because 1.416 is not greater than 1.43, we do not reject the null hypothesis that the "before" and "after" variances are equal.

15. A. We have a "not equal to" alternative hypothesis:

$$H_0: \rho = 0 \text{ versus } H_a: \rho \neq 0$$

B. We would use the nonparametric Spearman rank correlation coefficient to conduct the test.

C. Mutual fund expense ratios are bounded from above and below, and in practice there is at least a lower bound on alpha (as any return cannot be less than −100 percent). These variables are markedly non-normally distributed, and the assumptions of a parametric test are not likely to be fulfilled. Thus a nonparametric test appears to be appropriate.

D. The calculation of the Spearman rank correlation coefficient is given in the following table.

Mutual Fund	1	2	3	4	5	6	7	8	9
Alpha (X)	−0.52	−0.13	−0.60	−1.01	−0.26	−0.89	−0.42	−0.23	−0.60
Expense Ratio (Y)	1.34	0.92	1.02	1.45	1.35	0.50	1.00	1.50	1.45
X Rank	5	1	6.5	9	3	8	4	2	6.5
Y Rank	5	8	6	2.5	4	9	7	1	2.5
d_i	0	−7	0.5	6.5	−1	−1	−3	1	4
d_i^2	0	49	0.25	42.25	1	1	9	1	16

$$r_S = 1 - \frac{6 \sum d_i^2}{n(n^2 - 1)} = 1 - \frac{6(119.50)}{9(81 - 1)} = 0.0042$$

We use Table 7-11 to tabulate the rejection points for a test on the Spearman rank correlation. Given a sample size of 9 in a two-tailed test at a 0.05 significance level, the upper-tail rejection point is 0.6833 (we use the 0.025 column). Thus we reject the null hypothesis if the Spearman rank correlation coefficient is less than −0.6833 or greater than 0.6833. Because r_S is equal to 0.0042, we do not reject the null hypothesis.

CHAPTER 8

CORRELATION AND REGRESSION

SOLUTIONS

1. The four variables Y_1 through Y_4 have a zero correlation with X. Notice that although Y_3 and Y_4 are clearly nonlinearly related to X (decreasing and then increasing as the value of X increases), their overall linear relationship with X is zero. Variable Y_5 has a correlation of 1.0 with X.

2. A. The sample mean, variance, and standard deviation of X are

$$\overline{X} = \sum_{i=1}^{n} X_i/n = 220/11 = 20$$

$$s_X^2 = \sum_{i=1}^{n} (X_i - \overline{X})^2/(n-1) = 440/10 = 44$$

$$s_X = \sqrt{s_X^2} = \sqrt{44} = 6.633$$

B. The sample mean, variance, and standard deviation of Y are

$$\overline{Y} = \sum_{i=1}^{n} Y_i/n = 385/11 = 35$$

$$s_Y^2 = \sum_{i=1}^{n} (Y_i - \overline{Y})^2/(n-1) = 1120/10 = 112$$

$$s_Y = \sqrt{s_Y^2} = \sqrt{112} = 10.583$$

C. The sample covariance between X and Y is

$$\text{Cov}(X, Y) = \sum_{i=1}^{n} [(X_i - \overline{X})(Y_i - \overline{Y})]/(n-1) = -568/10 = -56.8$$

D. The sample correlation between X and Y is

$$r = \frac{\text{Cov}(X, Y)}{s_X s_Y} = \frac{-56.8}{6.633 \times 10.583} = -0.809$$

3. A. The sample variances and standard deviations are

$$s_X^2 = \sum_{i=1}^{n} (X_i - \overline{X})^2/(n-1) = 769.081/59 = 13.035$$

$$s_X = \sqrt{13.035} = 3.610$$

$$s_Y^2 = \sum_{i=1}^{n} (Y_i - \overline{Y})^2/(n-1) = 1243.309/59 = 21.073$$

$$s_Y = \sqrt{21.073} = 4.591$$

$$s_Z^2 = \sum_{i=1}^{n} (Z_i - \overline{Z})^2/(n-1) = 183.073/59 = 3.103$$

$$s_Z = \sqrt{3.103} = 1.762$$

B. The sample covariances are

$$\mathrm{Cov}(X, Y) = \sum_{i=1}^{n} (X_i - \overline{X})(Y_i - \overline{Y})/(n-1) = 720.535/59 = 12.212$$

$$\mathrm{Cov}(X, Z) = \sum_{i=1}^{n} (X_i - \overline{X})(Z_i - \overline{Z})/(n-1) = 231.007/59 = 3.915$$

$$\mathrm{Cov}(Y, Z) = \sum_{i=1}^{n} (Y_i - \overline{Y})(Z_i - \overline{Z})/(n-1) = 171.816/59 = 2.912$$

C. The sample correlations are

$$r_{XY} = \frac{\mathrm{Cov}(X, Y)}{s_X s_Y} = \frac{12.212}{(3.610)(4.591)} = 0.737$$

$$r_{XZ} = \frac{\mathrm{Cov}(X, Z)}{s_X s_Z} = \frac{3.915}{(3.610)(1.762)} = 0.615$$

$$r_{YZ} = \frac{\mathrm{Cov}(Y, Z)}{s_Y s_Z} = \frac{2.912}{(4.591)(1.762)} = 0.360$$

4. Sample mean sales are $(50 + 70 + 80 + 60)/4 = 260/4 = 65$.
Sample mean interest rate is $(8.0 + 7.0 + 6.0 + 7.0)/4 = 28.0/4 = 7.0$.
Sample variance of sales is $[(50 - 65)^2 + (70 - 65)^2 + (80 - 65)^2 + (60 - 65)^2]/3 = 500/3 = 166.7$.
Sample standard deviation of sales is the square root of the variance, or 12.91.
Sample variance of interest rates is $[(8 - 7)^2 + (7 - 7)^2 + (6 - 7)^2 + (7 - 7)^2]/3 = 2/3 = 0.666667$.
Sample standard deviation of interest rates is the square root of this result, or 0.8165.
Sample covariance between sales and interest rates is $[(50 - 65)(8 - 7) + (70 - 65)(7 - 7) + (80 - 65)(6 - 7) + (60 - 65)(7 - 7)]/3 = -30/3 = -10$.

Sample correlation is the covariance divided by the product of the standard deviations:

$$r = \frac{\text{Cov}(X, Y)}{s_x s_y} = \frac{-10}{(12.91)(0.8165)} = -0.9487$$

5. The critical t-value for $n - 2 = 34$ df, using a 5 percent significance level and a two-tailed test, is 2.032. First, take the smallest correlation in the table, the correlation between Fund 3 and Fund 4, and see if it is significantly different from zero. Its calculated t-value is

$$t = \frac{r\sqrt{n - 2}}{\sqrt{1 - r^2}} = \frac{0.3102\sqrt{36 - 2}}{\sqrt{1 - 0.3102^2}} = 1.903$$

This correlation is not significantly different from zero. If we take the next lowest correlation, between Fund 2 and Fund 3, this correlation of 0.4156 has a calculated t-value of 2.664. So this correlation is significantly different from zero at the 5 percent level of significance. All of the other correlations in the table (besides the 0.3102) are greater than 0.4156, so they too are significantly different from zero.

6. A. The negative correlation, as Osterburg hypothesizes, is consistent with reversals. An above-average return tends to be followed by a below-average return. Similarly, a below-average return tends to be followed by an above-average return.

   B. The null hypothesis, H_0, is that the correlation is 0 ($\rho = 0$); the alternative hypothesis, H_a, is that the correlation is different from 0 ($\rho \neq 0$). We can test this hypothesis with a t-test. The calculated value of the t-test is as follows:

$$t = \frac{r\sqrt{n - 2}}{\sqrt{1 - r^2}} = \frac{-0.0641\sqrt{59 - 2}}{\sqrt{1 - (-0.0641)^2}} = -0.485$$

   This test statistic has a t-distribution with $n - 2 = 59 - 2 = 57$ df, so the critical t-value (for a two-tailed test and 5 percent significance) is approximately 2.00. So we cannot reject the hypothesis that $\rho = 0$ with 95 percent confidence. We thus cannot reject Martinez's opinion that the returns are random.

7. The null hypothesis, H_0, is that the correlation is 0 ($\rho = 0$); the alternative hypothesis, H_a, is that the correlation is different from 0 ($\rho \neq 0$). The calculated value of the t-test for the S&P 500 is

$$t = \frac{r\sqrt{n - 2}}{\sqrt{1 - r^2}} = \frac{0.0034\sqrt{347 - 2}}{\sqrt{1 - 0.0034^2}} = 0.063$$

The t-values for the other indices are calculated similarly, as follows:

MSCI Europe   0.623
MSCI Pacific   2.095
MSCI Far East   1.965

The critical t-value for $n - 2 = 347 - 2 = 345$ df is approximately 1.65. At a 10 percent significance level (two-tailed test with 345 df), the correlations for the S&P 500 and MSCI Europe are not significantly different from zero. The MSCI Pacific and MSCI Far East correlations apparently are significantly different from zero.

8. The following table provides several useful calculations:

Year i	Exchange Rate X_i	Sales Y_i	$(X_i - \overline{X})^2$	$(Y_i - \overline{Y})^2$	$(X_i - \overline{X})(Y_i - \overline{Y})$
1	0.4	20	0.0016	36	-0.24
2	0.36	25	0.0000	1	0.00
3	0.42	16	0.0036	100	-0.60
4	0.31	30	0.0025	16	-0.20
5	0.33	35	0.0009	81	-0.27
6	0.34	30	0.0004	16	-0.08
Sum	2.16	156	0.0090	250	-1.39

A. The sample mean and standard deviation of the exchange rate are

$$\overline{X} = \sum_{i=1}^{n} X_i/n = 2.16/6 = 0.36$$

and

$$s_X = \sqrt{\sum_{i=1}^{n}(X_i - \overline{X})^2/(n-1)} = \sqrt{0.009/5} = 0.042426$$

The sample mean and standard deviation of sales are

$$\overline{Y} = \sum_{i=1}^{n} Y_i/n = 156/6 = 26$$

and

$$s_Y = \sqrt{\sum_{i=1}^{n}(Y_i - \overline{Y})^2/(n-1)} = \sqrt{250/5} = 7.0711$$

B. The sample covariance between the exchange rate and sales is

$$Cov(X, Y) = \sum_{i=1}^{n}(X_i - \overline{X})(Y_i - \overline{Y})/(n-1) = -1.39/5 = -0.278$$

C. The sample correlation between the exchange rate and sales is

$$r = \frac{Cov(X, Y)}{s_X s_Y} = \frac{-0.278}{(0.042426)(7.0711)} = -0.927$$

D. We want to estimate a regression equation of the form $Y_i = b_0 + b_1 X_i + \varepsilon_i$. The estimates of the slope coefficient and the intercept are

$$\hat{b}_1 = \frac{\sum_{i=1}^{n}(Y_i - \overline{Y})(X_i - \overline{X})}{\sum_{i=1}^{n}(X_i - \overline{X})^2} = \frac{-1.39}{0.009} = -154.44$$

and

$$\hat{b}_0 = \overline{Y} - \hat{b}_1 \overline{X} = 26 - (-154.44)(0.36) = 26 + 55.6 = 81.6$$

So the regression equation is $Y_i = 81.6 - 154.44 X_i$.

9. A. The coefficient of determination is

$$\frac{\text{Explained variation}}{\text{Total variation}} = \frac{60.16}{140.58} = 0.4279$$

   B. For a linear regression with one independent variable, the absolute value of correlation between the independent variable and the dependent variable equals the square root of the coefficient of determination, so the correlation is $\sqrt{0.4279} = 0.6542$. (The correlation will have the same sign as the slope coefficient.)

   C. The standard error of the estimate is

$$\left(\sum_{i=1}^{n} \frac{(Y_i - \hat{b}_0 - \hat{b}_1 X_i)^2}{n-2} \right)^{1/2} = \left(\frac{\text{Unexplained variation}}{n-2} \right)^{1/2} = \sqrt{\frac{80.42}{60-2}} = 1.178$$

   D. The sample variance of the dependent variable is

$$\sum_{i=1}^{n} \frac{(Y_i - \overline{Y})^2}{n-1} = \frac{\text{Total variation}}{n-1} = \frac{140.58}{60-1} = 2.3827$$

   The sample standard deviation is $\sqrt{2.3827} = 1.544$.

10. A. The degrees of freedom for the regression is the number of slope parameters in the regression, which is the same as the number of independent variables in the regression. Because regression df $= 1$, we conclude that there is one independent variable in the regression.

   B. Total SS is the sum of the squared deviations of the dependent variable Y about its mean.

   C. The sample variance of the dependent variable is the total SS divided by its degrees of freedom ($n - 1 = 5 - 1 = 4$ as given). Thus the sample variance of the dependent variable is $95.2/4 = 23.8$.

   D. The Regression SS is the part of total sum of squares explained by the regression. Regression SS equals the sum of the squared differences between predicted values of the Y and the sample mean of Y: $\left[\sum_{i=1}^{n} (\hat{Y}_i - \overline{Y}) \right]^2$. In terms of other values in the table, Regression SS is equal to Total SS minus Residual SS: $95.2 - 7.2 = 88$.

   E. The F-statistic tests whether all the slope coefficients in a linear regression are equal to 0.

   F. The calculated value of F in the table is equal to the Regression MSS divided by the Residual MSS: $88/2.4 = 36.667$.

   G. Yes. The significance of 0.00904 given in the table is the p-value of the test (the smallest level at which we can reject the null hypothesis). This value of 0.00904 is less than the specified significance level of 0.05, so we reject the null hypothesis. The regression equation has significant explanatory power.

11. A. For the large-cap fund, the predicted rate of return, $\hat{Y}$, is

$$\hat{Y} = \hat{b}_0 + \hat{b}_1 X = -0.287 + 0.802(8.00) = 6.129$$

B. The estimated variance of the prediction error, s_f^2, of Y, given X, is

$$s_f^2 = s^2 \left[1 + \frac{1}{n} + \frac{(X - \overline{X})^2}{(n-1)s_x^2} \right]$$

$$= 4.243^2 \left[1 + \frac{1}{12} + \frac{(8.00 - 2.30)^2}{(12-1)(38.51)} \right] = 20.884$$

The standard deviation of the prediction error is the square root of this number: 4.57. For 10 degrees of freedom, the critical t-value is 2.228. A 95 percent prediction interval is $\hat{Y} \pm t_c s_f$, or $6.129 \pm 2.228(4.57)$, or 6.129 ± 10.182.

$$\text{Prob}(-4.053 < Y < 16.311) = 0.95$$

12. A. For a sentiment index of 90, predicted auto sales, $\hat{Y}$, are $\hat{Y} = \hat{b}_0 + \hat{b}_1 X = 6.071 + 0.09251(90) = 14.397$ (about 14.4 million vehicles). The estimated variance of the prediction error, s_f^2, of Y, given X, is

$$s_f^2 = s^2 \left[1 + \frac{1}{n} + \frac{(X - \overline{X})^2}{(n-1)s_x^2} \right]$$

$$= 0.81325^2 \left[1 + \frac{1}{120} + \frac{(90 - 91.0983)^2}{(120-1)(137.3068)} \right] = 0.66694$$

The standard deviation of the prediction error is the square root of this number: 0.8167. For 118 degrees of freedom and a 0.05 level of significance, the critical t-value is approximately 1.98. The 95 percent prediction interval for $X = 90$ is $\hat{Y} \pm t_c s_f$, or $14.397 \pm 1.98(0.8167)$, or 14.397 ± 1.617.

$\text{Prob}(12.780 < Y < 16.014) = 0.95$

B. For a sentiment index of 100, predicted auto sales, $\hat{Y}$, are

$$\hat{Y} = \hat{b}_0 + \hat{b}_1 X = 6.071 + 0.09251(100) = 15.322$$

The estimated variance of the prediction error, s_f^2, of Y, given X, is

$$s_f^2 = s^2 \left[1 + \frac{1}{n} + \frac{(X - \overline{X})^2}{(n-1)s_x^2} \right]$$

$$= 0.81325^2 \left[1 = \frac{1}{120} + \frac{(100 - 91.0983)^2}{(120-1)(137.3068)} \right] = 0.67009$$

The standard deviation of the prediction error is the square root of this number: 0.81859. For 118 degrees of freedom, the critical t-value is approximately 1.98. A 95 percent prediction interval would be $\hat{Y} \pm t_c s_f$, or $15.322 \pm 1.98(0.81859)$, or 15.322 ± 1.621.

$\text{Prob}(13.701 < Y < 16.943) = 0.95$

13. A. The sample size is $n = 9$.

For X, the sample mean is $\overline{X} = \sum_{i=1}^{n} X_i/n = 81/9 = 9$, the sample variance is

$$s_X^2 = \sum_{i=1}^{n} (X_i - \overline{X})^2/(n-1) = 60/8 = 7.5, \text{ and the sample standard deviation is}$$

$s_X = \sqrt{7.5} = 2.7386.$

For Y, the sample mean is $\overline{Y} = \sum_{i=1}^{n} Y_i/n = 144/9 = 16$, the sample variance is

$$s_Y^2 = \sum_{i=1}^{n} (Y_i - \overline{Y})^2/(n-1) = 144/8 = 18, \text{ and the sample standard deviation is}$$

$s_Y = \sqrt{18} = 4.2426.$

B. The sample covariance is

$$\text{Cov}(X, Y) = \sum_{i=1}^{n} (X_i - \overline{X})(Y_i - \overline{Y})/(n-1) = 84/8 = 10.5$$

The sample correlation between X and Y is

$$r = \frac{\text{Cov}(X, Y)}{s_X s_Y}$$

$$= \frac{10.5}{(2.7386)(4.2426)} = 0.9037$$

C. The coefficients for the regression equation are

$$\hat{b}_1 = \frac{\sum_{i=1}^{n} (Y_i - \overline{Y})(X_i - \overline{X})}{\sum_{i=1}^{n} (X_i - \overline{X})^2} = \frac{84}{60} = 1.4, \text{ and}$$

$$\hat{b}_0 = \overline{Y} - \hat{b}_1 \overline{X} = 16 - 1.4(9) = 3.4$$

So the regression equation is $\hat{Y}_i = 3.4 + 1.4X_i$.

D. The total variation is $\sum_{i=1}^{n} (Y_i - \overline{Y})^2 = 144$, and the unexplained variation is $\sum_{i=1}^{n} (Y_i - \hat{b}_0 - \hat{b}_1 X_i)^2 = 26.4$. So the explained variation is $144 - 26.4 = 117.6$.

E. The coefficient of variation, the R-squared, is

$$\frac{\text{Explained variation}}{\text{Total variation}} = \frac{117.6}{144} = 0.81667$$

F. The standard error of the estimate is

$$\text{SEE} = \left[\sum_{i=1}^{n} \frac{(Y_i - \hat{b}_0 - \hat{b}_1 X_i)^2}{n-2} \right]^{1/2}$$

$$= \left(\frac{26.4}{9-2} \right)^{1/2} = 1.942$$

14. The R-squared (**X1**) is the explained variation/total variation $= 14.246/60.139 = 0.2369$. The Multiple R (**X2**) is the correlation between the two variables, which is the square root of the R-squared, or $\sqrt{0.2369} = 0.4867$. The standard error (**X3**) is the square root of unexplained variation divided by $(n - 2)$, which is $\sqrt{45.893/(1819 - 2)} = 0.1589$.

The Total df, **X4**, is the sample size minus 1, or $n - 1 = 1,819 - 1 = 1,818$. The Regression df (**X5**) is equal to the number of independent variables, which is 1. The Residual df (**X6**) is the difference between the Total df and Regression df, which is also $n - (k + 1)$ where n is the sample size (1,819) and k is the number of independent variables (1). X6 is $1,819 - (1 + 1) = 1,817$. MSS is the "mean square," which is the sum of squares divided by the degrees of freedom. For **X7**, the MSS regression is $14.246/1 = 14.246$. For **X8**, the MSS residual is $45.893/1,817 = 0.025258$. The F (**X9**) is testing the hypothesis that the regression coefficient equals zero, and it is equal to MSS regression/MSS residual, or $14.246/0.025258 = 564.02$. This F has 1 df in the numerator and 1817 df in the denominator. This value for F is extremely large, and the probability of an F this large is practically zero.

X10, the calculated t-value for the slope coefficient, is the coefficient divided by its standard error: $t = -0.04375/0.00184 = -23.75$. This is an extremely large negative t, with a probability of practically zero. (Notice that the square root of the F is equal to the t for a regression with one independent variable.) Finally, **X11** and **X12** are the upper and lower bounds for a 95 percent confidence interval for the slope coefficient. The critical t for a two-tailed test at the 5 percent significance level with 1,817 degrees of freedom is approximately 1.96. The lower bound, **X11**, is $\hat{b}_1 - t_c s_{\hat{b}_1} = -0.04375 - 1.96(0.001842) = -0.04736$. The upper bound, **X12**, is $\hat{b}_1 + t_c s_{\hat{b}_1} = -0.04375 + 1.96(0.001842) = -0.04014$.

15. The Month 2 data point is an outlier, lying far away from the other data values. Because this outlier was caused by a data entry error, correcting the outlier improves the validity and reliability of the regression. In this case, the true correlation is reduced from 0.996 to 0.824. The revised R-squared is substantially lower (0.678 versus 0.992). The significance of the regression is also lower, as can be seen in the decline of the F-value from 500.79 to 8.44 and the decline in the t-statistic of the slope coefficient from 22.379 to 2.905.

The total sum of squares and regression sum of squares were greatly exaggerated in the incorrect analysis. With the correction, the slope coefficient changes from 1.069 to 0.623. This change is important. When the index moves up or down, the original model indicates that the portfolio return goes up or down by 1.069 times as much, while the revised model indicates that the portfolio return goes up or down by only 0.623 times as much. In this example, incorrect data entry caused the outlier. Had it been a valid observation, not caused by a data error, then the analyst would have had to decide whether the results were more reliable including or excluding the outlier.

16. A. If FEE $= 0\%$, RETURN $= -3.021 + 7.062(0) = -3.021\%$
    If FEE $= 1\%$, RETURN $= -3.021 + 7.062(1) = 4.041\%$

    B. The calculated t-value for the coefficient of FEE is 14.95. The critical t-value for 58 degrees of freedom, a two-tailed test, and a 5 percent significance level is 2.00. Because the calculated t exceeds the critical t, we may conclude that the coefficient of FEE is not equal to zero and that the relationship between RETURN and FEE is significant.

    C. Smith's analysis is inadequate to conclude that high fees are good. Clearly, high returns cause high fees (because of the compensation contract that Diet Partners has with its clients). The regression may be recognizing this relationship. Unfortunately, the reverse may not be true—that fees cause returns. As an analogy, assume that income taxes are a function of income. A regression of income as a function of income taxes would find a strong positive relationship. Does this mean that taxes cause income, or the reverse? Smith's experiment is too simplistic to address the issue of whether a particular compensation contract is good or bad for client returns.

17. 17-1. B is correct. The coefficient of determination is the same as R-squared.

    17-2. C is correct. Deleting observations with small residuals will degrade the strength of the regression, resulting in an *increase* in the standard error and a *decrease* in R-squared.

    17-3. D is correct. For a regression with one independent variable, the correlation is the same as the Multiple R with the sign of the slope coefficient. Because the slope coefficient is positive, the correlation is 0.8623.

    17-4. B is correct. This answer describes the calculation of the F-statistic.

    17-5. D is correct. To make a prediction using the regression model, multiply the slope coefficient by the forecast of the independent variable and add the result to the intercept.

    17-6. D is correct. The p-value reflects the strength of the relationship between the two variables. In this case the p-value is less than 0.05, and thus the regression of the ratio of cash flow from operations to sales on the ratio of net income to sales is significant at the 5 percent level.

18. 18-1. B is correct because the calculated test statistic is

$$ t = \frac{r\sqrt{n-2}}{\sqrt{1-r^2}} $$

$$ = \frac{-0.1452\sqrt{248-2}}{\sqrt{1-(-0.1452)^2}} = -2.3017 $$

Because the absolute value of $t = -2.3017$ is greater than 1.96, the correlation coefficient is statistically significant. For a regression with one independent variable, the t-value (and significance) for the slope coefficient (which is -2.3014) should equal the t-value (and significance) of the correlation coefficient. The slight difference between these two t-values is caused by rounding error.

    18-2. A is correct because the data are time series, and the expected value of the error term, $E(\varepsilon)$, is 0.

    18-3. D is correct. From the regression equation, Expected return $= 0.0138 + -0.6486$ $(-0.01) = 0.0138 + 0.006486 = 0.0203$, or 2.03 percent.

    18-4. C is correct. R-squared is the coefficient of determination. In this case, it shows that 2.11 percent of the variability in Stellar's returns is explained by changes in CPIENG.

    18-5. A is correct, because the standard error of the estimate is the standard deviation of the regression residuals.

    18-6. C is the correct response, because it is a false statement. The slope and intercept are both statistically significant.

CHAPTER 9

MULTIPLE REGRESSION AND ISSUES IN REGRESSION ANALYSIS

SOLUTIONS

1. A. $R_{it} = b_0 + b_1 R_{Mt} + b_2 \Delta X_t + \epsilon_{it}$

   B. We can test whether the coefficient on the S&P 500 Index returns is statistically significant. Our null hypothesis is that the coefficient is equal to 0 ($H_0: b_1 = 0$); our alternative hypothesis is that the coefficient is not equal to 0 ($H_a: b_1 \neq 0$). We construct the t-test of the null hypothesis as follows:

   $$\frac{\hat{b}_1 - b_1}{s_{b_1}} = \frac{0.5373 - 0}{0.1332} = 4.0338$$

   where

   $\hat{b}_1 =$ the regression estimate of b_1

   $b_1 =$ the hypothesized value of the coefficient (here, 0)

   $s_{\hat{b}_1} =$ the estimated standard error of $\hat{b}_1$

   Because this regression has 156 observations and three regression coefficients, the t-test has $156 - 3 = 153$ degrees of freedom. At the 0.05 significance level, the critical value for the test statistic is between 1.98 and 1.97. The absolute value of the test statistic is 4.0338; therefore, we can reject the null hypothesis that $b_1 = 0$.

   Similarly, we can test whether the coefficient on the change in the value of the U.S. dollar is statistically significant in this regression. Our null hypothesis is that the coefficient is equal to 0 ($H_0: b_2 = 0$); our alternative hypothesis is that the coefficient is not equal to 0 ($H_a: b_2 \neq 0$). We construct the t-test as follows:

   $$\frac{\hat{b}_2 - b_2}{s_{b_2}} = \frac{-0.5768 - 0}{0.5121} = -1.1263$$

   As before, the t-test has 153 degrees of freedom, and the critical value for the test statistic is between 1.98 and 1.97 at the 0.05 significance level. The absolute value of the test statistic is 1.1263; therefore, we cannot reject the null hypothesis that $b_2 = 0$.

Based on the above t-tests, we conclude that S&P 500 Index returns do affect ADM's returns but that changes in the value of the U.S. dollar do not affect ADM's returns.

C. The statement is not correct. To make it correct, we need to add the qualification "holding ΔX constant" to the end of the quoted statement.

2. A. $R_i = b_0 + b_1(\text{B/M})_i + b_2\text{Size}_i + \epsilon_i$

B. We can test whether the coefficients on the book-to-market ratio and size are individually statistically significant using t-tests. For the book-to-market ratio, our null hypothesis is that the coefficient is equal to 0 (H_0: $b_1 = 0$); our alternative hypothesis is that the coefficient is not equal to 0 (H_a: $b_1 \neq 0$). We can test the null hypothesis using a t-test constructed as follows:

$$\frac{\hat{b}_1 - b_1}{s_{\hat{b}_1}} = \frac{-0.0541 - 0}{0.0588} = -0.9201$$

where

$\hat{b}_1$ = the regression estimate of b_1

b_1 = the hypothesized value of the coefficient (here, 0)

$s_{\hat{b}_1}$ = the estimated standard error of $\hat{b}_1$

This regression has 66 observations and three coefficients, so the t-test has $66 - 3 = 63$ degrees of freedom. At the 0.05 significance level, the critical value for the test statistic is about 2.0. The absolute value of the test statistic is 0.9201; therefore, we cannot reject the null hypothesis that $b_1 = 0$. We can conclude that the book-to-market ratio is not useful in explaining the cross-sectional variation in returns for this sample.

We perform the same analysis to determine whether size (as measured by the log of the market value of equity) can help explain the cross-sectional variation in asset returns. Our null hypothesis is that the coefficient is equal to 0 (H_0: $b_2 = 0$); our alternative hypothesis is that the coefficient is not equal to 0 (H_a: $b_2 \neq 0$). We can test the null hypothesis using a t-test constructed as follows:

$$\frac{\hat{b}_2 - b_2}{s_{\hat{b}_2}} = \frac{-0.0164 - 0}{0.0350} = -0.4686$$

where

$\hat{b}_2$ = the regression estimate of b_2

b_2 = the hypothesized value of the coefficient (here, 0)

$s_{\hat{b}_2}$ = the estimated standard error of $\hat{b}_2$

Again, because this regression has 66 observations and three coefficients, the t-test has $66 - 3 = 63$ degrees of freedom. At the 0.05 significance level, the critical value for the test statistic is about 2.0. The absolute value of the test statistic is 0.4686; therefore, we cannot reject the null hypothesis that $b_2 = 0$. We can conclude that asset size is not useful in explaining the cross-sectional variation of asset returns in this sample.

3. A. The estimated regression is (Analyst following)$_i$ $= -0.2845 + 0.3199$Size$_i - 0.1895$ (D/E)$_i + \epsilon_i$. Therefore, the prediction for the first company is

$$(\text{Analyst following})_i = -0.2845 + 0.3199(\ln 100) - 0.1895(0.75)$$

$$= -0.2845 + 1.4732 - 0.1421 = 1.0466$$

Recalling that (Analyst following)$_i$ is the natural log of $(1 + n_i)$, where n_i is the number of analysts following company i; it follows that $1 + n_1 = e^{1.0466} = 2.848$, approximately. Therefore, $n_1 = 2.848 - 1 = 1.848$, or about two analysts. Similarly, the prediction for the second company is as follows:

$$(\text{Analyst following})_i = -0.2845 + 0.3199(\ln 1,000) - 0.1895(0.75)$$

$$= -0.2845 + 2.2098 - 0.1421 = 1.7832$$

Thus, $1 + n_2 = e^{1.7832} = 5.949$, approximately. Therefore, $n_2 = 5.949 - 1 = 4.949$, or about five analysts.

The model predicts that $5 - 2 = 3$ more analysts will follow the second company than the first company.

   B. We would interpret the *p*-value of 0.00236 as the smallest level of significance at which we can reject a null hypothesis that the population value of the coefficient is 0, in a two-sided test. Clearly, in this regression the debt-to-equity ratio is a highly significant variable.

4. The estimated model is

$$\text{Percentage decline in TSE spread of company } i = -0.45 + 0.05\text{Size}_i$$
$$- 0.06(\text{Ratio of spreads})_i + 0.29(\text{Decline in Nasdaq spreads})_i$$

Therefore, the prediction is

$$\text{Percentage decline in TSE spread} = -0.45 + 0.05(\ln 900,000) - 0.06(1.3)$$
$$+ 0.29(1) = -0.45 + 0.69 - 0.08 + 0.29 = 0.45$$

The model predicts that for a company with average sample characteristics, the spread on the TSE declines by 0.45 percent for a 1 percent decline in Nasdaq spreads.

5. A. To test the null hypothesis that all the slope coefficients in the regression model are equal to 0 (H_0: $b_1 = b_2 = 0$) against the alternative hypothesis that at least one slope coefficient is not equal to 0, we must use an *F*-test.

   B. To conduct the *F*-test, we need four inputs, all of which are found in the ANOVA section of the table in the statement of the problem:

   i. total number of observations, n
   ii. total number of regression coefficients to be estimated, $k + 1$
   iii. sum of squared errors or residuals, $\sum_{i=1}^{n}(Y_i - \hat{Y}_i)^2$ abbreviated SSE, and
   iv. regression sum of squares, $\sum_{i=1}^{n}(\hat{Y}_i - \overline{Y})^2$, abbreviated RSS

C. The F-test formula is

$$F = \frac{\text{RSS}/k}{\text{SSE}/[n - (k + 1)]} = \frac{0.0094/2}{0.6739/[66 - (2 + 1)]} = 0.4394$$

The F-statistic has degrees of freedom $F\{k, [n - (k + 1)]\} = F(2, 63)$. From the F-test table, for the 0.05 significance level, the critical value for $F(2, 63)$ is about 3.15, so we cannot reject the hypothesis that the slope coefficients are both 0. The two independent variables are jointly statistically unrelated to returns.

D. Adjusted R^2 is a measure of goodness of fit that takes into account the number of independent variables in the regression, in contrast to R^2. We can assert that adjusted R^2 is smaller than $R^2 = 0.0138$ without the need to perform any calculations. (However, adjusted R^2 can be shown to equal -0.0175 using an expression in the text on the relationship between adjusted R^2 and R^2.)

6. A. You believe that opening markets actually reduces return volatility; if that belief is correct, then the slope coefficient would be negative, $b_1 < 0$. The null hypothesis is that the belief is not true: $H_0: b_1 \geq 0$. The alternative hypothesis is that the belief is true: $H_a: b_1 < 0$.

B. The critical value for the t-statistic with $95 - 2 = 93$ degrees of freedom at the 0.05 significance level in a one-sided test is about 1.66. For the one-sided test stated in Part A, we reject the null hypothesis if the t-statistic on the slope coefficient is less than -1.66. As the t-statistic of $-2.7604 < -1.66$, we reject the null. Because the dummy variable takes on a value of 1 when foreign investment is allowed, we can conclude that the volatility was lower with foreign investment.

C. According to the estimated regression, average return volatility was 0.0133 (the estimated value of the intercept) before July 1993 and $0.0058 (= 0.0133 - 0.0075)$ after July 1993.

7. A. The appropriate regression model is $R_{Mt} = b_0 + b_1 \text{Party}_t + \epsilon_t$

B. The t-statistic reported in the table for the dummy variable tests whether the coefficient on Party_t is significantly different from 0. It is computed as follows:

$$\frac{\hat{b}_1 - b_1}{s_{\hat{b}_1}} = \frac{-0.0570 - 0}{0.0466} = -1.22$$

where

$\hat{b}_1$ = the regression estimate of b_1

b_1 = the hypothesized value of the coefficient (here, 0)

$s_{\hat{b}_1}$ = the estimated standard error of $\hat{b}_1$

To two decimal places, this value is the same as the t-statistic reported in the table for the dummy variable, as expected. The problem specified two decimal places because the reported regression output reflects rounding; for this reason, we often cannot exactly reproduce reported t-statistics.

C. Because the regression has 77 observations and two coefficients, the t-test has $77 - 2 = 75$ degrees of freedom. At the 0.05 significance level, the critical value for the two-tailed test statistic is about 1.99. The absolute value of the test statistic is

1.2242; therefore, we do not reject the null hypothesis that $b_1 = 0$. We can conclude that the political party in the White House does not, on average, affect the annual returns of the overall market as measured by the S&P 500.

8. A. The regression model is as follows:

$$\text{(Analyst following)}_i = b_0 + b_1 \text{Size}_i + b_2 \text{(D/E)}_i + b_3 \text{S\&P}_i + \epsilon_i$$

where $\text{(Analyst following)}_i$ is the natural log of $(1+$ number of analysts following company $i)$; Size_i is the natural log of the market capitalization of company i in millions of dollars; (D/E)_i is the debt-to-equity ratio for company i, and $\text{S\&P}_i$ is a dummy variable with a value of 1 if the company i belongs to the S&P 500 Index and 0 otherwise.

B. The appropriate null and alternative hypotheses are $H_0: b_3 = 0$ and $H_a: b_3 \neq 0$, respectively.

C. The t-statistic to test the null hypothesis can be computed as follows:

$$\frac{\hat{b}_3 - b_3}{s_{\hat{b}_3}} = \frac{0.4218 - 0}{0.0919} = 4.5898$$

This value is, of course, the same as the value reported in the table. The regression has 500 observations and 4 regression coefficients, so the t-test has $500 - 4 = 496$ degrees of freedom. At the 0.05 significance level, the critical value for the test statistic is between 1.96 and 1.97. Because the value of the test statistic is 4.5898 we can reject the null hypothesis that $b_3 = 0$. Thus a company's membership in the S&P 500 appears to significantly influence the number of analysts who cover that company.

D. The estimated model is

$$\text{(Analyst following)}_i = -0.0075 + 0.2648 \text{Size}_i - 0.1829 \text{(D/E)}_i$$
$$+ 0.4218 \text{S\&P}_i + \epsilon_i$$

Therefore the prediction for number of analysts following the indicated company that is not part of the S&P 500 Index is

$$\text{(Analyst following)}_i = -0.0075 + 0.2648(\ln 10,000) - 0.1829(2/3) + 0.4218(0)$$
$$= -0.0075 + 2.4389 - 0.1219 + 0 = 2.3095.$$

Recalling that $\text{(Analyst following)}_i$ is the natural log of $(1 + n_i)$, where n_i is the number of analysts following company i; it ensues (coding the company under consideration as 1) that $1 + n_1 = e^{2.3095} = 10.069$, approximately. Therefore, the prediction is that $n_1 = 10.069 - 1 = 9.069$, or about nine analysts.

Similarly, the prediction for the company that is included in the S&P 500 Index is

$$\text{(Analyst following)}_i = -0.0075 + 0.2648(\ln 10,000) - 0.1829(2/3) + 0.4218(1)$$
$$= -0.0075 + 2.4389 - 0.1219 + 0.4218 = 2.7313$$

Coding the company that does belong to the S&P 500 as 2, $1 + n_2 = e^{2.7313} = 15.353$. Therefore, the prediction is that $n_2 = 15.353 - 1 = 14.353$, or about 14 analysts.

E. There is no inconsistency in the coefficient on the size variable differing between the two regressions. The regression coefficient on an independent variable in a multiple regression model measures the expected net effect on the expected value of the dependent variable for a one-unit increase in that independent variable, after accounting for any effects of the other independent variables on the expected value of the dependent variable. The earlier regression had one fewer independent variable; after the effect of S&P 500 membership on the expected value of the dependent variable is taken into account, it is to be expected that the effect of the size variable on the dependent variable will change. What the regressions appear to indicate is that the net effect of the size variable on the expected analyst following diminishes when S&P 500 membership is taken into account.

9. A. In a well-specified regression, the differences between the actual and predicted relationship should be random; the errors should not depend on the value of the independent variable. In this regression, the errors seem larger for smaller values of the book-to-market ratio. This finding indicates that we may have conditional heteroskedasticity in the errors, and consequently, the standard errors may be incorrect. We cannot proceed with hypothesis testing until we test for and, if necessary, correct for heteroskedasticity.

B. A test for heteroskedasticity is to regress the squared residuals from the estimated regression equation on the independent variables in the regression. As seen in Section 4.1.2, Breusch and Pagan showed that, under the null hypothesis of no conditional heteroskedasticity, $n \times R^2$ (from the regression of the squared residuals on the independent variables from the original regression) will be a χ^2 random variable, with the number of degrees of freedom equal to the number of independent variables in the regression.

C. One method to correct for heteroskedasticity is to use robust standard errors. This method uses the parameter estimates from the linear regression model but corrects the standard errors of the estimated parameters to account for the heteroskedasticity. Many statistical software packages can easily compute robust standard errors.

10. The test statistic is nR^2, where n is the number of observations and R^2 is the R^2 of the regression of squared residuals. So, the test statistic is $52 \times 0.141 = 7.332$. Under the null hypothesis of no conditional heteroskedasticity, this test statistic is a χ^2 random variable. There are three degrees of freedom, the number of independent variables in the regression. Appendix C shows that for a one-tailed test, the test statistic critical value for a variable from a χ^2 distribution with 3 degrees of freedom at the 0.05 significance level is 7.815. The test statistic from the Breusch–Pagan test is 7.332. So, we cannot reject the hypothesis of no conditional heteroskedasticity at the 0.05 level. Therefore, we do not need to correct for conditional heteroskedasticity.

11. A. The test statistic is nR^2, where n is the number of observations and R^2 is the R^2 of the regression of squared residuals. So, the test statistic is $750 \times 0.006 = 4.5$. Under the null hypothesis of no conditional heteroskedasticity, this test statistic is a χ^2 random variable. Because the regression has only one independent variable, the number of degrees of freedom is equal to 1. Appendix C shows that for a one-tailed test, the test statistic critical value for a variable from a χ^2 distribution with one degree of freedom at the 0.05 significance level is 3.841. The test statistic is 4.5. So, we can reject the

hypothesis of no conditional heteroskedasticity at the 0.05 level. Therefore, we need to correct for conditional heteroskedasticity.

B. Two different methods can be used to correct for the effects of conditional heteroskedasticity in linear regression models. The first method involves computing robust standard errors. This method corrects the standard errors of the linear regression model's estimated parameters to account for the conditional heteroskedasticity. The second method is generalized least squares. This method modifies the original equation in an attempt to eliminate the heteroskedasticity. The new, modified regression equation is then estimated under the assumption that heteroskedasticity is no longer a problem.

Many statistical software packages can easily compute robust standard errors (the first method), and we recommend using them.

12. A. Because the value of the Durbin–Watson statistic is less than 2, we can say that the regression residuals are positively correlated. Because this statistic is fairly close to 2, however, we cannot say without a statistical test if the serial correlation is statistically significant.

B. From January 1987 through December 2002, there are 16 years, or $16 \times 12 = 192$ monthly returns. Thus the sample analyzed is quite large. Therefore, the Durbin–Watson statistic is approximately equal to $2(1 - r)$, where r is the sample correlation between the regression residuals from one period and those from the previous period.

$$DW = 1.8953 \approx 2(1 - r)$$

So, $r \approx 1 - DW/2 = 1 - 1.8953/2 = 0.0524$. Consistent with our answer to Part A, the correlation coefficient is positive.

C. Appendix E indicates that the critical values d_l and d_u for 100 observations when there is one independent variable are 1.65 and 1.69, respectively. Based on the information given in the problem, the critical values d_l and d_u for about 200 observations when there is one independent variable are about 1.74 and 1.78, respectively. Because the DW statistic of 1.8953 for our regression is above d_u, we fail to reject the null hypothesis of no positive serial correlation. Therefore, we conclude that there is no evidence of positive serial correlation for the error term.

13. A. This problem is known as multicollinearity. When some linear combinations of the independent variables in a regression model are highly correlated, the standard errors of the independent coefficient estimates become quite large, even though the regression equation may fit rather well.

B. The choice of independent variables presents multicollinearity concerns because market value of equity appears in both variables.

C. The classic symptom of multicollinearity is a high R^2 (and significant F-statistic) even though the t-statistics on the estimated slope coefficients are insignificant. Here a significant F-statistic does not accompany the insignificant t-statistics, so the classic symptom is not present.

14. A. To test the null hypothesis that all of the regression coefficients except for the intercept in the multiple regression model are equal to 0 (H_0: $b_1 = b_2 = b_3 = 0$) against the alternative hypothesis that at least one slope coefficient is not equal to 0, we must use an F-test.

$$F = \frac{RSS/k}{SSE/[n - (k + 1)]} = \frac{0.1720/3}{0.8947/[156 - (3 + 1)]} = 9.7403$$

The F-statistic has degrees of freedom $F\{k, [n - (k + 1)]\} = F(3, 152)$. From the F-test table, the critical value for $F(3, 120) = 2.68$ and $F(3, 152)$ will be less than $F(3, 120)$, so we can reject at the 0.05 significance level the null hypothesis that the slope coefficients are all 0. Changes in the three independent variables are jointly statistically related to returns.

B. None of the t-statistics is significant, but the F-statistic is significant. This suggests the possibility of multicollinearity in the independent variables.

C. The apparent multicollinearity is very likely related to the inclusion of *both* the returns on the S&P 500 Index *and* the returns on a value-weighted index of all the companies listed on the NYSE, AMEX, and Nasdaq as independent variables. The value-weighting of the latter index, giving relatively high weights to larger companies such as those included in the S&P 500, may make one return series an approximate linear function of the other. By dropping one or the other of these two variables, we might expect to eliminate the multicollinearity.

15. A. Your colleague is indicating that you have omitted an important variable from the regression. This problem is called the omitted variable bias. If the omitted variable is correlated with an included variable, the estimated values of the regression coefficients would be biased and inconsistent. Moreover, the estimates of standard errors of those coefficients would also be inconsistent. So, we cannot use either the coefficient estimates or the estimates of their standard errors to perform statistical tests.

B. A comparison of the new estimates with the original estimates clearly indicates that the original model suffered from the omitted variable bias due to the exclusion of company size from that model. As the t-statistics of the new model indicate, company size is statistically significant. Further, for the debt-to-equity ratio, the absolute value of the estimated coefficient substantially increases from 0.1043 to 0.1829, while its standard error declines. Consequently, it becomes significant in the new model, in contrast to the original model, in which it is not significant at the 5 percent level. The value of the estimated coefficient of the S&P 500 dummy substantially declines from 1.2222 to 0.4218. These changes imply that size should be included in the model.

16. A. You need to use a qualitative dependent variable. You could give a value of 1 to this dummy variable for a listing in the United States and a value of 0 for not listing in the United States.

B. Because you are using a qualitative dependent variable, linear regression is not the right technique to estimate the model. One possibility is to use either a probit or a logit model. Both models are identical, except that the logit model is based on logistic distribution while the probit model is based on normal distribution. Another possibility is to use discriminant analysis.

CHAPTER 10

TIME-SERIES ANALYSIS

SOLUTIONS

1. A. The estimated forecasting equation is $UER_t = 5.5098 - 0.0294(t)$. The data begin in January 1996, and July 1996 is period 7. Thus the linear trend model predicts the unemployment rate to be $UER_7 = 5.5098 - 0.0294(7) = 5.3040$ or approximately 5.3 percent.

   B. The DW statistic is designed to detect positive serial correlation of the errors of a regression equation. Under the null hypothesis of no positive serial correlation, the DW statistic is 2.0. Positive serial correlation will lead to a DW statistic that is less than 2.0. From the table in Problem 1, we see that the DW statistic is 0.9099. To see whether this result is significantly less than 2.0, refer to the Durbin–Watson table at the end of the book, in the column marked $k = 1$ (one independent variable) and the row corresponding to 60 observations. We see that $d_l = 1.55$. Because our DW statistic is clearly less than d_l, we reject the null hypothesis of no serial correlation at the 0.05 significance level.

   The presence of serial correlation in the error term violates one of the regression assumptions. The standard errors of the estimated coefficients will be biased downward, so we cannot conduct hypothesis testing on the coefficients.

2. The difference between UER and its forecast value, PRED, is the forecast error. In an appropriately specified regression model, the forecast errors are randomly distributed around the regression line and have a constant variance. We can see that the errors from this model specification are persistent. The errors tend first to be above the regression line and then, starting in 1997, they tend to be below the regression line until 2000 when they again are persistently above the regression line. This persistence suggests that the errors are positively serially correlated. Therefore, we conclude that the model is not appropriate for making estimates.

3. A log-linear model captures growth at a constant rate. The log-linear model $\ln (Sales_t) = b_0 + b_1 t + \epsilon_t$ would be the simplest model consistent with a constant growth rate for monthly sales. Note that we would need to confirm that the regression assumptions are satisfied before accepting the model as valid.

4. A. The plot of the series ΔUER_t seems to fluctuate around a constant mean; its volatility appears to be constant throughout the period. Our initial judgment is that the differenced series is covariance stationary.

   B. The change in the unemployment rate seems covariance stationary, so we should first estimate an AR(1) model and test to see whether the residuals from this model have significant serial correlation. If the residuals do not display significant serial correlation, we should use the AR(1) model. If the residuals do display significant serial correlation, we should try an AR(2) model and test for serial correlation of the residuals of the AR(2) model. We should continue this procedure until the errors from the final AR(p) model are serially uncorrelated.

5. The DW statistic cannot be appropriately used for a regression that has a lagged value of the dependent variable as one of the explanatory variables. To test for serial correlation, we need to examine the autocorrelations.

6. When a covariance-stationary series is at its mean-reverting level, the series will tend not to change until it receives a shock (ϵ_t). So, if the series ΔUER_t is at the mean-reverting level, $\Delta UER_t = \Delta UER_{t-1}$. This implies that $\Delta UER_t = -0.0405 - 0.4674\Delta UER_t$, so that $(1 + 0.4674)\Delta UER_t = -0.0405$ and $\Delta UER_t = -0.0405/(1 + 0.4674) = -0.0276$. The mean-reverting level is -0.0276. In an AR(1) model, the general expression for the mean-reverting level is $b_0/(1 - b_1)$.

7. A. The predicted change in the unemployment rate for next period is -5.45 percent, found by substituting 0.0300 into the forecasting model: $-0.0405 - 0.4674(0.03) = -0.0545$.

   B. If we substitute our one-period-ahead forecast of -0.0545 into the model (using the chain rule of forecasting), we get a two-period ahead forecast of -0.0150 or -1.5 percent.

   C. The answer to Part B is quite close to the mean-reverting level of -0.0276. A stationary time series may need many periods to return to its equilibrium, mean-reverting level.

8. The forecast of sales is $4,391 million for the first quarter of 2002 and $4,738 million for the second quarter of 2002, as the following table shows.

Date	Sales (millions)	Log of Sales	Actual Values of Changes in the Log of Sales $\Delta \ln (Sales_t)$	Forecast Values of Changes in the Log of Sales $\Delta \ln (Sales_t)$
1Q:2001	$6,519	8.7825	0.1308	
2Q:2001	$6,748	8.8170	0.0345	
3Q:2001	$4,728	8.4613	-0.3557	
4Q:2001	$4,298	8.3659	-0.0954	
1Q:2002	$4,391	8.3872		0.0213
2Q:2002	$4,738	8.4633		0.0761

We find the forecasted change in the log of sales for the first quarter of 2002 by inputting the value for the change in the log of sales from the previous quarter into the equation $\Delta \ln (Sales_t) = 0.0661 + 0.4698\Delta \ln (Sales_{t-1})$. Specifically, $\Delta \ln (Sales_t) = 0.0661 + 0.4698(-0.0954) = 0.0213$, which means that we forecast the log of sales in the first quarter of 2002 to be $8.3659 + 0.0213 = 8.3872$.

Next, we forecast the change in the log of sales for the second quarter of 2002 as $\Delta \ln (Sales_t) = 0.0661 + 0.4698(0.0213) = 0.0761$. Note that we have to use our first-quarter 2002 estimated value of the change in the log of sales as our input for $\Delta \ln (Sales_{t-1})$ because we are forecasting past the period for which we have actual data.

With a forecasted change of 0.0761, we forecast the log of sales in the second quarter of 2002 to be $8.3872 + 0.0761 = 8.4633$.

We have forecasted the log of sales in the first and second quarters of 2002 to be 8.3872 and 8.4633, respectively. Finally, we take the antilog of our estimates of the log of sales in the first and second quarters of 2002 to get our estimates of the level of sales: $e^{8.3872} = 4,391$ and $e^{8.4633} = 4,738$, respectively, for sales of \$4,391 million and \$4,738 million.

9. A. The RMSE of the out-of-sample forecast errors is approximately 27 percent. Out-of-sample error refers to the difference between the realized value and the forecasted value of $\Delta \ln (\text{Sales}_t)$ for dates beyond the estimation period. In this case, the out-of-sample period is 1Q:2001 to 4Q:2001. These are the four quarters for which we have data that we did not use to obtain the estimated model $\Delta \ln (\text{Sales}_t) = 0.0661 + 0.4698 \Delta \ln (\text{Sales}_{t-1})$.

The steps to calculate RMSE are as follows:

   i. Take the difference between the actual and the forecast value. This is the error.
   ii. Square the error.
   iii. Sum the squared errors.
   iv. Divide by the number of forecasts.
   v. Take the square root of the average.

We show the calculations for RMSE in the table below.

Actual Value of Changes in the Log of Sales $\Delta \ln (\text{Sales}_t)$	Forecast Value of Changes in the Log of Sales $\Delta \ln (\text{Sales}_t)$	Error (Column 1 −Column 2)		Squared Error (Column 3 Squared)
0.1308	0.1357	−0.0049		0.0000
0.0345	0.1299	−0.0954		0.0091
−0.3557	0.1271	−0.4828		0.2331
−0.0954	0.1259	−0.2213		0.0490
			Sum	0.2912
			Mean	0.0728
			RMSE	0.2698

B. The lower the RMSE, the more accurate the forecasts of a model in forecasting. Therefore, the model with the RMSE of 20 percent has greater accuracy in forecasting than the model in Part A, which has an RMSE of 27 percent.

10. A. Predictions too far ahead can be nonsensical. For example, the AR(1) model we have been examining, $\Delta \text{UER}_t = -0.0405 - 0.4674 \Delta \text{UER}_{t-1}$, taken at face value, predicts declining civilian unemployment into the indefinite future. Because the civilian unemployment rate will probably not go below 3 percent frictional unemployment and cannot go below 0 percent unemployment, this model's long-range forecasts are implausible. The model is designed for short-term forecasting, as are many time-series models.

B. Using more years of data for estimation may lead to nonstationarity even in the series of first differences in the civilian unemployment rate. As we go further back in time, we increase the risk that the underlying civilian unemployment rate series has more than one regime (or true model). If the series has more than one regime, fitting one model to the entire period would not be correct. Note that when we have good reason to believe that a time series is stationary, a longer series of data is generally desirable.

11. A. The graph of ln (Sales$_t$) appears to trend upward over time. A series that trends upward or downward over time often has a unit root and is thus not covariance stationary. Therefore, using an AR(1) regression on the undifferenced series is probably not correct. In practice, we need to examine regression statistics to confirm visual impressions such as this.

B. The most common way to transform a time series with a unit root into a covariance-stationary time series is to difference the data—that is, to create a new series Δ ln (Sales$_t$) = ln (Sales$_t$) − ln (Sales$_{t-1}$).

12. The plot of the series Δ ln (Sales$_t$) appears to fluctuate around a constant mean; its volatility seems constant throughout the period. Differencing the data appears to have made the time series covariance stationary.

13. A. In a correctly specified regression, the residuals must be serially uncorrelated. We have 108 observations, so the standard error of the autocorrelation is $1/\sqrt{T}$, or in this case $1/\sqrt{108} = 0.0962$. The t-statistic for each lag is significant at the 0.01 level. We would have to modify the model specification before continuing with the analysis.

B. Because the residuals from the AR(1) specification display significant serial correlation, we should estimate an AR(2) model and test for serial correlation of the residuals of the AR(2) model. If the residuals from the AR(2) model are serially uncorrelated, we should then test for seasonality and ARCH behavior. If any serial correlation remains in the residuals, we should estimate an AR(3) process and test the residuals from that specification for serial correlation. We should continue this procedure until the errors from the final AR(p) model are serially uncorrelated. When serial correlation is eliminated, we should test for seasonality and ARCH behavior.

14. A. The series has a steady upward trend of growth, suggesting an exponential growth rate. This finding suggests transforming the series by taking the natural log and differencing the data.

B. First, we should determine whether the residuals from the AR(1) specification are serially uncorrelated. If the residuals are serially correlated, then we should try an AR(2) specification and then test the residuals from the AR(2) model for serial correlation. We should continue in this fashion until the residuals are serially uncorrelated, then look for seasonality in the residuals. If seasonality is present, we should add a seasonal lag. If no seasonality is present, we should test for ARCH. If ARCH is not present, we can conclude that the model is correctly specified.

C. If the model Δ ln (Sales$_t$) = $b_0 + b_1[\Delta$ ln (Sales$_{t-1}$)] + ϵ_t is correctly specified, then the series Δ ln (Sales$_t$) is covariance stationary. So, this series tends to its mean-reverting level, which is $b_0/(1 - b_1)$ or $0.0661/(1 - 0.4698) = 0.1247$.

15. The quarterly sales of Avon show an upward trend and a clear seasonal pattern, as indicated by the repeated regular cycle.

16. A. A second explanatory variable, the change in the gross profit margin lagged four quarters, ΔGPM_{t-4}, was added.

    B. The model was augmented to account for seasonality in the time series (with quarterly data, significant autocorrelation at the fourth lag indicates seasonality). The standard error of the autocorrelation coefficient equals 1 divided by the square root of the number of observations: $1/\sqrt{40}$ or 0.1581. The autocorrelation at the fourth lag (0.8496) is significant: $t = 0.8496/0.1581 = 5.37$. This indicates seasonality, and accordingly we added ΔGPM_{t-4}. Note that in the augmented regression, the coefficient on ΔGPM_{t-4} is highly significant. (Although the autocorrelation at second lag is also significant, the fourth lag is more important because of the rationale of seasonality. Once the fourth lag is introduced as an independent variable, we might expect that the second lag in the residuals would not be significant.)

17. A. The table shows strong seasonal autocorrelation of the residuals. The bottom portion of the table shows that the fourth autocorrelation has a value of 0.6030 and a t-statistic of 4.9728. With 68 observations and two parameters, this model has 66 degrees of freedom. The critical value for a t-statistic is about 2.0 at the 0.05 significance level. Given this value of the t-statistic, we must reject the null hypothesis that the fourth autocorrelation is equal to 0 because 4.9728 is larger than the critical value of 2.0. At this significance level, we can also conclude that the second autocorrelation does not equal 0. Because the second and fourth autocorrelations do not equal 0, this model is misspecified and the estimates for b_0 and b_1 are invalid.

    B. We should estimate a new autoregressive model and test the residuals for serial correlation. In this model, the fourth autocorrelation is the seasonal autocorrelation because this AR(1) model is estimated with quarterly data. We should use an autoregressive model with a seasonal lag because of the seasonal autocorrelation. We are modeling quarterly data, so we need to estimate ln (Sales$_t$) − ln (Sales$_{t-1}$) = $b_0 + b_1$[ln (Sales$_{t-1}$) − ln (Sales$_{t-2}$)] + b_2[ln (Sales$_{t-4}$) − ln (Sales$_{t-5}$)] + ϵ_t.

18. A. In order to determine whether this model is correctly specified, we need to test for serial correlation among the residuals. We want to test whether we can reject the null hypothesis that the value of each autocorrelation is 0 against the alternative hypothesis that each is not equal to 0. At the 0.05 significance level, with 68 observations and three parameters, this model has 65 degrees of freedom. The critical value of the t-statistic needed to reject the null hypothesis is thus about 2.0. The absolute value of the t-statistic for each autocorrelation is below 0.60 (less than 2.0), so we cannot reject the null hypothesis that each autocorrelation is not significantly different from 0. We have determined that the model is correctly specified.

    B. If sales grew by 1 percent last quarter and by 2 percent four quarters ago, then the model predicts that sales growth this quarter will be $0.0121 - 0.0839(0.01) + 0.6292(0.02) = 0.0238$ or 2.38 percent.

19. We should estimate the regression $\Delta UER_t = b_0 + b_1 \Delta UER_{t-1} + \epsilon_t$ and save the residuals from the regression. Then we should create a new variable, $\hat{\epsilon}_t^2$, by squaring the residuals. Finally, we should estimate $\hat{\epsilon}_t^2 = a_0 + a_1 \hat{\epsilon}_{t-1}^2 + u_t$ and test to see whether a_1 is statistically different from 0.

20. The t-statistic for the coefficient on $\hat{\epsilon}_{t-1}^2$ is clearly not significant, indicating that we cannot reject the hypothesis that a_1 is 0 in the regression $\hat{\epsilon}_t^2 = a_0 + a_1 \hat{\epsilon}_{t-1}^2 + u_t$. Therefore, we conclude that the regression $\Delta UER_t = b_0 + b_1 \Delta UER_{t-1} + \epsilon_t$ for this time period is free from ARCH.

21. To determine whether we can use linear regression to model more than one time series, we should first determine whether any of the time series has a unit root. If none of the time series has a unit root, then we can safely use linear regression to test the relations between the two time series. Note that if one of the two variables has a unit root, then our analysis would not provide valid results; if both of the variables have unit roots, then we would need to evaluate whether the variables are cointegrated.

CHAPTER 11

PORTFOLIO CONCEPTS

SOLUTIONS

1. The expected return is $0.75E$(return on stocks) $+0.25E$(return on bonds)

$$= 0.75(15) + 0.25(5)$$
$$= 12.5 \text{ percent}$$

The standard deviation is

$$\sigma = [w_{stocks}^2\sigma_{stocks}^2 + w_{bonds}^2\sigma_{bonds}^2 + 2w_{stocks}w_{bonds}$$
$$\text{Corr}(R_{stocks}, R_{bonds})\sigma_{stocks}\sigma_{bonds}]^{1/2}$$
$$= [0.75^2(225) + 0.25^2(100) + 2(0.75)(0.25)(0.5)(15)(10)]^{1/2}$$
$$= (126.5625 + 6.25 + 28.125)^{1/2}$$
$$= (160.9375)^{1/2}$$
$$= 12.69\%$$

2. Use the expression

$$\sigma_p^2 = \sigma^2 \left(\frac{1-\rho}{n} + \rho \right)$$

The square root of this expression is standard deviation. With variance equal to 625 and correlation equal to 0.3,

$$\sigma_p = \sqrt{625 \left(\frac{1-0.3}{100} + 0.3 \right)}$$
$$= 13.85\%$$

3. Find portfolio variance using the following expression

$$\sigma_p^2 = \sigma^2 \left(\frac{1-\rho}{n} + \rho \right)$$
$$= 625[(1-0.3)/24 + 0.3] = 205.73$$

With 24 stocks, variance of return is 205.73 (equivalent to a standard deviation of 14.34 percent). With an unlimited number of securities, the first term in square brackets is 0 and the smallest variance is achieved:

$$\sigma^2_{\min} = \sigma^2 \rho = 625(0.30) = 187.5$$

This result is equivalent to a standard deviation of 13.69 percent. The ratio of the variance of the 24-stock portfolio to the portfolio with an unlimited number of securities is

$$\frac{\sigma^2_p}{\sigma^2_{\min}} = \frac{205.73}{187.5} = 1.097$$

The variance of the 24-stock portfolio is approximately 110 percent of the variance of the portfolio with an unlimited number of securities.

4. Define

R_p = return on the portfolio

R_1 = return on the risk-free asset

R_2 = return on the risky asset

w_1 = fraction of the portfolio invested in the risk-free asset

w_2 = fraction of the portfolio invested in the risky asset

Then the expected return on the portfolio is

$$E(R_p) = w_1 E(R_1) + w_2 E(R_2)$$
$$= 0.10(5\%) + 0.9(13\%) = 0.5 + 11.7 = 12.2\%$$

To calculate standard deviation of return, we calculate variance of return and take the square root of variance:

$$\sigma^2(R_P) = w_1^2 \sigma^2(R_1) + w_2^2 \sigma^2(R_2) + 2w_1 w_2 \text{Cov}(R_1, R_2)$$
$$= 0.1^2(0^2) + 0.9^2(23^2) + 2(0.1)(0.9)(0)$$
$$= 0.9^2(23^2)$$
$$= 428.49$$

Thus the portfolio standard deviation of return is $\sigma(R_P) = (428.49)^{1/2} = 20.7$ percent.

5. According to the market model, $\text{Var}(R_p) = \beta_p^2 \sigma_M^2 + \sigma_{\epsilon_p}^2$. The S&P 500 index fund should have a beta of 1 with respect to the S&P 500. By moving 10 percent of invested funds from the index fund to a security with a beta of 2, we necessarily will increase $\beta_p^2 \sigma_M^2$ (systematic risk) for the portfolio. An individual asset will also have higher nonsystematic risk (residual risk) than the highly diversified index fund, so $\sigma_{\epsilon_p}^2$ will increase as well. Thus the new portfolio cannot have a lower standard deviation of return than the old portfolio.

6. A. With R_T the return on the tangency portfolio and R_F the risk-free rate,

$$\text{Expected risk premium per unit of risk} = \frac{E(R_T) - R_F}{\sigma(R_T)} = \frac{14 - 6}{24} = 0.33$$

B. First, we find the weight w of the tangency portfolio in the investor's portfolio using the expression $\sigma(R_P) = w\sigma(R_T)$,
so

$$w = (20/24) = 0.8333$$

Then

$$E(R_p) = wE(R_T) + (1 - w)R_F = 0.833333(14\%) + 0.166667(6\%) = 12.67\%$$

7. A. According to the Markowitz decision rule, Martinez should prefer Portfolio B to Portfolio C because B has the same expected return as C with lower standard deviation of return than C. Thus he can eliminate C from consideration as a stand-alone portfolio. The Markowitz decision rule is inconclusive concerning the choice between A and B, however, because although A has higher mean return, it also has higher standard deviation of return.

   B. With a risk-free asset, we can evaluate portfolios using the Sharpe ratio (the ratio of mean return in excess of the risk-free rate divided by standard deviation of return). The Sharpe ratios are

$$\text{Portfolio A: } (12 - 2)/15 = 0.67$$

$$\text{Portfolio B: } (10 - 2)/8 = 1.00$$

$$\text{Portfolio C: } (10 - 2)/9 = 0.89$$

   With risk-free borrowing and lending possible, Martinez will choose Portfolio B because it has the highest Sharpe ratio.

8. The quantity (Sharpe ratio of existing portfolio) × (Correlation of U.S. bonds with existing portfolio) = 0.15(0.20) = 0.03. Because U.S. bonds' predicted Sharpe ratio of 0.10 exceeds 0.03, it is optimal to add them to the existing portfolio.

9. With R_M the return on the market portfolio, and all the other terms as defined in previous answers, we have

$$E(R_p) = wE(R_M) + (1 - w)R_F$$

$$17 = 13w + 5(1 - w) = 8w + 5$$

$$12 = 8w$$

$$w = 1.5$$

Thus $1 - 1.5 = -0.5$ of initial wealth goes into the risk-free asset. The negative sign indicates borrowing: $-0.5(\$1 \text{ million}) = -\$500,000$, so the investor borrows $500,000.

10. We start from the definition of correlation (first line below). In the numerator, we substitute for covariance using Equation 11-14; in the denominator we use Equation 11-13 to substitute for the standard deviations of return.

$$\text{Corr}(R_1, R_2) = \frac{\text{Corr}(R_1, R_2)}{\sigma_1 \sigma_2}$$

$$= \frac{\beta_1 \beta_2 \sigma_M^2}{\sqrt{\beta_1^2 \sigma_M^2 + \sigma_{\epsilon_1}^2} \sqrt{\beta_2^2 \sigma_M^2 + \sigma_{\epsilon_2}^2}}$$

$$= \frac{1.5(1.2)(8)^2}{\sqrt{1.5^2(8)^2 + 2^2} \sqrt{1.2^2(8^2) + 4^2}}$$

$$= 0.91$$

11. $\beta_{adj} = 0.33 + (0.67)(1.2)$
    $= 0.33 + 0.80$
    $= 1.13$

    $E(R_p) = E(R_i) = R_F + \beta_i[E(R_M) - R_F]$
    $= 5\% + 1.13(8.5\%)$
    $= 14.6\%$

12. The surprise in a factor equals actual value minus expected value. For the interest rate factor, the surprise was 2 percent; for the GDP factor, the surprise was −3 percent.

    $R = $ Expected return − 1.5(Interest rate surprise) + 2(GDP surprise)

    + Company-specific surprise

    $= 11\% - 1.5(2\%) + 2(-3\%) + 3\%$

    $= 5\%$

13. Portfolio inflation sensitivity is the weight on Manumatic stock multiplied by its inflation sensitivity, plus the weight on Nextech stock multiplied by its inflation sensitivity: $0.5(-1) + 0.5(2) = 0.5$. So a 1 percent interest rate surprise increase in inflation is expected to produce a 50 basis point increase in the portfolio's return.

14. The arbitrage portfolio must have zero sensitivity to the factor. We first need to find the proportions of A and B in the short position that combine to produce a factor sensitivity equal to 0.45, the factor sensitivity of C, which we will hold long. Using w as the weight on A in the short position,

    $$2w + 0.4(1 - w) = 0.45$$

    $$2w + 0.4 - 0.4w = 0.45$$

    $$1.6w = 0.05$$

    $$w = 0.05/1.6 = 0.03125$$

Hence, the weights on A and B are −0.03125 and −0.96875, respectively. These sum to −1. The arbitrage portfolio has zero net investment. The weight on C in the arbitrage portfolio must be 1, so that combined with the short position, the net investment is 0. The expected return on the arbitrage portfolio is $1(0.08) - 0.03125(0.15) - 0.96875(0.07) = 0.08 - 0.0725 = 0.0075$ or 0.75 percent. For \$10,000 invested in C, this represents a $\$10,000 \times 0.0075 = \$75$ arbitrage profit.

15. A. Tracking risk or active risk is the square root of active risk squared. For Manager A, it is $(36)^{1/2} = 6$ percent; for Manager B, it is $(40)^{1/2} = 6.32$ percent.

    B. Although Manager A assumed very slightly more active specific risk than Manager B, B assumed more active factor risk than A, resulting in higher active risk squared for B. Looking at the components of active factor risk, we see that although B was essentially industry neutral to the benchmark (active industry factor risk of 2), B tilted his risk indexes exposures substantially away from those of the benchmark (active risk indexes risk of 25, which is 5% per annum).

    C We can use the information ratio (IR, the ratio of mean active return to active risk) to evaluate the two managers' risk-adjusted performance. The mean active return of A was $12\% - 10.5\% = 1.5\%$. Thus A's IR was $1.5\%/6\% = 0.25$. The mean active return of B was $14\% - 10.5\% = 3.5\%$. Thus B's IR was $3.5\%/6.32\% = 0.55$. Because B gave more mean active return per unit of active risk than A, his risk adjusted performance was superior.

16. A. i. The factors are mutually uncorrelated. Then we have the equation: Active factor risk for a factor = (Active sensitivity to the factor)^2 (Factor variance)

    $$\text{Duration: } (6.00 - 5.00)^2(121) = 121.0$$

    $$\text{Steepness: } (0.50 - 0.35)^2(64) = 1.44$$

    $$\text{Curvature: } (-0.15 - 0.30)^2(150) = 30.375$$

    ii. The sum of the individual factor risks is $121.0 + 1.44 + 30.375 = 152.815$. We add to this sum active specific risk to obtain active risk squared of $152.815 + 25 = 177.815$. Thus the factors' marginal contributions to active risk squared (FMCAR) for the factors are as follows:

    $$\text{Duration: } 121.0/177.815 = 0.68$$

    $$\text{Steepness: } 1.44/177.815 = 0.0081$$

    $$\text{Curvature: } 30.375/177.815 = 0.1708$$

    B. The bet in which Sherman took a longer-duration position than the benchmark accounted for about 68 percent of active risk squared, a much larger share than any of the two other factor bets. Also, active specific risk accounted for $25/177.815 = 0.1406$ or about 14 percent of active risk squared. Thus Sherman's largest bet against the benchmark was on the duration factor.

    C. Tracking risk was $(177.815)^{1/2} = 13.33$ percent. Average active return was -0.2%. Thus Sherman's IR was $-0.2\%/13.33\% = -0.015$. A negative IR means that Sherman did not produce any increase in active return for the active risk undertaken. Based only on this piece of information, we would conclude that her performance was unsatisfactory.

17. We need to combine Portfolios K and L in such a way that sensitivity to the inflation factor is zero. The inflation sensitivities of Portfolios K and L are 0.5 and 1.5, respectively.

With w the weight on Portfolio L, we have

$$0 = 0.5(1 - w) + 1.5w$$
$$0 = 0.5 - 0.5w + 1.5w$$
$$0 = 0.5 + w$$
$$w = -0.5$$

The weight on Portfolio L in the new portfolio is -0.5, and the weight on Portfolio K is $1.5(-0.5 + 1.5 = 1)$. For every \$1.50 invested in Portfolio K, the institution shorts \$0.50 of Portfolio L. The new portfolio's return is

$$R = 0.125 + 0.25F_{\text{GDP}}$$

The intercept is computed as $(1.50 \times 0.12) + (-0.5 \times 0.11) = 0.125$, and the sensitivity to the GDP factor is computed as $(1.50 \times 1.0) + (-0.5 \times 2.5) = 0.25$.

18. $E(R_A) = 6 + 0.5\lambda = 10.25$
    $E(R_B) = 6 + 1.2\lambda = 16.2$
    Using either equation, we can calculate the price of factor risk as

$$\lambda = \frac{10.25 - 6}{0.5} = \frac{16.2 - 6}{1.2} = 8.5$$

The risk premium for each unit of factor risk, or price of risk, is 8.5 percent.

19. With w the weight on Portfolio A, $(1 - w)$ the weight on Portfolio B, and 1.71 the sensitivity of the S&P 500 to the business cycle factor, we have

$$2.25w + 1.00(1 - w) = 1.71$$
$$2.25w + 1 - w = 1.71$$
$$1.25w = 0.71$$

Thus

$$w = 0.568, \text{ weight on Portfolio A}$$
$$1 - w = 0.432, \text{ weight on Portfolio B}$$

With a weight of 0.568 on A and 0.432 on B, the resulting inflation factor sensitivity is $0.568(-0.12) + 0.432(-0.45) = -0.263$.

20. If the average investor has income from employment, then this income makes this investor recession sensitive. Hence, the average investor requires a risk premium to hold recession-sensitive securities. The average investor's need for a risk premium for these stocks influences their prices. Cyclical stocks and high-yield bonds are both very sensitive to economic conditions. For example, the debt-paying ability of high-yield bond issuers is strongly affected by recessions. The wealthy investor with no labor income can take the recession risk for which she would receive a premium (pay a lower price than would be the case if the average investor were not recession sensitive). The high-wealth investor can afford to take the risk because she does not face recession risk from labor income.

PART II

SOLUTIONS

ABOUT THE CFA PROGRAM

The Chartered Financial Analyst® designation (CFA®) is a globally recognized standard of excellence for measuring the competence and integrity of investment professionals. To earn the CFA charter, candidates must successfully pass through the CFA Program, a global graduate-level self-study program that combines a broad curriculum with professional conduct requirements as preparation for a wide range of investment specialties.

Anchored by a practice-based curriculum, the CFA Program is focused on the knowledge identified by professionals as essential to the investment decision-making process. This body of knowledge maintains current relevance through a regular, extensive survey of practicing CFA charterholders across the globe. The curriculum covers 10 general topic areas ranging from equity and fixed-income analysis to portfolio management to corporate finance, all with a heavy emphasis on the application of ethics in professional practice. Known for its rigor and breadth, the CFA Program curriculum highlights principles common to every market so that professionals who earn the CFA designation have a thoroughly global investment perspective and a profound understanding of the global marketplace.

www.cfainstitute.org

0-470-05220-1 • Cloth
US$95.00/ CAN$113.99/UK£65.00

Tap into the minds of leading
industry professionals and academics
and learn Quantitative Investment
Analysis from the inside out.

wiley.com

    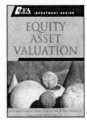

CPSIA information can be obtained at www.ICGtesting.com
Printed in the USA
BVOW02n0135250713

326869BV00001BA/2/P